23/2/17

UAT

Please renew or return items by the date
shown on your receipt

www.hertsdirect.org/libraries

Renewals and   0300 123 4049
enquiries:

Textphone for hearing   0300 123 4041
or speech impaired

'What makes this book so enthralling is the way that film sequences bring alive the magic and structure of parents and infants communicating. It takes a special mind to draw important general truths from a lifetime of expert observations, and to make scientific principles transparent to the everyday reader. Lynne Murray succeeds superbly.'

Professor John Duncan FRS, FBA, of the Medical Research Council's
Cognition and Brain Unit at Cambridge, and Department of Psychology,
University of Oxford

'This wonderful book is a compelling sequel to *The Social Baby*. As its subtitle explains it is about how relationships support development and it provides an extremely lucid and accessible exposition of the latest research that shows how critical the earliest relationships are to the child's social, emotional and cognitive development. It is copiously illustrated with annotated stills from videos of parents with their infants, which bring vividly alive the lessons from research. It will be an invaluable resource to all professionals working with infants and young children, compiling as it does the learning contained in articles in scholarly journals that would otherwise not be widely available. It shows how "it is the context of social relationships that almost all other skills are fostered" – a message that needs to be heard by all involved in the early child care and development field for its important implications for where support and intervention needs to be targeted.'

Paul Barrows Consultant Child and Adolescent Psychotherapist;
former Chair of the UK Association for Infant Mental Health;
former editor of the Journal of Child Psychotherapy and of
the Newsletter of the World Association for Infant Mental Health

'This is a beautiful and exciting book; years of careful, evaluated research into the psychology of babies is generously shared with parents and professionals. The key point that babies develop within relationships is brilliantly illustrated with captivating photos that show each stage of an interaction between parent and baby. The evidence that parents and babies affect each other and that emotional and cognitive development grows from this is clearly shown. It will help parents give meaning to their baby's behaviour and support their confidence in responding. For professionals, these photos back up theory, and looking at the sequence together with parents will help a shared understanding of babies.

'This is perhaps the most successful format so far in bringing together the methods of observation of Child Development Research and Psychoanalytic Infant Observation. These "snapshots" provide visual confirmation of detail observed in the moment that back up the evidence from long-term observation of a baby's emotional development within its family.'

Dilys Daws, Hon Consultant Child Psychotherapist, Tavistock Clinic

'The Psychology of Babies is a landmark publication. Lynne Murray guides her readers effortlessly through the wondrous world of early relationships and development. Stunning frame-by-frame photography brings vividly to life the rich insights and discoveries of a whole generation of ground-breaking research. This is essential reading.'

Chris Cuthbert, Head of Strategy & Development, NSPCC

'This beautifully written and generously illustrated book combines the great qualities of presenting research-based information while being in tune with parents' needs and concerns. Alongside all of that, page after page shows us how babies experience the world; what they get (and what they need) from their parents and other carers.'

Mary Newburn, Head of Research and Quality, NCT

'The author has poured a lifetime of hers and others' detailed research into this fascinating book which should be read by all new parents, and all those who work with parents and their infants, including health visitors. It comprehensively and clearly demonstrates, with the support of stills from films, the unique qualities of the very young infant to both communicate with and react to their emotional environment and the relationships they encounter therein. The reader is systematically introduced to the emotional world of the baby, and most importantly, to how positive relationships can shape their understanding of this world. I am sure many parents who have to return to work will appreciate the chapter on settling infants into day care, and the understanding of the emotions related to this often challenging time, likewise the content on settling babies to sleep.'

Cheryll Adams, Director, Institute of Health Visiting

'As Chair of Home-Start UK, I know how much support parents often need in today's world. This beautiful and wise book will surely enrich and deepen parents' natural understanding of the wonderful process of their children's development. It will also remind us all that parents and parenting should be valued above everything else in our society.'

James Sainsbury OBE, Chair of Home-Start UK

The Psychology of Babies

How relationships support development
from birth to two

Lynne Murray

ROBINSON

Constable & Robinson Ltd.
55–56 Russell Square
London WC1B 4HP
www.constablerobinson.com

First published in the UK by Robinson,
an imprint of Constable & Robinson Ltd., 2014

A copy of the British Library Cataloguing in
Publication Data is available from the British Library

ISBN: 978-1-84901-293-5 (flexiback)
ISBN: 978-1-84901-957-6 (ebook)

Printed and bound in China

1 3 5 7 9 10 8 6 4 2

www.psychology-of-babies.co.uk

Contents

3 Self-regulation and control

Acknowledgements

I owe a debt of gratitude to many people for their various contributions to this book, but I am particularly grateful to Colin Guilford and Kyla Vaillancourt, who both provided invaluable help with the collection and processing of video-material. I am similarly extremely grateful to all the parents who participated with their babies, and who bravely opened up their lives to the scrutiny of a video camera, whether in their homes, playgroup or nursery, and allowed themselves to be filmed, sometimes at challenging moments, without constraint, and without knowing what the end product would be.

I am also indebted to many colleagues and friends who have provided inspiration and valuable discussion on the issues underpinning this book. Among those whose influence was formative are Colwyn Trevarthen, Margaret Donaldson, Ed Tronick and the late Dan Stern, all giants in the field of infant development with whom it has been a great privilege to work. I have also gained much from the work of Andy Meltzoff and from sharing ideas about the social lives of babies with Beatrice Beebe, Bhisma Chakrabarti, Dilys Daws, John Davis, John Duncan, Judy Dunn, Jonathan Hill, Juliet Hopkins, Claire Hughes, Vasu Reddy and James Sainsbury, and from the stimulation and support received while working closely with Peter Cooper, Alan Stein, Pasco Fearon, Mark Tomlinson, Marc de Rosnay, Sarah Halligan, Adriane Arteche, Rosario Montirosso and Pier Ferrari. Peter, Pier, Pasco and Rosario kindly gave me detailed and extremely helpful feedback on the text of the current book, and I am also very grateful for generous feedback from Michael Lamb, Carmel Houston-Price, Graham Schafer, Nick Holmes, Andrew Bremner, Chloe Campbell, Mark Hunter, and Pete Lawrence. I would like to thank Kate Arnold-Forster, who kindly arranged for me to have access to the playgroup at the Museum of English Rural Life at the University of Reading, where Bekky Moran facilitated the observations of the children, as well as all the staff at Mongewell Park Nursery (of the Bright Horizons group) who similarly allowed their daily work with babies to be filmed. Both institutions are admirable models of how babies' and young children's emotional and attachment needs can be supported in the context of providing rich and stimulating environments for cognitive and wider social development. I also thank Liz White, Leonardo De Pascalis and Laura Bozicevic, who provided assistance with some of the figures and referencing, and Andrew Glennerster and Philip Barnard for their helpful encouragement. Not least, I am enormously grateful to Louise Dalton and Cathy Creswell for their unstinting support throughout.

It has been a real pleasure to work with the team at Constable & Robinson. I feel particularly privileged to have been very closely supported by the late Nick Robinson, and have enormously appreciated his active involvement, and his whole-hearted enthusiasm and encouragement. Nick was crucial in getting this book off the ground, and I am pleased that he was able to see the final draft before his untimely death in the summer of 2013. I am also extremely grateful to Fritha Saunders, Duncan Proudfoot and Andrew McAleer for their support and guidance, to Peggy Sadler for her work on the design, and in particular to Jan Chamier for her highly expert and sensitive work on textual editing, and for steering the book through to its conclusion.

Finally, I would like to thank all my family for their encouragement and interest, and especially my husband, for his unerring and invaluable support on every front.

LM

Foreword

Lynne Murray is a professor of psychology and an internationally respected researcher on infant development, known for her special knowledge of the importance of affectionate parental care. She is also a teacher and a writer whose earlier book, The Social Baby, has given families pleasure and confidence in sharing life with young children. She has worked in Africa, as well as in Europe, to help parents care for and communicate with their children. Being a mother and grandmother, she knows first hand the joy of play, of new experiences for parents in warm attachment with their sons and daughters.

As she explains in the introduction to this book, she has reviewed up to date research which has transformed scientific understanding of young children's vitality and needs. This will be an important source for students. But the book's most impressive message is the story of family life, presented in brilliant photographs and pictures from videos of real-life creative communication – usually taking place not in the laboratory, but at home, in the garden, on the beach, or in a place of daycare, by people who know and love young children. We see the hopes and feelings of the babies and their parents and other companions, as well as their affection for one another and appeals for attention or help when they need it.

The author first summarizes and illustrates the steps by which an alert newborn baby, dependent on intimate care and protection, becomes a mobile and self-confident, even super-confident, two-year-old, eager to know the world and to be a strong player in it. Developments in body and mind bring discoveries and challenges, sometimes troublesome doubts and fears. At every stage a need for company is expressed – a partner who responds with sensitivity and shares joys and concerns. That is what love is about and how it sustains

relationships. Lynne Murray gives a clear account of work on attachment relations and the evidence that what aids parents best to provide for security in their babies is 'helping parents to think about their babies' experience,' – perhaps reflecting on their feelings about the care they themselves received in childhood. Video feedback can greatly help carers 'see things afresh from their baby's point of view . . . seeing strengths in the relationship with their baby that they had not appreciated before.' That is the refreshing message throughout – babies are individuals with their own point of view and their own hopes to do interesting and enjoyable things for themselves and in warm friendship.

There is a well-informed and thoughtful account of provision for out-of-home care for babies and toddlers, and the benefits of high-quality care – 'a high staff-to-baby ratio, good staff training and higher rates of pay all contribute to high staff morale, a sense of professionalism and a low staff turnover.' Attachments to parents and care staff have to be supported, and changes managed sensitively. There is concern about inequalities of availability and quality of care: 'Given the importance of sensitive parental support for the baby's development, it is critical that government policy should support both good quality daycare and the ability of parents with young babies to work fewer and more flexible hours.' This is an urgent message for countries such as the UK and the USA. Particularly interesting is that good care out of home for babies and toddlers can lead to the development of rich new relationships between the children, which benefit adaptation later to school and a wider group of peers.

Discussing the development of emotional self-regulation skills, Professor Murray does not assume that babies' emotions are entirely self-related – even 'primitive' expressions of distress of a hungry, uncomfortable, sleep-needing newborn are offers of communication with another person. The development of well-being and well-feeling of a child is a life process that is guided by the affectionate, sensitive and playful care and the companionship of parents and family: the book highlights this subtle and important principle. There are delightful examples of how in more vigorous games with a baby, 'managing to enjoy the game and not become distressed can exercise both his own and his parent's regulation skills.' A key factor of interpersonal timing is illustrated with Lynne Murray's own studies of the effects of a parent withholding response to the baby's offers of communication, or of dis-coordinated behaviour, both of which may be disturbing for a baby when a parent is suffering from some emotional disorder and may seem 'withdrawn', 'intrusive' or 'overprotective and unencouraging'. For babies, as for anybody, responsive, emotional attunement is important for confirming a relationship and for learning in it. The author describes how development of conversational 'narratives' of living and learning help parents 'socialize' a child and 'convey the values of the family and the wider community' – from a newborn being settled into a comfortable sleep routine, to a two-year-old's 'helping' at the table or in the garden, or sharing imaginative play with other children.

The final chapter is on a favourite topic of psychologists and brain scientists – cognition or intelligence. Our culture has long given great importance to 'brainy' discrimination of facts and formal transmission of knowledge and understanding. These are skills that have been generally understood to be outside the life of babies. But both kinds of science have had to come to terms with clear evidence that we come into the world with intentions and conscious interest in goals and projects of our movements, and brains that are especially sensitive to meanings of other people's behaviours, especially when these are directed towards ourselves, to be shared. Once more, Lynne Murray expands our appreciation of this native cleverness and its development in relationships, with pictures that show intimate details of how conscious interests about the physical world, and making sense of others' actions, are communicated by and for babies. The ways a teacher may assist early learning, and the special value of book-sharing are all made clear. The most important conclusions are that, 'from birth, babies actively push their cognitive development forward, experimenting to find out what they can do, and how the world works,' and 'for their natural abilities to flourish social relationships are of key importance. . . where the partner is responsive to the baby's efforts, and in particular to his interests and direction of attention.'

This is a book by a thoughtful and experienced expert about the mutual support between human natures in intimate relationships, and what they need to grow strong. It tells a beautifully illustrated story of the psychology of babies and their devoted company.

*Colwyn Trevarthen, PhD, FRSEProfessor
(Emeritus) of Child Psychology and Psychobiology,
The University of Edinburgh*

About the author

Lynne Murray is currently Professor of Developmental Psychology
at the University of Reading and is Professor Extra-ordinary at
Stellenbosch University, South Africa. Before this, she studied at
Edinburgh University, and was a Research Fellow at Cambridge.
Her research, principally funded by the Medical Research Council
(UK), has focused on how social relationships influence child
development. She has a particular interest in young children's
development in the presence of difficult circumstances, for example
where mothers are depressed or anxious, where the child has a cleft
lip, or where families live in conditions of economic hardship. She
has also carried out research on how child development may be
helped by supporting parents' understanding and communication
with their child. She is the author of *The Social Baby,* and has
published almost 200 journal articles and book chapters.

To all the babies in the book

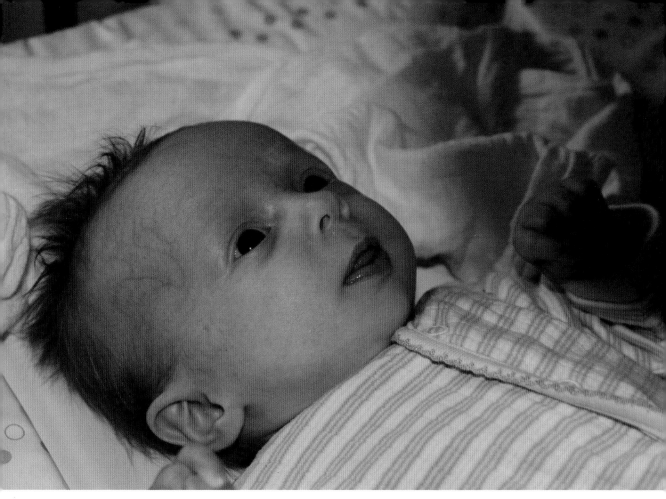

Introduction

Much of what is written about early child development either covers the first few months and deals with issues of caring, or else focuses on the developing skills of the preschool child from two to five years. My previous book, *The Social Baby*, falls into the first group and, in the context of babies' early communication skills, largely covers the main areas of caretaking that face parents through the first 3–4 months – feeding, sleeping, crying and so on. While parents and healthcare professionals who know the book have been very positive about it, I am often asked, 'Why did you stop there?' People feel they need something about development beyond this stage. This book fills the gap. It is not intended to replace *The Social Baby*, since much of the detail about understanding babies' cues in the very early stages is not duplicated here – instead it takes a much wider and longer-term look at the psychological development of babies right through their first two years and sets out how it can be supported by social relationships.

In those first two years there is particularly rapid brain growth and babies are highly sensitive to their social environment. Enormous strides are made in psychological development: this includes major advances in how babies understand other people, as well as important developments in their wider cognitive abilities, their language, and their emotional and behavioural self-control. It is also during this period that the pattern of the baby's attachments to their carers becomes established. In all these areas of development, the nature of the baby's interactions with others plays a fundamental role. The first two years is a vitally important period, since the baby's development in each

of these realms can have a profound and lasting effect on their later functioning.

This book is firmly grounded in research, and accounts of the key studies are given throughout. What distinguishes it from a standard text book, however, is that this general scientific evidence is very fully illustrated by the results of close observations of individual babies, both in everyday life and in selected experiments. The effect is livelier and I hope will help to make the scientific findings more accessible to parents as well as to clinicians or other professionals working with parents and young babies, and to students who are primarily interested in the research. In fact, the technique of taking film or video footage, and then subjecting it to frame-by-frame analysis, has a long tradition in the study of child psychology. Indeed, my very first job as a junior researcher was to sit in a darkened room (no doubt ruining my eyesight), tracing out by hand in fractions of a second, cine film projections of the arm, head and leg movements of a newborn baby as he watched a coloured ball dangling before him. The main value of this approach is that, unlike in real time when either as observers, or even more as participants, events simply flash by, the frame-by-frame unpacking of an action sequence allows us to see its natural structure in a way that might otherwise escape us. What we might treat, then, as trivial or even random baby behaviour can suddenly be revealed as something remarkable and systematic. So powerful is this technique of highlighting key moments of unfolding events, especially with a commentary to alert the viewer to critical details, that my students and clinical audiences overwhelmingly ask for presentations

like this even in preference to seeing real-time sequences, since they say it gives them unique access to the psychological experience of the baby. The principle applies no less to observations of other people's interactions with the baby: much of what we do when we engage with babies is outside our conscious awareness and, even if we do think about it, can seem merely accidental or unimportant. But once we know more about babies' processing of experiences from experimental studies, and put that knowledge together with fine-grained observations of what happens when a parent interacts with their baby, we can see that what we do intuitively is often very complex and tuned to the baby's abilities in a way that precisely supports their development.

But if parenting is done largely intuitively and in any case supports babies' development, as such observations suggest, then what is the advantage of having it spelled out for us in a book? There are three main ways in which setting out the research evidence and observations can be valuable. First, there is the simple, intrinsic fascination of learning more about the remarkable capacities of young infants – of realizing, for example, that what might seem simple 'mucking about' is actually a baby making an important discovery. As a result of such understanding, our experience and enjoyment of being with a baby can be vastly enriched. Similarly, when we understand more of what is going on and realize that babies' behaviour has its own sense and logic, it gives us a heightened respect for them; we see that their behaviour is not simple, random or passive, but that they are actively and effectively forging their own development.

The second value in a greater understanding of babies' development is that it can encourage parents to trust their intuitions, supported by knowing that what they do naturally is actually important in fostering their baby's development. In a sophisticated world, parents' intuition can all too easily be undermined. They may feel embarrassed, for example, to speak in 'baby talk', but if they understand that this style of speech has universal features that are precisely tuned to babies'

sensitivities, and that these features are important in supporting language development, then they can put such worries aside. Such knowledge affirms the immense value of what parents do, day in day out, a role that can often be devalued by wider society.

Finally, knowledge is power: if we as parents are struggling with our baby's behaviour, as we can all do at times, or are serving in the role of clinicians or other professionals who support babies and parents, then the understanding we can gain from the extensive research on child development, coupled with an attitude of careful observation as illustrated in this book, may be an invaluable support in our difficulties. And even when everything is going well, the more we understand of our baby's development, the more we are empowered to make good choices about what we do.

One of the main conclusions to arise from recent research is that some of our previous accounts of parenting need to be refined. Through the last forty years or so, the overarching theme in descriptions of good parenting has been that of 'sensitivity'. While

no one would advocate not being sensitive to their child, it is (rather like 'love') such a general term that its usefulness is limited. Instead, what has increasingly emerged from studies is that different kinds of parental responsiveness, all of which might be considered 'sensitive', are associated with different developmental outcomes in the baby, something now generally referred to as the 'specificity' of effects. Often, the same parents who are able to give 'sensitive' responses to their baby's needs in one domain of development are also 'sensitive' in other domains, but this isn't always the case. So some parents who find it easy to give good cognitive stimulation (for example, supporting the baby to tackle shape puzzles, or encouraging his interest in picture books) may feel at a loss when it comes to managing a temper tantrum, and vice versa. This variability of response in different areas of parenting is particularly common where parents are experiencing difficulties such as depression or anxiety, but can happen to anyone. For this reason, it may be helpful to think in terms of separate areas of the baby's psychological development,

non-parental care and parents sometimes worry about its effects. This chapter therefore includes the research on daycare, with detailed observations of the related attachment issues.

Chapter 3 covers one of the most challenging developmental tasks for a baby, namely to regulate and manage difficult experiences and feelings and to learn self-control. Parents' support for their baby's self-regulation and control abilities often comes into play in the course of meeting attachment needs, but challenges to the baby's emotional and physical equilibrium occur in many other contexts too. How they are dealt with is particularly important for the development of both 'externalizing problems' like aggression, and 'internalizing problems' like very shy or inhibited behaviour. This area of self-regulation and control is one where the influence of individual differences in babies' natural tendencies is particularly clear, and such differences (for example, how sensitive the baby is to stimulation and the strength of their reactions) can have a real impact on the experience of parents. Perhaps more than in any other realm of development, then, the genuinely two-way nature of the parent–infant relationship is apparent here.

The final chapter considers babies' cognitive development. 'Cognitive' refers to a range of skills, including attention, learning, and language, as well as reasoning. While these are all 'mental' abilities, what is remarkable about young babies is that their physical (or motor) activities, like reaching, touching and moving, are key elements in their cognitive development. In this area it is particularly clear that babies push their own development forward, endlessly 'practising' their skills. But as in other areas, how parents adjust to the baby's initiatives can make an important contribution to their progress. There are many ways for parents to give support, including certain forms of play, but one particularly valuable activity is regular book-sharing. This activity appears to be of specific benefit to the baby's language development and even pre-literacy skills. Sadly, not all babies, particularly those in low-income parts of the world, have access to this kind of activity,

and the associated patterns of parenting that can support each of them. So although babies' different psychological abilities are largely intertwined, this book organizes development into distinctive key areas.

The first chapter tackles a theme that is at the core of the book, that is, the baby's social development, since it is in the context of social relationships that almost all other skills are fostered. Social development and understanding are completely transformed through the first two years, from the newborn baby's basic attraction to human features, to the two-year-old's ability to cooperate with others and to understand that someone else's experience might be quite different from their own.

The second chapter deals with an area that is of central importance in the baby's development – their attachment relationships. Attachment relationships centre on the baby's need for loving care and protection, and influence their sense of security. Although relationships with parents are normally of utmost importance for babies' attachment security, those with other carers are also relevant. Many babies experience

so as it is part of the mission of this book to enable such practices, a share of the proceeds will go to our research in Khayelitsha, a peri-urban settlement in South Africa where we have our 'Baby book-sharing' project.

Child development and parent–infant relationships encompass a vast number of topics. Even a simple count of references concerning 'mother–child relationships' in psychological journals over just the last fifteen years shows that almost 1000 papers have been published. It has been necessary, therefore, to be selective. The most striking omission will perhaps be the relative absence of reference to sex differences in development. This is of course an important topic, but it is also the case that individual differences between babies of the same sex are typically far greater than differences between 'average' male and female babies, and concentrating on observation of individual babies' responses goes some way to make up for this gap. The second aspect of selection has been to focus on babies' relationships with their adult carers: thus, although mention is made of relationships with siblings, and

other children in the daycare setting, there has not been space to capture the richness of the baby's wider social contacts. Finally, and due to a dearth of evidence rather than to any selection on my part, there is relatively little coverage of the variety of cultural differences in the context of babies' development. This lack is a shameful reflection of our ethnocentrism as researchers, since we have largely worked with populations that are easy for us to access: indeed, a recent WEIRD (Western Educated Industrialized Rich and Democratic societies) index calculation showed that over 95 per cent of what we learn about psychology from scientific journals is drawn from these countries – that is, from a small, skewed fraction of the world's population. This striking imbalance is beginning to be addressed, not before time.

Please note: I have tended to use just the masculine pronoun to refer to babies in this book, for brevity – I chose not to use just the female pronoun as it might be confusing since I have to refer to the baby's mother more often than the father.

Benjamin and his granny
make a cake.

1 Social understanding and cooperation

The first two years in a child's life sees dramatic advances in social development, starting with the newborn baby's basic attraction to other people and ending with the toddler being able to understand other people's experiences, cooperate with them, and play an active part in his family culture. This progression is marked by a series of shifts, each of which is accompanied by different kinds of social engagement, as the baby's carers intuitively adapt to his increasing capacities. This chapter sets out each of these phases, along with a description of the way in which the baby's social relationships can support their development.

Getting started: the newborn period and the first month

Young babies are totally dependent on others to care for them and the nature of the care they receive can have profound and long-lasting effects on their development. It is very important, then, that babies and their carers quickly become closely connected and attached to each other and, indeed, on each side there is a natural readiness to ensure that this happens within the first few days.

The parent's part: intuitive parenting

In human mothers, the same hormones and specialized brain circuits that are active when other mammals care for their young support a kind of mental absorption with the baby that has been called 'Primary Maternal Preoccupation'. This is a specific state of mind that normally develops in late pregnancy, where the mother becomes increasingly focused on thoughts and feelings about her baby to the relative exclusion of other concerns, and it lasts through the first few postpartum months. In any other circumstances this state of absorption or preoccupation might seem almost an illness, but in the parent of a young baby, it is just what is required, as it is precisely adapted to the baby's needs and means that much of the process of caring for the baby is done intuitively.

The natural human tendency to be attracted to babies is reflected in our very basic responses, such as those we have to baby faces. Human babies, like kittens, puppies, baby seals or chicks, have a number of special 'cute' facial features, like large foreheads, big, low-set eyes and full cheeks, which draw us to them and make us want to care for them. Indeed, when we see a baby's face, a very particular pattern of brain activity, quite distinct from the response to an adult face, occurs within just a fraction of a second in the part of the brain associated with experiencing pleasure, and triggers a readiness to interact with the baby.

Where our own babies are concerned, the automatic brain responses we have to them are even stronger, and trigger other specific kinds of brain activation as well. Seeing our baby's face, for example, sets off brain reactions that overlap with those occurring when we feel romantic love, with a particularly large increase in responses linked to the experience of reward. At the same time, there is a decrease in brain activity normally associated with making social judgements and evaluations. In effect, then, where both our romantic attachments and our babies are concerned, critical thought is suspended and, indeed, 'love is blind'.

One reason why babies prompt such intense feelings of preoccupation and caring is because the parts of our brain where these automatic responses are triggered are associated with the hormone oxytocin. Oxytocin is involved in very basic elements of care-giving in all mammals, and in humans is also linked to feelings of attachment, empathy and trust. It is produced, for example, within seconds of touching or suckling a young baby or even simply seeing or hearing a baby suckle. Levels of oxytocin also increase in both mothers and fathers following affectionate contact with their babies.

The baby's part: the social brain

Just as adults are instinctively drawn to care for babies, so babies too are geared up from the start to be in relationships with other people. The wealth of research in the last ten years or so on babies' remarkable responsiveness to others, shown in specific patterns of brain activity as well as their behaviour, has led researchers to refer to them as having a 'social brain'. Again, and just as for adults, faces are an important part of this. Babies show a clear preference for looking at face-like patterns, rather than patterns with the same elements scrambled up, within just days of birth. Considering that eye-contact is one of the most powerful ways we have of communicating with someone else, it is particularly striking that newborns are especially keen on looking at faces that signal readiness for engagement with them – that is, faces with open rather than closed eyes, and faces that look directly at them rather than looking to the side.

Very young babies are also sensitive to the human voice and will turn to hear someone speak in preference to listening to a non-human sound, even if it is of the same pitch and intensity. In addition, just as newborn babies are attracted to those facial features that are cues for social contact, they are exceptionally sensitive to the special speech that adults instinctively use to communicate with them ('baby-talk', sometimes known as 'parentese' or 'Infant Directed Speech' (IDS), see Chapter 4, p. 212). Remarkably, within a few weeks, they are even sensitive to the sound of their own name being called.

As well as showing this general tendency from birth to respond to human characteristics, especially those involved in making social connections, babies very quickly start to prefer the features of the people who care for them, such as their mother's face and voice, as well as her odour; it is as though they are ready, not simply to be generally social, but to form specific, close relationships.

Newborn imitation and mirror neurons

One of the newborn's most remarkable social capacities is an ability to imitate another person's facial movements and expressions. Since the baby has never seen his own face before, imitating someone else's action – for example, sticking his tongue out – depends on his being able to match what he sees the other person do with what he feels of his own facial movement. He has to sense some fundamental equivalence with the other person, to recognize they are somehow 'like him' (see Figure 1.1a, and also Chapter 4 on cognitive development, pp. 186–93). Although rigorously conducted studies have established this ability, newborn imitation is not always obvious and is best seen under conditions that are sensitively attuned to the baby, for example, when he is in a calm, alert state, in dimmed lighting and quiet conditions. Even then, not all babies will be inclined to imitate, and parents should not try to force a response, or worry if the baby does not seem to be interested.

In recent years, research with rhesus monkeys (whose newborn infants are also able to imitate others' facial movements, see Figure 1.1b) has shown that

Figures **1.1a and 1.1b**

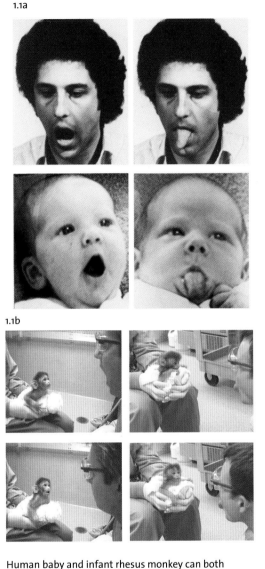

1.1a

1.1b

Human baby and infant rhesus monkey can both imitate the facial movements they see in another, even when newborn – here both are copying the human adult's mouth opening and tongue protrusion.

research shows that this automatic triggering of brain activity occurs, not just when watching or hearing the actions of others, but also when seeing or hearing their expressions of feeling. The mirror neuron system provides, then, a fundamental basis for connecting other people's experiences to our own, and for our feelings of empathy. Potentially, it plays an important part in assisting communication during early interactions and in the development of babies' social understanding.

Social interaction in the first month

In the first few weeks after birth, much parent–baby communication takes place through touching. Contact occurs throughout the day, as parents feed and bathe their baby, affectionately hold and stroke them, settle them to sleep, or soothe them if they are distressed. Although not obviously 'social', in the sense that they generally do not involve much face-to-face engagement (see picture sequence 1.1), there is nevertheless a kind of communicative exchange in these physical contacts, as parents adjust their touch to the baby's state and signals, and babies similarly adjust their behaviour in response. But even in these early days, there can be occasional opportunities for face-to-face social engagement when the baby is alert and calm. When the baby is in this state, parents intuitively tend to put themselves in his mid-line of view, at just the distance that the baby can see them clearly, and begin to talk to him. If the baby is in a comfortable position, with his head well supported, then he may start to look at the parent's face, scanning its contour or gazing at their eyes. At the point when the baby makes eye contact, parents will typically make a distinctive greeting signal, with an exaggerated facial expression and smile to affirm and encourage their baby's engagement. This greeting response to the baby's gaze is so universal and stereotyped that it is seen as belonging to what is called 'intuitive parenting'.

In these first few weeks, however, in spite of having the capacity to imitate others' facial movements, babies typically show rather little spontaneous imitation and do not take a very active social role during face-to-face

the basis for this imitative capacity is a special 'Mirror Neuron System' in the brain, whereby just the sight of someone performing an action automatically triggers in us the same brain responses that are involved when we produce the behaviour ourselves. Importantly,

1.1   Early fleeting contacts

Stanley, aged 2 weeks. In the first few weeks, babies' face-to-face social contacts are often only fleeting, and much communication is through touch. Here,

Stanley is settling to feed, but he makes brief eye-contact with his mother and seems to sense her presence as a social partner as he sucks.

1 Stanley is calm and wide awake as his mother prepares to feed him.

4 Although Stanley is busy feeding, he widens his eyes, as though also aware of his mother's voice and touch in the background.

2 He looks directly up to her face and makes eye-contact.

3 As he settles into the feed, Stanley's mother keeps up her engagement with him, talking softly, and stroking his head.

contacts. This suggests that newborns' imitation might play only a trivial role in naturally occurring face-to-face contact (a view consistent with the care and attention generally required on the part of researchers to elicit it) – its significance may lie more in what it says about the baby's fundamental capacity to link his own experience with that of others. Thus, while the baby may sometimes gaze intently at their parent's face and make tonguing and mouthing movements, these are generally somewhat formless – they are rarely responses to their parent's facial expressions and the baby seldom smiles, 'coos' or shows clear-cut, deliberate communicative bids. In turn, parents' responses during the first month are generally not socially playful; instead, they usually focus on the baby's physical experiences (like hiccupping, yawning or bringing back small amounts of

milk – known as 'posseting'), and on signs of change in their focus of interest or their emotional state (like starts of surprise or pouts reflecting discomfort). What these early face-to-face contacts do is help establish a sense of close emotional engagement and a 'conversational' setting, where the parent makes sense of their baby's expressiveness and communicates their empathy and understanding, laying the foundations for later, more obviously social, communication.

To summarize, newborn babies have a fundamental predisposition to respond to social signals, and they rapidly develop a specific attraction to their carers. This is matched by similar impulses on the part of parents, who want to engage with babies generally and their own baby in particular. Specific brain systems are active from birth, helping babies to relate to others and share their experiences. Together, these processes ensure that babies and their parents can quickly establish a close connection, and over the first month the foundations are laid for them to begin to communicate socially with each other.

The second month shift: the blossoming of Core Relatedness

From about the second month until the end of the fourth month has been called the period of 'Core Relatedness', or 'Primary Intersubjectivity'. These terms are used by specialists to reflect the purely social and emotionally intimate engagements that take place during this time, and the baby's striking drive towards and capacity for social communication. Over this period, the baby's active role in social engagement quickly picks up and the times when he is calm and alert grow longer. He will actively seek eye-contact, the length of time spent looking at his parent's face will increase and smiling starts to become clearly social. Rather than just gazing neutrally at his parent, the baby now becomes far more attentive and concentrates more; he will match the parent's expressions, and increasingly

follow his looks to them with smiles, vocalization and hand gestures, as well as the more deliberate and well-formed active mouth and tongue movements that are described as 'pre-speech' (see Figure 1.2, and picture sequence 1.2).

How the baby behaves with his parent in these engagements is now quite different from his behaviour towards objects – even including familiar dolls that are made to move responsively (see picture sequence 1.3 and Chapter 4, picture sequence 4.17). At this stage, it is common for parents to say that they notice an important change in their baby, often describing him as having become 'really human', or saying they have recognized a 'person' in their baby.

The parent's role

As the baby's interest and expressiveness during face-to-face interactions develop, so parents too become more actively engaged in supporting their baby's social engagement. Typically, the parent's gaze provides a kind of frame for the baby's attention, and the parent will only look away from their baby's face once he has broken gaze himself (see picture sequence 1.4).

Closely following the cues, and as illustrated in picture sequence 1.2 below of Stanley and his mother, parents often imitate or 'mirror' their baby's behaviour, using clear emotionally expressive signals which are often elaborations of the baby's own actions. This is particularly likely for potentially communicative behaviours, such as baby's vocalizations, smiles and clear 'pre-speech' mouth movements. As well as mirroring, parents also show facial 'marking' of their baby's signals. Unlike mirroring, these marking behaviours are not imitative, but they are nevertheless clear, expressive signals that highlight particular baby actions and affirm them (see picture sequence 1.5). Both mirroring and marking responses by the parents help to sustain the baby's involvement and enjoyment, but marking in particular is increasingly used to respond to the baby's facial movements and gestures as with a real conversational partner, giving him the space to express himself, and then making comments such

Figure **1.2**

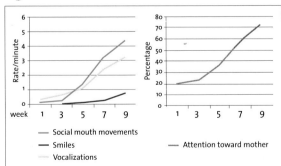

- Social mouth movements
- Smiles
- Vocalizations
- Attention toward mother

The graph on the left shows the number of times per minute babies express different social expressions over the period from 1 to 9 weeks, and the graph on the right shows the increase in the percentage time babies spend looking at their mother's face while being held in a face-to-face position for the same period.

1.2 Face-to-face interaction

Stanley, aged 9 weeks. During the second month, babies become more obviously social in face-to-face interactions. If their partner is attentive, and paces their behaviour so that it is responsive to the baby's own expressions and signals, babies will make eye-contact for sustained periods and show a wide range of communicative expressions, including active tonguing movements and shaping of their mouths, as well as smiles and vocalizations. Parents increasingly respond to these baby behaviours by mirroring their expressions, and marking them out as attempts to speak, and with each partner taking turns to be active or receptive, interactions take on a conversation-like form.

1 Stanley is very engaged with his mother, and has been making active movements of his tongue, as well as hand and arm gestures, while his mother watches attentively.

2 As Stanley's activity begins to subside, his mother mirrors back his tonguing in a clear, exaggerated form.

3 Stanley looks on, fascinated.

4 Now Stanley starts to get more active again, and it's his mother's turn to watch quietly.

5 His mother joins in with Stanley, as he opens his mouth wide . . .

6 . . . and both pause to enjoy the shared moment.

7 Then Stanley is off again, this time combining his mouthing with raising his index finger, as if making a conversational point, which his mother acknowledges.

8 As Stanley opens his mouth wide and vocalizes, his mother encourages and supports his efforts, as though he is really telling her something.

9 The two pause again and enjoy a quieter moment.

1.3 Behaviour towards objects

Astrid, aged 14 weeks. Although babies can be intently interested in objects if they are held near enough to focus on them, the quality of their attention and emotional responsiveness to them is usually quite distinct from their behaviour when they are engaged with another person.

1 Astrid is particularly attracted by her blue teddy, and she gazes at it intently as her father holds it up for her.

2 As it moves to and fro, Astrid follows it with interest, and her hands move towards it.

3 Astrid tracks the teddy with her gaze and is very absorbed, but she remains quiet and her expression is serious.

4 Astrid keeps up her concentration on the teddy for some time.

5 Eventually, her father gives her the teddy to hold. Astrid changes gear, shifting into social mode – her expression becomes animated and she shapes her mouth to communicate with her father.

as, 'Oh, I see' or 'Is that right?', as though highlighting his behaviour as significant and a real contribution to a two-way conversation. Such conversational marking responses also track the development of baby vocalizations so that, as the baby shifts from making only simple, vowel-like sounds such as 'ooo' to more complex, consonant-vowel forms like 'coo', parents become more discriminating, reserving what they treat as communications for these more advanced forms. In this way, they gradually help shape their baby's vocalizations in line with the structure of their own language.

These parental responses in face-to-face engagements, and particularly the tendency to imitate and elaborate on the baby's expressions, generally occur quite automatically. Although they might seem trivial, they support the baby's development in important ways that potentially involve the brain's mirror neuron system. The first concerns the creation of feelings of connectedness. As described on p. 9, when the baby simply watches someone make, say, a facial movement, his brain is activated in a very similar way to the activation that occurs when he performs that action himself. Similarly, when it is the baby who has performed the action first, there may be a kind of mental readiness, via the mirror neuron system, to detect the equivalent behaviour in someone else. His partner's subsequent imitation of him will therefore resonate with what he was predisposed to expect, providing a direct and immediate connection for him between his own experience and theirs. This is likely

1.4   Breaking and making eye-contact

Stanley, aged 9 weeks. Stanley and his mother are enjoying each other's company in the garden, when Stanley is distracted by the sound of a plane overhead. As is typical during interactions at this stage, it is Stanley who breaks gaze away from his mother, and she follows his look to see what it is that has caught his interest before they get back into social contact again.

1 Stanley and his mother enjoy a shared smile . . .

2 . . . and then Stanley sobers and turns as he hears the noise of a plane.

3 His mother follows to see the plane, and Stanley notices her shift in position.

4 Stanley glances up again to the where the noise came from, while his mother turns her attention back to him.

5 The engine noise has faded, and now that they are free to be social again, Stanley's expression changes back to one of bright interest, as his mother smiles at him.

6 Stanley enjoys watching as his mother starts to make a kissing sound . . .

7 . . . and they share broad smiles as she ends it.

8 Then it is Stanley's turn to take the initiative in the conversation.

1.5 Expressive 'marking'

Iris, aged 11 weeks. In early interactions, parents will often single out and highlight particular baby behaviours as being important, in what is called 'marking'. This involves very deliberate and clear facial expressions and vocalizations that convey the sense that something noteworthy has happened, and affirm what the baby has done. In this way, babies can gain a sense of the significance, or meaning, that their different behaviours have for their parents.

Here, Iris's mother encourages her daughter to copy her in sticking out her tongue during their play together. When Iris responds, her mother marks this out as something very special to be celebrated between them.

1 Iris pays close attention while her mother pushes out her tongue.

2 As Iris begins to stick her own tongue forward, her mother encourages her with a big smile and a look of anticipation.

3 Iris's tongue protrusion becomes stronger, and when her tongue is fully out, her mother 'marks' her daughter's achievement by flashing her eyebrows, nodding, smiling and saying 'oooh', all in combination.

4 Then Iris's mother follows through at the end of the tongue protrusion to praise her daughter again, and they both show their enjoyment at what they have shared.

to help forge close, intimate links between the two of them, as is evident from babies' tendency to stay engaged for longer and show more enjoyment when they are imitated compared to when engagement is active, but not imitative. These same mirroring parental responses have also been thought to help the baby develop a solid and coherent 'sense of self', or 'core self', as his own initiatives are affirmed by what his parent does.

Finally, because parents' mirroring responses often build on and elaborate the baby's original behaviour – for instance, they may add an eyebrow flash and an expressive sound to their imitation of the baby's mouth opening – the baby's experience of the links between his own and his partner's action is accordingly enriched. In the parent's more elaborate responses, the manner of their expression, especially the intensity and emotional tone, carries important cues about what significance they give to the baby's behaviour. For example, their response might communicate feelings of sympathy if they see the baby's expression as reflecting discomfort, or feelings of pride at seeing an early smile. Through this process the baby can start to become attuned to the meaning his actions have in his relationship with his parents.

Different styles of interaction and other early 'meaning-making'

Research has shown the universality of many features of parent–baby relationships, but there is also considerable variability. So although responsiveness to the baby is common across different cultures, not all parents respond to the same baby behaviours and nor do they all respond in the same kinds of way. What the parent responds to and how they do it is likely to vary according to particular cultural values, as well as individual characteristics. Some cultures (for example, the US and many North European countries) greatly value babies' independence. These parents tend to use the high levels of facial and vocal expressiveness described above to respond to and imitate their babies' signals in face-to-face play, and this style of responsiveness has been found to predict earlier signs of self-awareness in the baby (that is, they learn to recognize themselves in a mirror, see pp. 44–8). Others (for example, in Japan and some rural African societies) place much more value on babies' affiliation and compliance, and on sharing and cohesiveness within the society. These parents, although similarly responsive to their babies, may pick up on different baby cues, and

Figure 1.3a

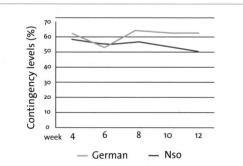

This graph shows the levels of contingent (that is, immediate) responses of parents in two different cultures, one in rural Africa (the Nso), the other German, to babies' vocalizations during the first 3 months. Even though the two cultures differ from each other in the style of their responses, their level of contingent responsiveness to the babies is very similar.

Figure 1.3b

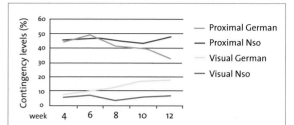

The Nso and German parents show very similar levels of close physical (proximal) responses to their babies' vocal expressions at first, and the two cultures are also similar to each other in the amount of visual contact they make with their babies at four weeks. But as time goes on, the way the two groups respond to their babies begins to diverge. Nso mothers continue to use close physical responses, whereas these begin to drop off in the German group. By contrast, visual responses remain constant in Nso mothers, but increase in those from Germany. The babies' own behaviour develops according to the type of contingent responsiveness of their parents to their cues – for example, German babies seem to increasingly imitate their mothers' smiles during face-to-face interactions over the first 3 months, but the Nso babies do not.

are more likely to use close physical contact to respond to them, perhaps kissing, or rhythmically patting them, but showing far less vocal and facial imitation (see Figures 1.3a left and 1.3b above). In turn, babies' own behaviour during interactions in those cultures develops in different ways: one study comparing Nso mothers and babies (a rural society in the Cameroon) with those in Germany, for example, found that most of the German babies increasingly imitated their mothers' smiles during face-to-face interactions over the first three months, a pattern that did not occur in the Nso babies (see Figure 1.3b).

Even within one culture, there is considerable variability in the way parents respond to their baby's social signals, and such differences are also likely to reflect parents' individual feelings and values, and the meaning they attribute to their baby's behaviour.

For example, some parents might particularly enjoy their baby's exuberance and mirror or mark out his excited smiles in an intensified way, encouraging his expressiveness; others in the same situation might feel their baby is becoming overexcited, so they respond in a more muted fashion in an effort to dampen down his responses. In each case, the baby's experience of what it is like to smile with another person, akin to a basic sense of the 'meaning' of the event, will be markedly different. Individual babies will then respond in their own way to their parents' reactions, so that unique patterns of mutual responsiveness are gradually built up between parent and baby which become more predictable and settled over time.

The baby's growing social sensitivity

During this period of the second to fourth month, as the baby matures and gains experience, he becomes more sensitized to the nature of face-to-face interactions. Experimental studies show that babies are increasingly affected by abnormal or unexpected behaviour on the part of their social partner. For example, if their parent stops interacting normally and suddenly becomes silent and unresponsive while still looking at them, babies will react with protest and mild distress. They also fail to show their normal smiles if the sequence of steps in a familiar game, like 'Peek-a

boo', is changed, or if the adult ends the game with an inappropriate emotion (for example, looking sad, angry or fearful). By contrast, when more natural changes in contact occur as, for example, when the adult simply turns away to talk to someone, or to look at something nearby, the baby is unperturbed, and generally watches with quiet, positive interest (see two stills from picture sequence 1.6 and also Chapters 3 and 4 for examples of babies' responses to the unnatural behaviour of their partner and, by contrast, sequence 1.7). In abnormal and normal changes to social contacts, then, the baby processes cues about his partner's direction of attention and the changes in their social and emotional expressions, and he responds in a way that appears emotionally and socially appropriate.

As well as becoming more discriminating in relation to such social cues in general over the first four months, the baby also grows increasingly attuned to the particular style of his parents' interactions. If he has been used, for example, to his parent being highly responsive to him during social interactions, then he will be more sensitive to differences in other people's responsiveness than babies who have not had this experience. Further, babies generally prefer the style of responsiveness they are used to and will engage more with people whose behaviour is similar to that of their parents. Over time, as the pattern of

1.6   The face-to-face 'still-face' experiment

William, aged 11 weeks. Two- to three-month-old babies are highly sensitive to the way their partner behaves in a social interaction. This is vividly illustrated in experimental studies in which the parent is asked briefly to stop responding and instead adopt a still, or blank, face – the baby's behaviour changes almost immediately.

1 Normal interaction.

2 Mother's 'still face'.

1.7 A natural interruption

Astrid, aged 14 weeks. Parents cannot always be engaged with their babies and other agendas regularly take over. Within the first three to four months, babies seem to have a sense of what is a natural, as opposed to an unnatural, break in contact from their parents.

Here, Astrid's mother receives a call which she needs to attend to. While Astrid looks on, her mother talks to her friend, and as she does so her behaviour and emotional expression change. Astrid is quite unperturbed by this natural interruption and quietly watches her mother. None of the protests, bids for contact, or withdrawal, occur that are seen in more unnatural breaks. Nevertheless, as soon as her mother finishes her call, Astrid becomes animated and signals her readiness to engage again.

1 Astrid and her mother have been playing, when a call comes through that her mother needs to take.

2 As she starts the conversation with her friend, Astrid's mother warmly smiles at her daughter, as though reassuring her that she will still be aware of her presence.

3 Now Astrid's mother needs to concentrate, as arrangements have to be made: she turns away and her face sobers. Astrid continues to look on, one hand opening out in her mother's direction.

4 Astrid still watches quietly, as her mother thinks about the time that will be needed for her friend to reach them …

6 As Astrid sees her mother turn back to her, she immediately raises her arms in greeting, and is keen to play again.

5 . … and then her mother winds up the call.

interaction between baby and parent becomes more predictable and settled, it begins to transfer to the way he interacts with others. In turn, the style of responding that the baby has developed will influence the way other people respond to him, so that they may find themselves unconsciously drifting towards the parent's way of interacting in order to engage the baby effectively. It is as though the baby's way of experiencing social interactions is gradually 'sculpted' and refined in line with his family's own style of expressiveness, and becomes part of how he engages with the world in general.

By the time the baby is four months old he has become a sophisticated social partner: he is highly motivated to engage socially with others, is sensitive to the quality of his partner's engagement, and has a rich repertoire of gestures, and vocal and facial expressions that he uses actively and appropriately in face-to-face communication. With this solid basis for social understanding now in place, the baby's developmental agenda shifts, and with it, the nature of the social interactions that take place.

Four to five months: moving into the wider world and Topic-based Relatedness

At around three to four months, babies' visual acuity improves dramatically. Whereas previously they were able to see objects clearly in focus around 22–30cm away (the distance at which people naturally place their faces), a baby's vision by this time is approximately the same as an adult's, and by four and a half months marked improvements occur in the baby's ability

1.8   Play, with a topic

Astrid, aged 4.5 months. Around 3–4 months, when the baby's gaze to distant objects and his reaching and grasping improves, the nature of social interactions changes. Instead of the earlier face-to-face engagements, when communication is about just 'being together', play typically has some topic – sometimes a toy, or the parent making a funny sound to entertain the baby or, quite often, body games. These tend to involve a predictable sequence of actions that the parent performs on the baby's body, finishing with a climax that the baby becomes able to anticipate.

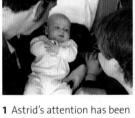

2 She starts to play a tickling game that they have by now enjoyed many times before, and Astrid's look brightens.

1 Astrid's attention has been caught by her mother, as she approaches and greets her daughter.

3 As her mother's tickling fingers advance towards her neck, Astrid becomes more animated, anticipating what will happen next.

4 She squirms with excitement and pleasure as her mother tickles her, shutting her eyes at the climax . . .

5 . . . and then sharing a smile with her mother.

to reach out and grasp things. In line with these advances, the baby's interests and motives during social engagements change, and spurred on by these developments parents find different techniques to communicate with them. Babies cease, for example, to engage in the same high level of eye-contact with their parent, and will enjoy looking around, perhaps becoming absorbed in exploring something within reach, like a strap on their chair, or gazing at something at a distance that has caught their attention. Parents adapt to this change in several ways – for example, by developing body games, often with a musical, rhythmic structure and a climactic end point that focuses on some part of the baby's body (such as 'Round and round the garden' or 'Pat-a-cake'), or by bringing objects into play, or even by making a playful 'object' of some

Figure 1.4

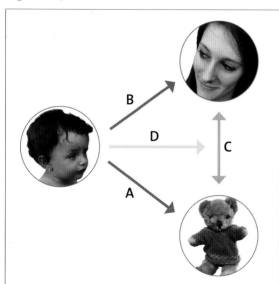

Connected-up relatedness. At around 9–10 months, babies start to integrate their different experiences in new ways: thus, their interest in the world (path A), their ability to communicate (path B), and their knowledge of others' experience of the world (path C) all become connected up (path D). Having done this, the baby can then, for example, deliberately signal to his parent that he wants them to get him the teddy that is out of reach.

action, perhaps using a stylized noise like blowing a raspberry to entertain the baby (see picture sequence 1.8 and sequences 3.5 and 4.18 in Chapters 3 and 4). Communication has now expanded from the 'core relatedness' or 'primary intersubjective' experience of just being together and sharing feelings and expressiveness, to the inclusion of some separate focus or topic.

Moving from Topic-based to nine-month Connected-up Relatedness

A striking feature of the baby's growing interest in play that has a topic, such as a toy, is that the remarkable social communication seen during early face-to-face interactions is not integrated in any obvious way into this new kind of activity. For example, if the five-month-old baby wants his teddy and it is out of reach, he will simply express his desire for it, perhaps leaning out towards it, looking at it intently and grunting with effort, and anyone else present will be left to read his cues and act on them. What he does not do at this phase is to look directly at the other person and actively signal to them that he wants them to help get his teddy for him.

This last kind of behaviour generally does not start to emerge until around 9–10 months, and represents an important shift in social development as the baby moves into a stage of more connected-up communication (known to professionals as the 'Joint Attention' or 'Secondary Intersubjectivity' phase). As well as his core communication skills and his developing competence in the physical world, making this shift requires two other important developments: first, the baby needs to develop greater understanding of other people's experience of the world (in this example, that the adult could reach across to the teddy); and second, he needs to be able to connect up others' experience of the world with his own (that is, he needs to recognize that the adult could help him by passing him what he wants, and be able to communicate this to them) (see Figure 1.4 and picture sequence 1.9).

Other signs of this key developmental shift to a more connected-up social understanding include the baby's

1.9   The shift to more connected-up understanding

Ben, aged 10 months. Around this time, babies start to join up their different skills and experiences in new ways, also showing a growing awareness of other people's take on the world and of how this connects with their own experience.

Here, in a classic example of this development, Ben shows his mother that he would like her to get his tractor for him.

1 Ben's mother is busy getting a spoonful of food ready for him when he spots his toy tractor on a shelf nearby.

2 Ben's keen to have his tractor, and he shapes his hand and fingers into a kind of reach or point towards it. Younger babies might also do this when they want something, with the adult being left to pick up on their cues and fetch the baby what he wants.

3 Now, though, Ben shows his new, more connected-up, understanding – he turns deliberately to his mother and directly requests her to reach it for him with his expression.

4 His mother responds, reaching across as Ben stretches towards it again.

5 Ben's mother places the tractor on the table so that he can see it easily as he eats.

6 Ben is delighted – his communication to his mother has worked, and he can enjoy his meal with one of his favourite toys nearby.

taking a more reciprocal role in his play with others – he will, for example, start to pass things to and fro, or perhaps take the role previously played only by his parent in a game of peek-a-boo (see picture sequences 1.10 and 1.11).

1.10   Giving and sharing

Benjamin, aged 10 months. One aspect of the shift to more connected understanding is when the baby begins wanting to give things to others. This linking up of their own activity with someone else's experience, and sharing awareness of what is happening, seems to bring them great satisfaction and enjoyment. Here, Benjamin has discovered the joys of giving, and wastes no opportunity to practise this new way of relating with his father and his great-granny.

1 Benjamin has been having a drink of water, watched over by great-granny, when his father joins them. Benjamin immediately holds out his bottle to his father …

2 …and, as his father gratefully accepts it, Benjamin looks very pleased.

3 Benjamin's father gives the bottle back, and suggests that great-granny might like a turn too.

4 Benjamin can easily follow his father's suggestion now, and he readily turns to great-granny, offering her a drink as well.

5 Great-granny is also pleased to be offered the bottle, and Benjamin seems to relish this giving game …

6 …banging his hands on the table as his father applauds him for being kind …

7 …and then enjoying sharing clapping himself with great-granny.

1.11   Reciprocal play

Ben, aged 12 months. The kind of 'connected-up' understanding that babies have developed by around 10 months is also shown in the way they take a more reciprocal part in playing. Before this stage, it is normally parents who set the scene for a game and orchestrate the moves, but now babies begin to take on the same roles as their playmate and show greater awareness of the other person's experience. Here, Ben has just finished his lunch and his mother uses the cloth she had for wiping up to start a game of peek-a-boo. Ben becomes very involved and, with his mother's support, takes on the different roles of the game himself, and contributes creatively to the unfolding action.

1.11   **Reciprocal play** continued

1 Ben watches closely as his mother hides her face from him.

2 He stays very concentrated as she reveals herself and says 'boo'.

3 Ben's mother marks the end of the sequence with a smile, while Ben looks down at the cloth.

4 Now Ben reaches across for the cloth …

5 … and begins to hide his own face, his mother shifting a little to one side to help achieve the 'hidden' effect for him.

6 Ben's fully engaged in hiding now, and his mother supports the game structure with a big, anticipatory 'aaahh' …

7 … before sharing the 'boo' with a delighted Ben.

8 Now Ben passes the cloth over to his mother, inviting her to hide again …

9 … and the two enjoy another round.

10 'Boo!'

11 Ben's mother hides herself again …

12 … and now Ben varies the game, and starts to pull the cloth away …

13 … to reveal his mother waiting for him …

14 … and they share the hilarity of her reappearance.

1.12   Sharing interests

Ben, aged 13 months. One sign that the baby is developing a shared understanding of the world and knows something about other people's attention and interest, is the act of pointing. Pointing can be done in several ways – the baby can point to show his partner that he wants something (sometimes called an 'imperative' point), or it can be used to draw his partner's attention to something interesting (a 'declarative' point). Pointing can be used to help give another person information, say by showing them where something is that they are looking for. It can also be used simply to share experiences, and this kind of pointing typically continues beyond the moment when the baby has attracted his partner's attention to the object or event of interest.

Here, Ben points at a poster on the wall in order to direct his mother's attention and then enjoys a game, playing at monkeys with her.

1 Ben wants to draw his mother's attention to a poster of animals on the wall behind her, and gives a clear point to where she should look.

2 As Ben's mother follows his signal and turns to the poster, Ben continues pointing, and starts to make the sound he uses for the monkey's call.

3 His mother joins in the pointing, as well as the 'whooping' noise the monkey makes.

4 Ben is delighted; he carries on pointing and joins in with more whooping.

5 Just sharing such simple activities with someone now gives Ben immense pleasure and fun.

At this same stage, the baby will also begin to follow others' suggestions and cooperate more effectively with them (see too Chapter 3, picture sequence 3.9, Ben wiping up spilt milk). He will also look to his parent's face when he is uncertain about what is going on as though seeking information from them to guide him (see also Chapter 3 on referencing, pp. 148–9) and, at least by one year, he will often point to draw his partner's attention to something interesting that he wants to share with them (see picture sequence 1.12). Alongside these new changes in social understanding, the baby's awareness of more emotional aspects of his relationships is developing, reflected in behaviour such as 'separation anxiety' or 'stranger fear' (see Chapter 2 on attachment), and what has been called the 'capacity for concern' – that is, when the baby may show comforting behaviour towards someone else.

How Connected-up Relatedness develops 1: babies' implicit understanding of other people

Developing a sense of the connections between one's own experience and other people's, as described above, is fundamental to mature, social understanding; yet how babies get to this point is not entirely understood. Unlike the social understanding of older children, which can largely be discerned from what they say, babies' developing understanding of other people is generally not expressed explicitly. This means that it often needs quite sensitive methods to be revealed, such as measuring subtle signs of the baby's attention (see text box A), or their brain responses as they process different events. In fact, studies using methods like these have shown us that the very beginnings of the baby's understanding of others' experience of the world are in place as early as the first two to three months. So before babies can see well at a distance or focus clearly on what someone else is looking at, they already show a basic readiness to respond to others' experience of their surroundings, turning, for example, in the same general direction when their social partner turns. It is as though the baby is geared up from very early on to share his experience with others. This action of turning to see exactly what it is that someone is attending to steadily develops and becomes more precise over the following year. Thus, during the first four to six months babies need objects to be quite close, readily visible, and in an uncluttered, simple setting in order to follow someone's gaze to them; whereas by the end of the first year they can follow someone's gaze in more complex conditions, and will look to distant objects that are far to the side of their line of view (see picture sequence 1.13).

As well as detecting other people's simple interest, babies also start to grasp their desires and their goals from the way they look and behave. Within the first

A Measuring signs of interest and understanding through eye movement

Human eye movements, compared to those of other creatures, are particularly good at showing what we are interested in, since the whites of our eyes are relatively large and contrast sharply with the dark of our irises. Thus when we turn our eyes to look at something it is very obvious, with the movement acting as a kind of pointer so that others can see what it is we are attending to, and one way babies can try to find out what someone is interested in is by following their line of gaze.

Many studies make precise recordings of the baby's eye movements while he watches someone either looking at objects and events, or performing different actions in relation to them (such as grasping, pointing or reaching out to them). Two kinds of eye movement are particularly useful for showing how the baby understands others' behaviour and, in particular, their goals or intentions. These are, first, 'anticipatory looks', where the baby's gaze darts ahead to the place where he expects someone's action will finish, and second, 'violation of expectation' looks, where the baby looks for longer than usual in order to process something that he did not expect to see.

6–10 months, for example, the baby's gaze will dart ahead in anticipation of where someone's action (like reaching out to something) will finish, as though he realizes what the end point of the action is. Similarly, babies will seem surprised if they see someone showing an interest in one object (looking at it or pointing to it), and then apparently changing their goal by picking up and holding a different object. Within this period, babies also start to be able to tell the difference between an event that is caused deliberately, and a very similar one happening accidentally. They will respond differently, for example, to someone 'accidentally'

1.13   Gaze following

Iris, aged 14 months. The fact that babies want to share their experience with others is seen in their following the direction of someone else's gaze, as well as their pointing. The nearer the object of the other person's attention, and the more striking it is, the more likely it is that the baby will turn to look at it. Babies are also more likely to follow someone's attention if the other person engages with them socially, and signals their interest.

Here, Iris sits on her mother's lap, while the researcher greets her and then turns first one way then the other, to look at two attractive toys placed on either side of the table.

1 The researcher catches Iris's interest, making eye-contact and smiling. Iris immediately pays close attention.

2 The researcher turns to one side and looks at the red car while Iris happily watches.

3 Now Iris turns herself to see what the researcher was looking at.

4 Iris then turns back, and looks to the researcher's face again.

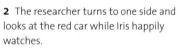

5 Now the researcher turns in the other direction to look at the second toy.

6 Iris, too, turns, to see what the new object of the researcher's interest is.

dropping a toy they want, as opposed to moving it out of their reach. They even seem to realize that different people might have different goals and intentions.

Importantly, much of the baby's understanding of the intentions behind what other people do develops in line with his ability to do the same things himself. Thus, once babies start to grab hold of things, or begin pointing, they become able to see the goal of others' grasping and pointing; when they can crawl themselves, they can anticipate another crawling baby's path of movement; and once they are able to achieve their own goals in a 'planful' way (for example, knowing that if they pull a cloth on which there is a toy that they want, this will bring the toy within their reach), they are able to see the plan in someone else's behaviour. The baby's own experience, then, of actively engaging with his environment and increasing the scope of what he can do, feeds directly into his growing understanding of similar behaviour in others. What also needs to be put in place, though, for full 'connected-up relatedness' is a more active linking of his own experience of the world with his knowledge of how others experience it too (see link D in Figure 1.4, p. 20). An important way for this further element to be developed is through particular types of play and social interaction.

How Connected-up Relatedness develops 2: the role of social interaction

Supporting a shared interest As noted above, at the point when the baby's interest in pure face-to-face play begins to wane, around 3–4 months, parents intuitively adjust by shifting the form of their engagement. The techniques they now start using to engage their baby – following his focus of interest in other things and bringing them into play, or using body games – all effectively create a shared focus, or topic, and (critically for the development of 'connected-up relatedness' or Secondary Intersubjectivity) they can strengthen the baby's awareness of a link between his own interest in something and actions involving that thing done by another person. His awareness of these links can also be increased by particular kinds of parental expressiveness in play. One of these is sometimes known as 'motionese'. This is an action equivalent of 'baby talk', where different physical phases of play are highlighted through the timing and intensity of communication. Motionese is often used in nursery rhymes such as 'Round and round the garden', or 'Pat-a-cake', where the rhythmical movements and musical quality make the topic clear for the baby and easy to share. When the baby's own actions or body parts are the focus of play, this offers another opportunity for him to develop his self-awareness, as well as linking his actions to his playmate's (see picture sequence 1.14).

One other notable feature of parents' communication with their baby during interactions that have a topic, is

called the 'ostensive' quality, where distinct facial and vocal cues are used to show, or teach, the baby about the world. This behaviour is rather similar to the clear 'marking' expressions that parents use in earlier face-to-face interactions when they single out and emphasize some aspect of the baby's own communication for comment (see p.11 and again picture sequence 1.5 above of Iris's mother marking her daughter's tongue protrusion). In this case, however, the 'ostensive marking' alerts the baby to the fact that something else of potential importance is going on, and it engages him emotionally, making it easier for him to follow the adult's further cues to the topic of interest (see picture sequence 1.15).

Younger babies seem to gain particular benefit from such ostensive signals. Three- to six-month-olds, for example, orient themselves more quickly, and are more likely to follow someone shifting their gaze, or their point to an object, if the adult first establishes eye-contact with them and greets them in an enthusiastic 'baby talk' voice, or flashes their eyebrows and smiles at them, as though signalling that something interesting is about to happen. In addition, exactly how babies respond to things around them reveals their sensitivity to others' interest in those same things: four- to nine-month-olds, for example, show more efficient brain processing of an object if they have seen someone else look in its direction beforehand, while by one year, just the physical presence of someone who previously gazed at an object, but is no longer doing so, causes the baby to pay more attention to it. Finally, social connections also affect babies' memory: for example, if an adult makes eye-contact with the baby and smiles at him, the baby will be more likely to recognize that person's face later on.

In other words, babies do not simply register their environment according to its physical features, rather, their response to the world is enriched by connecting up with someone else and sharing their experience. Indeed, research tracking babies' development from the early months shows that parents' support for the baby's interests in the form of such expressive ostensive

1.14   Coordinating body movements

Saavan, aged 6.5 months. Body games become more frequent from 4 to 5 months as babies start to lose interest in simple face-to-face interactions and parents find themselves having to use new techniques to engage them. Saavan and his mother have developed a routine of 'stretching up and standing', after Saavan has had his nappy changed.

Saavan is now very familiar with this game, and anticipates each step. At this point, his mother can play around with the precise timing of her moves with small variations to make the game more interesting for Saavan and to give him practice in reading his mother's intentions and in coordinating his own actions with hers.

1 Saavan is already anticipating the game he plays with his mother after being changed, reaching up his arms to her as she finishes dressing him.

2 Saavan is keen to get going, looking up to his mother's face with excitement as she signals her preparations to lift him.

3 Saavan's mother cheers to mark out his effort in standing right up.

4 Saavan has a clear sense of what comes next, and his mother pauses to watch him as he takes the initiative to move on to the next step and prepares to lower himself.

5 This round of the game is over, and both Saavan and his mother share a quiet moment to mark the transition.

6 Then they both signal their readiness for another round, and the game continues.

marking and teaching is particularly valuable in fostering the kind of connected-up social understanding that emerges at around nine to ten months.

Coordinating actions In many body games, the baby's and adult's actions need to be closely coupled for the game to work, and as the baby gets used to particular routines parents typically create moments when they play around with the baby's anticipation just when the climax is imminent, establishing, and then reinforcing the baby's awareness of the common goal and their parent's intentions (see again picture sequence 1.14,

1.15 'Ostensive marking'

Isabel, aged 9 months. Babies can be helped to understand someone else's goals and interests in relation to particular objects or events by the adult using 'ostensive marking'. This means establishing the baby's interest and then giving clear signals at key points of the action – the signals can be a combination of different forms of expressiveness, such as eyebrow flashes, smiles, gasping or breath holding, and vocalizations that all help to mark out the connections between events and the important moments. This behaviour is a kind of 'teaching' about the social meaning of what is happening and it assists the baby in making sense of his world.

1 Isabel is enjoying chewing on a rusk; her mother is preparing some fruit juice for her and holds up the piece of melon she is peeling for Isabel to see, explaining what she is doing.

2 She shows Isabel what the melon looks like once it is peeled.

3 Now she cuts the melon slice into smaller pieces, giving a running commentary to her daughter on what is happening – Isabel is fascinated and watches intently throughout.

4 Isabel's mother holds up a piece of the cut melon and suggests Isabel might like to try it.

5 She passes it over, and Isabel explores the feel of it.

6 Now Isabel's mother shows her that she needs to put the cup under the spout of the juicer.

7 As she moves to press the button and start the fruit going through, Isabel's mother signals that this next part is going to be really interesting.

8 As the machine whirrs away and the juice starts to pour out, Isabel's mother marks what's happening with strong signs of excitement.

9 Now Isabel's mother shows her daughter the final stage of the juice making, pouring the juice into Isabel's bottle, so that Isabel can have a clear sense of each step.

where Saavan is stretching up). Aside from play, the everyday, repeated, caretaking activities like getting dressed or having a nappy change also present opportunities for the baby to gain an implicit sense of how his actions and his parent's need to be coordinated towards a common goal in order to get the job done smoothly (see picture sequence 1.16). In effect, and without even being aware of it, parents provide their

1.16   Coordinating actions

Iris, aged 12 months. Everyday routines, like getting dressed, seem very simple on the surface, but actually give babies important opportunities for reading their parent's intentions and coordinating their own behaviour with the parent's actions.

Here, Iris's mother removes her daughter's top while Iris plays with a ball. Iris is very used to having her clothes removed by her mother, so she can smoothly adjust to the sequence of moves, holding on to her ball throughout, in an early form of cooperation.

1 Iris looks up to her mother's face, as her mother begins to slip off her sleeve, holding on to her ball with her other hand.

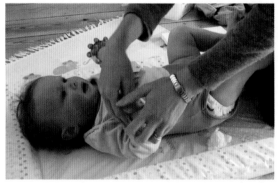

2 Now her right hand has become free, Iris uses it to grasp the ball.

3 She is very familiar with this routine, and takes the ball in her right hand to leave her left hand free for her mother.

4 Now her mother can easily remove Iris's other sleeve.

5 Iris makes these adjustments to her mother undressing her very smoothly and without any obvious effort.

6 With both hands free, she holds her ball comfortably between them.

7 Iris looks up to her mother to share a smile as her top is finally removed.

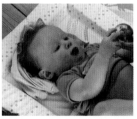

8 Then she turns back to enjoy exploring her ball, while her mother moves on to the next step of changing her clothes.

baby with constant rehearsals of experiences that support his development of connected-up relating.

Social interactions with three or more While one-to-one contacts play a central role in the development of social understanding, babies' social interactions very often take place with at least two other people present. Studies of these engagements, known to specialists as 'triadic', and generally involving the baby and both his parents, show that they play a key part in the baby's developing awareness of other people's intentions and relationships with the wider world. A three- or four-month-old baby will, for example, look to and fro between his parents, alternately watching and making emotionally expressive bids to join in, as though he understands their state of engagement and is genuinely sharing in the interaction. Interestingly, this kind of behaviour in the baby is more common when the parents themselves have a harmonious relationship (see picture sequence 1.17).

Even if one of the adults sits back and stops actively engaging, the baby seems to sense their continuing potential involvement and will still glance over to them, as though interested in their response and welcoming their inclusion in the triad. Parents can take advantage of the fact that the baby's interests now extend beyond one-to-one play by constructing more active triadic games, including complex sequences of anticipation and surprise. When he is sensitively supported by his parents, such play can bring particularly rich opportunities for the baby to experience the ebb and flow of others' intentions, and join them up with his own (see picture sequence 1.17).

The baby puts himself in the picture during social interactions As well as the contribution that parents make to their baby's social understanding, babies generate experiences themselves that connect up their own attention and interests with those of others, and they creatively play around with their own actions as a topic of shared interest. From their earliest interactions, as the baby's partner watches him and responds to

1.17   Three is company – triadic interactions 1

Astrid, aged 4.5 months. Babies can take an active part in developing their awareness of other people's interests and experience, and the connections between them, through early 'triadic' interactions – that is, with not just one, but two other people.

Here, Astrid has just enjoyed the high point of a tickling game with her mother, but she seems to be aware of her father's presence and his potential involvement as well, and she seeks to share her experience with both her parents.

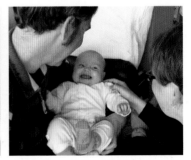

1 Astrid squeals with pleasure as her mother reaches the climax of the tickling game she has been playing.

2 Now she turns directly to look at her father, seeming to want him to share in the pleasure of the game as well.

3 Then she turns back again to include her mother once more.

1.17   Triadic interactions 2

Saavan, aged 6.5 months. Saavan enjoys a game of peek-a-boo with his father, while his mother is supporting his sense of anticipation and his pleasure in the game's highpoints.

1 Saavan's mother leans him over to peep beyond the door, letting Saavan know that his father is just about to emerge from the other side.

2 Saavan laughs, as his father pops his head round with a 'boo'.

3 Saavan has become very excited, and he briefly turns away as his father disappears again.

4 Saavan's mother prepares him for the next round, leaning Saavan away for a moment, and matching his father's withdrawal behind the door ...

5 ... before swinging him back into place to greet his father as he emerges again, while marking out this highpoint clearly for him with her own enthusiasm.

6 Saavan's pleasure increases as his father engages with him, while his mother enjoys watching the effect the game has.

his signals, he has the experience of being a focus of others' attention and shows a kind of awareness of this in his response. This typically occurs when someone starts or renews social contact by greeting the baby and smiling. At such moments, even two-month-old babies can show very similar behaviour to that of older children and adults when they are being 'coy' – half turning away with a slight smile and downturned gaze, and lifting an arm to the face, as though feeling self-conscious as attention is turned on them. Initially, such behaviour seems automatic, but as it is very engaging and adults respond positively, over time babies will use this coy display in a more playful, deliberate fashion, inviting attention.

The baby develops other behaviours, too, that support his growing awareness of himself as a focus of others' interest. Thus, just as adults use their own actions with the baby as a topic to share (see above p. 27), the six- to seven-month-old baby begins to develop a repertoire of his own party tricks and uses them in increasingly complex ways to negotiate his social interactions. Often, they start as slightly unusual, sometimes unintended movements that have perhaps evoked a parent's comment or response, like wagging his head or making funny sounds, but then the baby begins to use such actions deliberately to gain the adult's attention. A little later, around eight months, the baby can not only get others' attention, but he also starts to manipulate it by 'showing off', and even uses his clowning behaviour to win their approval, appreciation or amusement (see picture sequence 1.18).

By 9–10 months, the baby has gained considerable physical mastery of his environment and is reaching and grabbing, manipulating objects, and often crawling. Building on his fundamental capacity for communication, and supported in his interactions with others, he has also become able to grasp the essentials of other people's engagement with the environment, and to coordinate these with his own experiences. This achievement of more connected-up relatedness, or Secondary Intersubjectivity, has moved the baby a long way in his social development, and he now has a solid foundation for a fuller social understanding and cooperation with others.

1.18   Party tricks

Benjamin, aged 10 months. Benjamin has developed a party trick of 'head leaning' that he now does regularly in his play with others. He uses this special action to draw people into his games and to share a topic of interest with them. Here he plays it out with his father and great-granny.

1 Great-granny is giving Benjamin his food …

2 … when his father arrives. Benjamin greets him delightedly …

3 … and immediately launches into his new game of leaning over.

4 Ben's father joins in as Ben completes his trick.

1.18   **Party tricks** continued

5 Now Benjamin turns to great-granny to see if she wants to play too.

6 He starts to lean over again, and his great-granny follows on.

The second year: developing a 'bird's eye view' and Cooperative Relatedness

Although the skills shown by babies at 9–10 months represent a real advance in their social understanding, further key abilities still await development. These mainly involve coordinating different perspectives on the world, so that the baby can take more of a 'bird's eye view' and see things more objectively, and such abilities are also very important for his cognitive development (see Chapter 4). Later in childhood, the same skills extend to the ability to think about and reflect on one's own experience as a separate topic in itself, and similarly to reflect on other people's desires, knowledge and beliefs about the world, and how they might differ from one's own. These later skills are generally referred to as having a 'Theory of Mind', and without such understanding, a fully cooperative social life with others would be impossible.

Until relatively recently, many psychologists considered that the child's ability to appreciate that another person could hold a belief about the world that differs from what the child himself knows to be true (that is, that the other person could hold a 'false belief'), was achieved only at around 4 years of age – the age when children start to give correct answers to questions about other people's 'false beliefs' (see text box B

B **Theory of Mind and False Belief in older children**

Researchers often use 'False Belief' tasks to assess children of around 3–4 years for their ability to understand others' experiences and beliefs. In these tasks, the child is asked to predict what someone is going to do, based on that person's false belief about a situation. Typically, the child will be shown a scene with various props and two characters, for example a teddy and a doll. Then the teddy places an object in, say, a red box, closes the box and leaves the scene. In the teddy's absence, the doll removes the object, and then puts it away in a different place, say, a cupboard. When asked where the teddy will look for the object when he comes back, three-year-olds usually say that he will look in the cupboard, because that is where the child himself knows the object to be. Three-year-olds' answers, then, do not account for the fact that the teddy cannot know that the object is in the cupboard, and that he would believe, falsely, that it is still in the red box. Older children do take the teddy's false belief into account and correctly predict that he will look in the box.

for details of false belief understanding in children). However, this view is changing, and studies now show that within the first two years the baby not only becomes able to grasp important elements of others' experience, but towards the end of this period he has an intuitive sense of the fact that others may have different experiences from his own, including having 'false beliefs' about the world. In babies, of course, these skills are not expressed explicitly, such as in spoken answers to questions about what other people believe. Nevertheless, carefully designed experiments and detailed observation of babies' spontaneous interactions with others, show the period up to about two years to be marked by strikingly creative and rich behaviour that reflects an impressive, but still largely intuitive, understanding of others' contrasting perspectives, as well as a more objective take on his own experience. This intuitive understanding is very important too, since it predicts the Theory of Mind ability that will be held by the older child.

Signs of developing a bird's eye view and the capacity for Cooperative Relatedness

Teasing From around 9–10 months, babies play around and more actively experiment with the connections between their own and other people's experiences. They also begin to treat other people's mental states as special topics in themselves. One way the baby does this is to manipulate his partner through teasing and, by 11 months, this behaviour is common. The kernel of such play involves the baby deliberately setting up an expectation in his partner and then playfully violating it. For example, he might begin to pass them something, clearly inviting his partner to take it, but just at the point where they are poised to do so the baby will whip it away and laugh mercilessly at their partner's pretended surprise or disappointment (see Ben teasing, in picture sequences 1.19–1.21). Such sequences often get turned into routine games that the baby will repeat tirelessly, over and over again. Their success depends entirely on their partner entering into the spirit of the game, ideally showing mock shock or amazement. These responses make it clear to the baby that his partner's expectations have been thwarted and indeed, his having provoked such feelings is the high point and goal of his play. But the 'mock' element of the response also lets the baby know that his partner's disappointment is not real, and reinforces the collaborative spirit of the game (see also p. 55 for more on the role of pretend expressions).

1.19   Teasing 1

Ben, aged 11 months. When babies tease other people they show their awareness that the other person's experience is a topic of interest and something that can be manipulated. Ben starts to tease his father from around 11 months, using the same format repeatedly for many more months. The essence of the game is to set up an expectation in his father that Ben will give him something, but just as his father shows that he is keen to have it Ben tricks him by removing it. Essential to such games is the collaboration between the baby and his partner, with the adult typically giving clear signals in the form of pretend shock expressions, that their disappointment is not serious.

1 Ben has been looking at his picture book, and he passes it up to his father.

2 Ben's father reaches across and takes the book …

1.19 **Teasing 1** continued

3 ...and, having looked at it, he hands it back to Ben.

4 Ben swaps hands and offers the book to his father again.

5 But this time, as his father reaches out for it, Ben whips it away, watching his father's reaction ...

6 ...and Ben really laughs at his father's surprise.

1.20 **Teasing 2**

Ben, aged 14 months.

1 Ben is finishing his snack of tomatoes and reaches for the last one.

2 He offers it to his father.

3 Ben waits until his father has almost grasped the tomato ...

4 ...and then quickly withdraws his hand to eat it himself. His father stages an expression of mock shock and disappointment ...

5 ...and this sends Ben into peals of laughter.

1.21   Teasing 3

Ben, aged 23 months.

1 Ben's father has asked for a taste of Ben's broccoli, and Ben holds it out for him …

2 …but before his father has had a chance to reach out for it, Ben has whipped it away, and is laughing at his father's feigned surprise.

3 On this occasion, just the merest hint of his father's intention and disappointment are enough to have Ben in fits of laughter.

4 Ben starts the game up again, seeming to offer another taste to his father.

5 Now, his father carries over some of his 'mock' disbelief, pretending that, this time, he seriously wants some broccoli – but Ben stands his ground.

6 His father's apparent outrage again sends Ben into peals of laughter …

7 …and they both enjoy the joke.

Deception Aside from teasing, another way that babies will show their awareness of links between their own experience and that of other people is through deception. This can be playful as, for example, when the baby hides from a partner (see picture sequences 1.22 and 1.23 of Iris at 14 and 18 months), but it also happens when the baby wants to have something or do something that his partner might not want.

Before the end of the first year, this second kind of deception is usually passive, as when the baby, seemingly aware that what he wants to do will cause his parent to be cross, will wait until they are out of the room before doing it (see picture sequence 1.24).

1.22   Hiding 1

Iris, aged 14 months. Hiding from someone is a common way for babies to play around with other people's experiences and develop their awareness of the fact that others can have different perspectives from their own. The age when they start to enjoy such play is also the time when ideas about the physical world and the nature of the existence of objects begin to develop (see Chapter 4). As with teasing (see above), the fun of hiding games relies heavily on the collaboration of a partner – their exaggerated displays of puzzlement as to the baby's whereabouts during the hide, and surprise when the baby is revealed, are essential ingredients.

1 Iris has become keen on using her mother's jersey for her hiding game, and she gets ready to play.

2 Iris signals to her mother with an impish look that she is about to hide.

3 As soon as Iris has hidden, her mother joins in the game, asking 'Where's Iris, where can she be?' . . .

4 . . . and then, to Iris's great delight, shows her surprise and amazement when Iris reveals herself.

5 It is a game that can be endlessly repeated, and Iris has another go.

6 Again, her mother mimes puzzlement, wondering where Iris can have gone.

7 Iris enjoys surprising her mother with her reappearance.

1.23   Hiding 2

Iris, aged 18 months.

1 Iris now seems to know that if she stands behind her mother, her mother won't know where she is, even though Iris can see her, and her mother reinforces this message by wondering out loud where Iris is.

2 Iris enjoys her mother's puzzlement, but perhaps she wants to be found as well, or at least be close to her mother, and she comes up to touch her.

3 Iris watches her mother's face with its mixture of delight and surprise when she turns to see Iris.

4 Her mother talks to Iris about how she had wondered where Iris was, and Iris can now enjoy her mother's pleasure in finding her …

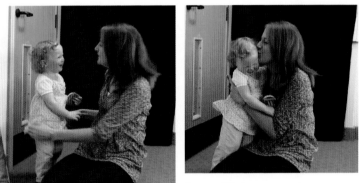

5 … and their warm reunion.

As the baby's awareness of others' perspectives develops, his attempts at deceit become more sophisticated and may involve actively concealing things from his partner, and even using distraction and trickery (see picture sequences 1.25 and 1.26). One technique commonly reported by parents is when the baby tries to distract them while he attempts to get something he is not meant to have. This often takes the form of him establishing eye-contact with the parent, and actively holding their gaze so that they do not look at what his hands are meanwhile doing. Over time, the baby's deception gradually extends to take account of other people being the focus of disapproval, rather than just himself – so by the time he is 18 months old, if he overhears someone else being reprimanded for doing something, he will refrain from doing that same thing himself as long as he knows the person who did the telling off can see him, but he will do it if they are looking the other way. Such strategies reflect quite sophisticated social understanding, since they involve the baby's deliberate efforts to manipulate other people's perspectives on his own behaviour. They reflect the baby's growing capacity to see his own behaviour more objectively, as others might see it, and to know that another person's take on the world can be different from his own.

1.24   Awareness of being naughty

Ben, aged 14 months. Ben is developing a sense of what it is to be naughty. Parents' disapproval of actions that give the baby great enjoyment can be valuable opportunities for babies to realize that another person may hold a different attitude from their own, which helps to develop their social understanding.

1 In a quiet moment when his mother is busy with other chores, Ben discovers the clothes rack, and tries to pull a pair of pants onto his head.

2 As this doesn't work, he starts to put them back on the rack …

3 … but it's tricky, and they fall off. Ben is quite interested in this, and it seems to prompt a good idea.

4 He gets another item from the rack …

5 … and drops it down too.

6 Next he flings down a sock with abandon …

7 … followed by another one.

8 Then he hears his mother say 'Ben, what are you doing?', and seems aware that what he had enjoyed so much might be something he shouldn't have done.

9 Ben crouches down, as if trying to hide from his mother's disapproval.

1.25   Concealing 'naughty' behaviour

Ben, aged 17 months. As the baby gains more experience of what his family's values are, he becomes able to anticipate their reactions to 'naughty' behaviour, and may try to do things he really wants to do secretly if his parent is likely to disapprove of them. This may, in part, reflect a simple wish to avoid the unpleasantness of a reprimand, but it can also reinforce his sense of there being different perspectives on events, and of his own possibilities for manipulating others' experience.

1 Ben's father sets him up to eat his lunch.

2 A little later, amidst a considerable amount of food on his table, Ben notices that some of it has fallen into his bib, and explores it with interest.

3 He seems to be aware that this is something his father might not like, and darts a glance over to check.

4 Ben's father seems not to have noticed, so now Ben deliberately spoons more food into his bib . . .

5 . . . checking again, as though to make sure all is still clear.

6 Ben enjoys putting more food in his bib . . .

7 . . . but checks once more to see if his father is looking.

8 This time, his father has seen what's going on, and he comes over to encourage Ben to eat properly.

9 Ben has a go . . .

1.25 Concealing 'naughty' behaviour continued

10 …but then the temptation of filling the bib takes over.

11 Ben looks across to his father again.

12 This time, his father notices immediately, and more firmly explains that this is not the way to treat his food.

14 This time, the food goes where it should, but Ben still keeps a watchful eye on his father.

13 Ben tackles his lunch again..

1.26 Strategic manipulations

Benjamin and Isabel, twins aged 20 months. One of the advantages of understanding another's person's experience is that it can help one get out of difficult situations. Benjamin and Isabel have just had a bath and finished their milk and they are about to go to bed with their 'clothies'. But they have accidentally been given the wrong ones. Isabel doesn't mind too much which one she has, but Benjamin has become very attached to one clothy in particular that has a rigid edging. He seems to realize that to get the one he wants, Isabel will have to give up the one she was given, and to make her do this, he'll need to make sure she has a substitute.

1 Benjamin looks a bit perturbed when he sees his sister with his favourite clothy.

1.26   **Strategic manipulations** continued

2 His first impulse is to stretch across to take it from her, but it's a bit too far for him to reach.

3 He looks intently at the one he has been given …

4 …and offers it to Isabel, as though realizing that if she accepts the one he's passing to her, he will get the one he wants.

5 Their father has noticed what's going on, and helps the swap, as Benjamin keeps a close eye on his clothy …

6 …and he seems relieved to have it at last.

7 Benjamin settles down to find the special edge that he likes to feel when he's tired, while Isabel plays with her own clothy.

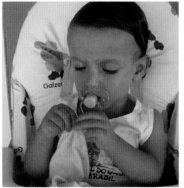

8 Benjamin begins to look dreamy as he fingers the rim of his clothy …

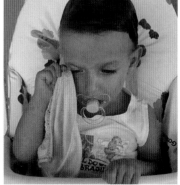

9 …and then, as he always does, he lifts it up to the side of his face to help himself finally settle.

Mirror recognition At the same time as these more complex deceptive strategies emerge, the baby is developing related behaviours that also reflect an increasing ability to see himself more objectively. A key sign is that he now learns to recognize himself in a mirror. Before one year, babies enjoy looking at their reflection, but will typically treat it as another baby and respond with smiling, curiosity and playfulness (see picture sequence 1.27).

As time goes on, however, the baby may also begin to look a little puzzled when he sees the mirror baby, perhaps searching behind the mirror, as though sensing that this is not an ordinary play situation. Such behaviour is typically followed, around 15–18 months, by responses that suggest more self-awareness as, for example, when the baby looks at his image with apparent admiration (see picture sequence 1.28).

1.27 Play with mirrors 1

Benjamin, aged nearly 10 months, is playing early one morning with his twin sister, Isabel. A duvet has been spread out across the stone floor and they find a mirror stand against the wall.

1 The babies are having fun crawling around. Benjamin discovers the mirror stand and pulls himself up to look at it.

2 He seems to treat his reflection as another baby, greeting and smiling at him.

3 Now he moves forward to give the mirror baby a kiss.

4 He performs one of his new 'party tricks' of blowing raspberries.

5 Then he turns back to play with his sister. Although one cannot know for sure that Benjamin doesn't recognize himself, there is nothing in his behaviour to suggest that his response is anything other than playful.

1.28   Play with mirrors 2: self-recognition

Ben, aged 17 months. Ben is having a snack on the kitchen floor at home, and he reacts to the reflective surface of the oven door as a mirror, in a way that shows his developing self-awareness.

1 Ben is busy having a snack on the kitchen floor.

2 As he is eating, he catches sight of his reflection in the oven door and points to it, as at an object of interest.

3 Now he begins a series of poses, as though trying out the idea that his actions might also be shown in the mirror.

5 …and now does something that looks like a real experiment – he starts to remove his bib, watching in the mirror carefully as he does so…

4 He takes a long hard look…

6 …then pulling the bib down into a different position.

7 Now he puts his bib back on, all the time keeping a close eye on his reflection.

1.28   **Play with mirrors 2: self-recognition** continued

8 Ben's father has noticed what's happening, and offers Ben a hat that he likes to use for dressing up.

9 Ben tries it on, still looking in the mirror.

10 And in another experiment, he watches the reflection as he lifts up the hat ...

11 ... and then lowers it again.

12 He seems to like what he sees and also to have discovered something important – he shouts out to his father to share it with him.

The classic test of whether or not the baby actually sees the reflection as himself is called the 'rouge test', where someone makes a mark on the baby's face, usually the tip of his nose, and then, having briefly distracted him, shows him a mirror. Before 15 months the baby usually shows no sign that he sees the mirror-image face with the mark as being his own, but from this age onward the baby will increasingly show signs of self-recognition, touching his nose as he looks at the image, saying his name, or pointing to himself. By two years almost all babies appear to recognize themselves

(see picture sequences 1.29 and 1.30). Interestingly, the development of the baby's ability to recognize himself in a mirror goes hand in hand with another sign that he sees himself more objectively – he will begin to use the pronouns 'me', 'my' and 'mine'.

Separating out the 'whys' and 'whats' and seeing sense
Babies have a strong impulse to imitate other people (see Chapter 4 on cognitive development) and, as they become more aware of people's goals and desires, their imitation changes accordingly, reflecting their new

1.29   The 'rouge' test 1

Iris, aged 14 months. Iris is in the research lab, where the 'rouge test' is used to see whether she recognizes her reflection as herself.

1 Iris's mother sets up the 'rouge test', making a red mark on the tip of her daughter's nose, as Iris plays in the research lab.

2 Iris notices the mirror on the wall behind her mother, and crawls over to it.

3 She pulls herself up and stands, placing her hand against the mirror.

4 Iris kisses the mirror baby.

5 She looks at her reflection, but shows no sign of self-recognition.

6 Indeed, she behaves as though there might be another baby behind the mirror, stretching up on tiptoe to look.

7 Not finding anything there, Iris loses interest and moves away to explore the toys.

1.30   The 'rouge test' 2

Iris, aged 18 months. Iris is back in the research lab where the 'rouge test' is repeated, and this time she clearly recognizes herself in the mirror.

1 Iris's mother has again marked the tip of her daughter's nose with some rouge. After some play, Iris spots the mirror and approaches it with interest.

2 Her response is quite different from last time, and she shows the classic sign of self-recognition, immediately touching her own nose.

3 She turns round to show her mother the mark, clearly understanding that it is her own reflection in the mirror.

social understanding. For instance, if the 18-month-old sees someone about to pull a toy barbell apart, but their hands slip and they fail, the baby will imitate what was intended and will proceed to successfully separate the parts of the toy, rather than copying the accidental behaviour (see Chapter 4, pp. 186–7 and picture sequence 4.11 of Iris's imitation). In this particular example of the barbell, the adult's goal is tightly coupled to their actual behaviour, with the effort to separate the parts of the toy being clearly evident in their facial expression and movements. In other cases, though, the adult's intention may be rather obscure, not connected in such a direct way to behaviour, and then the baby's job of identifying it is more challenging. Nevertheless, babies of 14 months can master some situations of this kind, and will imitate highly unusual or odd behaviours, so long as these behaviours seem to make sense (see text box C). Here, then, the baby is getting right behind the surface of what someone does and grasping that their purpose is something separate that can be decoupled from their actions.

Understanding contrasting perspectives From the end of the first year, the baby's growing tendency to treat the mental states of other people as topics of interest, and his developing awareness of himself shown in mirror recognition, is matched by his increasing understanding that his own experience can differ from that of others. As we have seen, the baby's growing sense of this difference is evident in the ever more sophisticated techniques he uses to deceive others. But other developments in his understanding go even further, requiring the baby to be able to see another's perspective in such an objective way that, when they consider it, they can put their own, contrasting, experience to one side. This ability can be seen, for example, in relation to likes and dislikes. So, whereas young babies do not make a distinction between their own and other people's tastes, if someone shows a baby of 14 months that they love a food that he himself strongly dislikes (say, broccoli or grapefruit), and that they also dislike one of the baby's favourite foods (say, biscuits), the baby will take the difference in tastes on board, and appropriately offer his partner their preferred food (see picture sequence 1.31).

C Rational understanding – imitation of unusual actions

In a pair of classic studies, two groups of babies each watch one of two rather unusual actions. In the first, an adult who is seated in front of a table with a light box on it, leans over and touches the top of the box with their forehead to make the light come on, their hands lying idly at their side. Here, then, it seems as though the adult must deliberately intend to make the light work in this particular way, since there is no other apparent reason for their odd behaviour.

In the other case, babies see the same head-touching-box action, but this time the behaviour is made to seem a necessary consequence of the situation, since the adult's hands are not idle but are holding a blanket around their shoulders, as though to keep warm. Unlike the first case, then, there isn't any implication here that the adult specifically wants to turn the light on with a head movement – it's just that this is the way they need to do it, because their hands are occupied.

The two groups of babies' behaviour was compared one week later, when they were placed at the table in front of the same light box themselves. This showed that babies in the first group turn the light on by imitating the head touch, presumably inferring that this is the sensible thing to do to make the light work, whereas those in the second group turn on the light by using their hands, presumably because they have realized that the head touch isn't an essential part of the light mechanism.

1.31   Awareness of others' experience

Iris, aged 18 months. In a classic experiment, babies of this age show awareness that other people's experience can be different from their own. The mother shows the baby two kinds of food – one that she knows the baby strongly dislikes and the other that she knows the baby likes a lot. She demonstrates that her own likes and dislikes are quite the opposite, and then asks the baby to give her something to eat. Young babies behave as though they don't distinguish their own experience from the other person's and will offer what they like themselves, but by 18 months, this is changing.

Here, Iris and her mother replicate this experiment using grapefruit vs. biscuits, and Iris clearly shows that she knows her mother's taste is different from her own.

1 Iris's mother shows two plates of food – grapefruit and biscuits. Grapefruit is something she knows Iris dislikes, while she also knows her daughter is very keen on biscuits.

2 Iris's mother picks up a piece of grapefruit.

1.31   **Awareness of others' experience** continued

3 She makes noises of pleasurable anticipation as she lifts it to her mouth, while Iris pays close attention.

4 'Mmm, delicious,' her mother says, with obvious lip-smacking noises.

5 Then Iris's mother tries a biscuit . . .

6 . . . and again Iris looks on attentively as her mother begins to eat it, in this case, with a frown.

7 'Oh, yuk,' her mother says, 'that's horrible,' with a clear grimace.

8 Iris's mother pushes the two plates towards her daughter.

9 Then she holds out her hands and asks Iris if she can have something to eat (not saying what she wants), and Iris immediately reaches for the grapefruit . . .

10 . . . and passes a piece to her mother.

11 'Mmm, yum,' her mother says . . .

12 . . . and asks for more to eat. Iris goes for the grapefruit again . . .

1.31   **Awareness of others' experience** continued

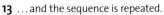

13 …and the sequence is repeated.

14 Her mother steadily eats the grapefruit pieces Iris provides…

15 …and soon there is just one left.

16 It's passed over too…

17 …and Iris's mother consumes it with relish.

18 Now what? As her mother asks for something to eat again, Iris's hand hovers over the biscuits…

19 …but then she checks back to the now empty grapefruit plate.

20 Iris looks flummoxed, and turns questioningly to her mother.

21 Her mother asks again if there's anything for her to eat and Iris's hand moves towards the biscuits again.

22 She seems just about to pick one up, but then changes her mind…

1.31   **Awareness of others' experience** continued

23 …and her hand shifts again to the empty grapefruit plate, as though she clearly knows that her mother would not want Iris's own favourite food.

24 Iris lifts the empty grapefruit plate to show it to her mother. Her mother resolves her daughter's difficult dilemma, reassuring her that actually she's had plenty to eat and that Iris need not worry any more.

At around the same age, when babies become very keen to be actively helpful, the particular conditions in which they give that help can be revealing about how they understand others' experience. Some of the helping behaviour is relatively straightforward and reflects babies' awareness that someone might simply lack knowledge. For example, if they watch someone 'accidentally' drop something they need or distractedly misplace it, and the person then appears puzzled, saying 'Hmm, that's strange . . . ' one-year-olds will readily point out the object for them. Over the next few months, however, babies' helping starts to reflect not only their understanding of other people's ignorance, but also the fact that another person's belief can actually be wrong. For example, if the baby is aware that someone last saw an object in one place and then, in their absence, the object is moved to a different place, the baby will show, in both his looking and his helping, that he understands that the other person believes something different from what the baby himself knows to be true – that is, he suspends his own perspective and understands the other's 'false belief' about the object's location. From one year to 18 months, the baby's understanding of the differences between his own and someone else's beliefs becomes increasingly complex. It extends beyond understanding another's false belief about an object's location, as just described,

to their false beliefs based on misleading appearances, and eventually to false beliefs based on confusions about the identity of things which may look exactly the same on the surface, but which differ in some hidden way.

Some of the developments in these abilities come about as babies' own experience of the world expands, and some experts have considered that they are influenced by important changes in brain development concerned with self-control and being able to hold back normal impulses (see more about this in Chapter 3, p. 142). This is clearly particularly relevant to 'false belief' situations where the baby has to put aside what he himself knows to be true, as well as to situations like the 'broccoli/biscuit' (or grapefruit/biscuit, as in our picture sequence) task described above. Further brain developments of this kind may also be important in explaining why it is that much older children have difficulties with the same kinds of problems when their responses are judged, not by what they do (like the helping and looking responses used in studies of babies), but by their being able to given spoken answers to false-belief questions, where a further layer of self-reflection and inhibition is involved. Nevertheless, alongside the way a growing maturity drives these developments, research also shows that the baby's social relationships play a significant part in fostering such skills.

The role of social interactions

Just as particular types of social experience support the development of babies' connected-up relatedness skills around 9–10 months, so other slightly different kinds of interaction can help in the continuing development of their more objective social understanding and cooperation. In particular, this is important for the baby's ability (described above) to disentangle someone's goals, desires and beliefs from their surface behaviour, and to grasp the fact that his own experience can be different from that of others.

Pretend play and conflicts   Pretend play, with its fundamental contrast between the imagined and the real, is particularly relevant to the developments in social understanding that take place through the second year. Indeed, it is no coincidence that babies with more complex pretend play show earlier mirror-self recognition. Babies increasingly engage in pretend play from around 12 months, and by 18 months they readily act out pretend scenes in which one object 'stands for' something else – using a coloured wooden brick, for example, as a sandwich to feed a teddy. By the age of two, such play is in full swing (see picture sequences 1.32 and 1.33).

1.32   Joint pretend play

Iris, aged 18 months. Pretend play is an important way in which babies can think about other people's experiences and the contrast between appearances and reality. As this kind of play is getting underway, it can be much richer and more helpful for later developments in social understanding if the baby is supported by a partner.

Here, Iris has come to the university research lab with her mother, and they play together at making food and feeding the teddy.

1 Iris has been playing with the pots and pans and toy food with her mother, and they are pretending to cook a toy sausage. Her mother talks about whether it is hot enough yet.

2 Iris takes the sausage out of the pan with her mother's help and they prepare to check whether it is cooked.

3 Iris lifts the sausage to her mouth, and looks directly to her mother to gauge her response as she pretends to test it, and they both make 'blowing' noises as though it is now hot.

4 Now the sausage cooking has finished, Iris looks interested in a toy banana. Her mother notices and passes the plate to her.

1.32   **Joint pretend play** continued

5 Iris's mother suggests to Iris that the teddy might like some banana . . .

6 . . . and Iris stretches over to pretend to feed him.

7 Iris takes the pretend feeding very seriously, carefully holding the banana in place, while her mother talks to her about how much teddy likes it.

8 Now Iris offers her mother the banana, and her mother thanks her and pretends to eat it.

1.33   **Solitary pretend play**

Ben, aged 24 months. Ben is playing with his Action Man figures. Drawing on his own experience, he enacts a nappy change for them, lining up wipes and cleaning them before trying to put their nappies on. It's not completely straightforward, but Ben constructively adapts his play to the situation.

1 Ben gets organized in the bathroom, getting baby wipes at the ready and lining up his Action Men.

2 He pulls a wipe from its packet . . .

3 . . . and cleans up the first man.

1.33   **Solitary pretend play** continued

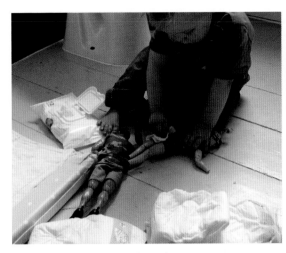

4 Now the second man is cleaned.

5 The next step is to put on the nappies.

6 It's very tricky when they are so large for the toy men.

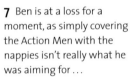

7 Ben is at a loss for a moment, as simply covering the Action Men with the nappies isn't really what he was aiming for . . .

8 . . . then he finds a solution, deciding that wrapping a nappy around each figure will be fine . . .

9 . . . and proudly shows his father what he has done.

Strikingly, the nature of the baby's pretending is much enriched if it is done together with someone else, whether an adult, older sibling or another baby. Furthermore, frequent social, as opposed to solitary, pretend play is significant as a predictor of children's later 'Theory of Mind' understanding and other perspective-taking skills. Parents typically use pretend play a great deal from the time their baby is one year old, and when they do so they stage a number of cues for the baby to help him appreciate the distinction between what is real and what is pretend. For example, they often make silly, exaggerated expressions and smile, and look to the baby's face more frequently

with longer, 'knowing' looks, as though checking that the baby has grasped the idea that the play is 'just' pretend. Other techniques parents frequently use to help the baby understand the real/pretend distinction are deliberate disruptions in the way the event is being enacted – for example, when pretending to eat a biscuit using a brick, the parent will typically bring the brick near to, but not actually touching, their mouth.

One form of pretend play that may be especially helpful in developing babies' abilities to see other people's different perspectives and cooperate with them is 'role play'. This is not just because of the nature of the play itself, but also because of the kinds of negotiations that typically take place in the run-up to it, where different roles and their associated actions and feelings are worked out. This kind of play is particularly likely between babies and their older siblings, who can support and structure the baby's experience (see picture sequence 1.34). Strikingly, research has also shown that the occurrence of conflict between babies and their siblings is predictive of a better understanding in Theory of Mind tasks (see picture sequence 1.35). This link is probably due to a similar process to the one involved in negotiating roles for pretend play, with conflicts pushing the baby to become aware that others can have very different perspectives from his own.

Conversations Developing language is an important reflection of the baby's ability to separate out signs and symbols from the real things and events that they refer to (see Chapter 4 on book-sharing for more on this topic). However, with regard to the development of social understanding and cooperation, it is not only the general ability to understand and use words themselves that helps. Rather, research has shown that specific kinds of talking with babies is important – not surprisingly, where parents talk to their babies about feelings and about the reasons for behaviour, the babies show better understanding of other people's feelings and perspectives in later childhood. How well-attuned and sensitive parents' talk is to the baby's experience is also key – where the baby's own feelings and intentions are accurately identified and responded to when parents talk to them, the more likely it is that babies will come to understand others' experiences, too, and behave in socially positive ways (see Chapter 2 on attachment for more on this topic).

Opportunities for cooperative projects As noted already, from towards the end of the first year babies generally start to enjoy getting involved in projects and actively joining in and helping (see picture sequence 1.36). Of course, this can mean that getting a job done takes the parent a good deal longer than if they simply did it themselves, but doing things together can be enormously enriching and enjoyable for the baby, and where parents are able and willing to do it such cooperative activities in infancy are a strong predictor of the child's later good adjustment and positive social behaviour (see Chapter 3 on self-regulation and control). Aside from the emotional satisfaction the baby can gain from helping, the long-term benefit may come about because it requires him to coordinate his actions with those of a partner and work towards a shared goal, thus increasing his awareness of another's perspectives and experience.

Performing useful routine tasks together is also something that gives the baby a sense of sharing values and wider goals. Through the second year babies are quick to pick up on conventional signs and symbols of these shared meanings and enjoy rehearsing them with others, actively taking their own part in their family's culture (see picture sequence 1.37).

1.34   Role play

Ben, aged 27 months, with his brother, Joe. Siblings often enact pretend play that involves negotiating different roles, and these are perfect opportunities for babies and toddlers to understand other people's experiences and perspectives. Here Ben and his brother play doctors.

1 Ben's brother, Joe, dressed in his doctor's coat, lifts Ben up on to the bed to examine him.

Role play continued

2 Ben says that his throat is very sore, an experience that he is familiar with.

3 Joe leans over to put the stethoscope to Ben's throat.

4 And Ben then opens his mouth wide so that Joe can shine the torch into it.

5 The bad news is that Ben has to have his tongue removed. Joe performs the operation very carefully, with Ben being a cooperative patient.

6 Now the doctor tells Ben that he will put in a new tongue and Ben waits at the ready.

7 The new tongue is inserted, and Ben's throat recovers.

8 Now it's Ben's turn to be the doctor.

9 He puts on his stethoscope, and tells his patient to get on to the bed.

By two years, babies have made great strides in social understanding, and they can perform the kinds of mental gymnastics that help them appreciate that others can have different experiences from their own. This gives them a range of new skills such as playing tricks and deceiving others and, more importantly, they are able to cooperate with others. While many kinds of engagement with babies help these developments, finding opportunities for babies to share in joint ventures, and engaging in pretend play and conversations with them about what people feel, and why they behave as they do, are particularly helpful.

1.35   Sibling conflict

Ben, aged 17 months. Brothers and sisters commonly squabble and fight: these experiences clearly let the baby know that other people can have different takes on the world from their own and can contribute something to the baby's social understanding that is not always provided by harmonious interactions.

1 Ben is busy drawing when his older brother, Joe, comes along.

2 Joe has his own idea of what to do with these drawings and moves in front of Ben, taking the pencil to show him.

3 Ben doesn't seem too bothered at first, and takes off his hat while Joe sketches.

4 But before Joe has finished with his plan, Ben wants to take back control.

5 The two tussle over the book, each with a very different goal …

6 … and Ben tries to pull his brother away as Joe begins to tear out the page.

7 Ben is outraged!

10 … and Ben adds his own design. The episode has given Ben direct experience of a clash of wills, but his brother's intervention has also shown him a different way of approaching things.

8 But as Joe folds up the paper and tells Ben what his plan is, Ben calms down a little and watches.

9 Joe gives the page back to Ben, now shaped as an aeroplane …

1.36   Cooperating in a project

Max, aged 19 months. Through their second year, babies increasingly enjoy helping and taking part in joint projects. Being involved in a task with someone else from beginning to end can support the baby's understanding of the overarching reasons for other people's behaviour, and also helps him take on board the wider social values of his family and their culture.

1 Max finds his father in the garden picking currants. His father asks him if he'd like to help …

2 …and shows him how to find the currants hidden behind the leaves.

3 Max stretches out to pick some …

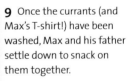

4 …and carefully places them in the bowl.

5 When the pair have gathered a good quantity, they both decide they should stop.

6 Max gazes down at his harvest …

7 …and proudly carries the bowl over to show his mother. She praises Max's hard work …

9 Once the currants (and Max's T-shirt!) have been washed, Max and his father settle down to snack on them together.

8 …rewarding him with a kiss.

1.37   Family culture

Ben, aged 18 months, with his family. As babies' social understanding develops through the second year, they become increasingly aware of the shared meanings and values in their family, and look for opportunities to express their own role in the family culture. In Ben's family, evening mealtimes are an important opportunity for everyone to come together around the kitchen table and share their experiences. Ben has recently become keen on connecting with his parents and brother through saying 'Cheers' to them.

1 Ben's father holds up his glass and calls 'Cheers' to Ben.

2 Ben responds with enthusiasm right away . . .

3 . . . and then looks across to his mother and invites her to do the same.

4 Ben's mother leans over to join him in 'Cheers'.

5 Now Ben turns to his brother, Joe, and wants him to join in as well.

6 Joe does 'Cheers' too . . .

7 . . . and then Ben gets ready for another round.

Summary of Chapter 1

Babies are geared up from birth to be social: they seek out human contact and are highly sensitive to how others communicate with them. Over the first two years, in tandem with developments in their cognitive and physical skills, the way in which babies relate to other people changes (see Table 1 for a schedule of these developmental shifts). Parents, and even other children, intuitively respond to these shifts and alter their behaviour accordingly. Although what parents do as they engage with babies might appear very ordinary, the subtle adjustments they make are nevertheless precisely adapted to the baby's growing social understanding, and they serve to support his development and help him eventually take his place in his wider community.

Table 1.1 Shifts in social relationships in babies through the first two years

Age at shift and phase	Nature of social relationships
Newborn/first month Attraction to people	Attraction to eyes, voice, maternal odour. Relatedness mainly through holding and touch.
2 months Core relatedness	Babies are highly motivated to respond socially; they sustain eye-contact, and show active social behaviours (e.g. smiles, vocalizations, gestures), and face-to-face interactions are close and emotionally expressive.
4–5 months Topic-based relatedness	Babies' vision improves and they begin to reach and grab things. Their interest shifts away from pure face-to-face contacts to focus on a topic. Interactions involve play with objects and body games.
9–10 months Connected-up relatedness	Babies connect up their interests in the world with their communication skills, and they communicate directly with others about their shared interests. Interactions involve joint, more reciprocal play.
18 months Cooperative relatedness	Babies recognize themselves in mirrors and understand that others' experiences can be different from their own. The distinction between real and pretend is well established. Social interactions can be genuinely cooperative and organized around shared goals and cultural values.

Iris needs her mother's steadying hand.

2 Attachment

One of the most important aspects of a baby's development is their attachment to those who care for them. Babies' attachment relationships are similar to their other emotional bonds with particular individuals, but special in that they centre around the baby's emotional and physical vulnerability and dependency – their need for protection, support and loving comfort from others. Attachment relationships differ, then, from those that may also be close but where issues of the baby's vulnerability and dependency do not apply – for instance in relationships with other children, which focus more on social playfulness.

The importance of a child's attachment relationships for their well-being and future development was first highlighted in 1952 by John Bowlby, who had studied the effects on young children of being separated from their parents during wartime evacuation, and the disrupted family backgrounds of children who became persistent delinquents. Together with evidence of how hospitalized babies reacted to what was in those days enforced separation from their parents, Bowlby's work provided the impetus for many studies into babies' and young children's attachments, as well as for improvements in policy regarding babies' care. Notably, these early findings on babies and young children chimed with results of research on rhesus monkeys, showing the importance for their emotional well-being, too, of providing close support and comfort, as well as basic physical care. With these findings in mind, Bowlby and other attachment researchers argued that an infant's (whether human or non-human primate) attachment relationship to their parent or other carer was of wide, evolutionary importance, because when such a relationship was in place it would help protect the infant from danger and ultimately help to ensure their survival.

Over the years, a number of core themes have emerged in attachment research. They include:

- the nature of babies' attachments – in particular the distinction between relationships that are secure and those that are insecure
- the influences on babies' security – in particular what kinds of care-giving lead to secure attachment
- the influences on parents' ability to provide care that promotes secure baby attachment
- the longer-term effects of early attachment relationships on child development

The nature of babies' attachment relationships

Typically, a baby will develop just a small number of attachment relationships. The main attachments are usually to their parents and other close family members who regularly care for them, such as grandparents, but attachment relationships may also develop between babies and professionals who are closely involved in their care. In this section, for brevity I have used the term 'parent', but that should be taken to stand for the baby's attachment figures in general.

Before we go on, it is important to note that not all aspects of care-giving are attachment-related, even in relationships that are strongly focused on the baby's attachment needs. Parents or other carers

2.1   Feeling ill

Babies' attachment needs vary according to the challenges present and how they feel at the time. When feeling ill or tired, for example, there is more need for close contact and comfort from an attachment figure, while the impulse to explore the environment and be independent is reduced. Here, 9-month-old twins Isabel and Benjamin are at their granny's house, where they have never been before. Isabel has been suffering from an ear infection and has a slight fever, while Benjamin is fit and well. With their mother present, Benjamin is happy to explore all the new toys and crawl around the play space. Isabel's first priority, by contrast, is to stay close to her mother, and she will only engage with the toys from the security of her mother's lap.

1 Benjamin, seated on the left, busily explores the various toys his granny has provided. Although Isabel is quite interested and watches what her brother is doing, she makes no move to explore the toys herself, but lies listlessly at her mother's feet.

2 Since Isabel has seemed quite interested in what her brother is doing, her mother picks her up . . . .

3 . . . and she shows Isabel how the small pan lid can spin round.

4 Isabel is interested enough to stretch out for it, while her mother stays in close contact, stroking Isabel's back with her hands.

5 But Isabel needs more comfort than this and she turns back to crawl onto her mother's lap. Meanwhile, Benjamin goes on examining each new toy.

6 Isabel's mother comforts her, realizing that she is just not ready to play without being in very close contact.

2.1 **Feeling ill** continued

8 Benjamin moves across the floor to explore something new, while Isabel watches him and, from the security of her mother's lap, tries out what the pan lid feels like to suck.

7 Once Isabel is settled comfortably in her mother's lap, she can enjoy exploring the pan lid. Benjamin's attachment needs are satisfied just by the presence of his mother nearby and he pays her little direct attention.

usually take on several roles with the baby, from being companionable and playful, to providing discipline and giving cognitive and learning support, as well as responding to attachment needs. Which of these roles is prominent at any one time will change with the situation and the baby's stage of development, as well as with the baby's current behaviour and emotional state. Aspects of care relevant to attachment will be most important in situations where there is some challenge that might frighten or distress the baby, or where the baby's state makes him more vulnerable, perhaps because he is tired, ill or, especially for very small babies, simply hungry. At these times the baby's attachment needs will be prominent and it is important that he receives support and comfort. At other times, however, for example if the baby is contented and in familiar, unthreatening surroundings, comfortable in the knowledge that their parent is available, their attachment needs will not be pressing. In this situation, the baby is likely to be more interested in exploring their environment, being playful, and in exercising their capacities to manage independently – these skills, too, are important for the baby's development, but are supported by different kinds of care-taking (see picture sequence 2.1).

Signs of attachment

Parents naturally start to give the kind of care that supports the development of the baby's attachment to them from birth, but it is generally not until the second half of the first year that the baby's strong emotional responses reflecting attachment to particular individuals start to become clear. From around this time, in line with their developing cognitive and social abilities, the baby appears to be more aware of their dependency on the parent. This is often first apparent in the home environment when a baby who has not previously seemed to mind if their parent leaves the room, now becomes distressed, as though they have a clearer sense that such an event marks the disappearance of someone who is important to them (see picture sequence 2.2). This phase is normally short-lived, as the baby becomes accustomed to the fact that brief separations are part of ordinary life and do not lead to unpleasant consequences. But their distress is significant as it reflects, not a backwards step to more immature behaviour, but the achievement of a new kind of awareness, indicating that they have established an attachment to a specific individual. Similarly, the growing sense of attachment to selected individuals can make a baby who has previously been happy in the company of unfamiliar people start to become much

2.2   Separation anxiety

One of the earliest signs that a baby is developing a clear sense of attachment to their parent is distress at separation from them. This even happens in the home, in the company of other people the baby knows well. Here, Lottie, aged 6 months, becomes rapidly upset as her attachment needs are challenged when her mother briefly leaves the room. Her new awareness of the special attachment to her mother means that she cannot be comforted, even by a close family friend. Lottie settles quickly, however, when her mother returns and Lottie can be close to her. Once reassured of her mother's presence, Lottie's attachment needs subside, and she can turn her attention to her little friend Astrid, who is playing nearby.

1 Lottie's mother is about to leave the room to make tea. She first makes sure that Lottie has something that she enjoys playing with and tells her that she will be back very soon.

2 For a few moments Lottie attends to her toy . . .

3 . . . but then she begins to look anxious.

4 Lottie starts to cry.

5 Her mother's friend tries to comfort her . . .

6 . . . but Lottie becomes more distressed . . .

7 . . . and being picked up by her mother's friend, even though a familiar visitor to the house, doesn't calm her.

8 Lottie's mother quickly returns . . .

2.2   Separation anxiety continued

9 ...and Lottie starts to calm as soon as her mother picks her up.

10 She is soon engaging happily with her mother.

11 Once settled again, Lottie can turn her attention back to the idea of playing, and looks with interest at what her little friend Astrid is doing.

more discriminating. They may show a new fearfulness and avoidance, not just of strangers, but even of people they know reasonably well (see picture sequence 2.3). Other clear signs of attachment are when a baby wants to be physically close to, and be comforted by particular people when they are feeling wary, frightened or distressed. This is often evident when a baby encounters some new, potentially challenging situation, when they will first seek contact, reassurance and support from their parent before gaining the confidence to move on to explore (see picture sequences 2.4 and 2.5).

2.3   Stranger fear

Babies' developing awareness of a special attachment to their parents is partly reflected in what is sometimes called 'stranger fear'. Here, children show a clear distinction between the people with whom they feel safe and secure – their attachment figures – and other, unfamiliar adults whom they treat much more warily.

Below, Ben, who was happy to be close to unfamiliar people through his first eight months or so, has lately started to become much more cautious. Now aged 10 months, he is very interested in the arrival of a family friend he hasn't met before, but his interest is mixed with apprehension. While he is securely held by his mother, his sociability and initial curiosity come to the fore, but as contact with the stranger increases Ben becomes more wary. And once he has left the safety of his mother's arms, nervousness takes over and he needs to be held by her again before he feels comfortable enough to engage with this new person.

1 When a family friend arrives, and Ben's mother introduces Ben to him, Ben readily reaches out to touch the friend's proffered hand.

2 The friend holds on to Ben's hand.

2.3   **Stranger fear** continued

3 But Ben seems to find this alarming, and he pulls his hand away, turning back to his mother.

4 He buries his face in her shoulder for reassurance.

5 Once Ben is settled, he feels a little braver, and turns back towards the new friend.

6 Encouraged by his mother, he is even willing to be passed over to the friend, despite giving him a searching look.

7 Ben is not quite sure about letting go of his mother, but she smiles encouragingly.

8 She supports his being held by her friend.

9 But being away from his mother is too much for Ben, and he pulls away from the friend to get back to her.

10 Once back in her arms, Ben's interest in the new person grows again.

11 But everyone decides it is better to take a bit more time before Ben ventures away from his mother again.

2.4 Meeting an unfamiliar dog

When a baby faces a new challenge, having an attachment figure present who is sensitively supportive can help the baby feel secure enough to overcome any wariness or fear, and have the confidence to explore. By contrast, facing such challenges with the support of an unfamiliar person, no matter how sensitive, can be more daunting.

Here, Benjamin, aged 9 months, meets an unfamiliar lady walking her dog. Benjamin is fascinated and would love to touch the dog, but he is able to do so only with the support of his father.

1 Benjamin and his father see a lady they haven't met before, out walking her dog. Benjamin is fascinated, but quite wary, sucking on his thumb as he gazes down at it.

2 Benjamin's father asks the owner if the dog is friendly, while Benjamin continues to watch closely as the dog sniffs his feet.

3 Benjamin's father bends right down, holding him close, and greets the dog, as the owner introduces him. Benjamin remains rather cautious, still sucking his thumb.

4 The dog owner comes down to Benjamin's level and shows him how much the dog likes to be stroked.

5 She offers to help Benjamin stroke the dog, holding out her hand to him.

6 While Benjamin smiles happily, he draws his hand back, not quite ready to accept the owner's offer.

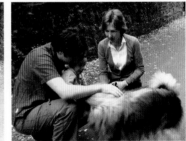

7 Benjamin's father now strokes the dog, talking to Benjamin about how soft his fur feels, and Benjamin is fascinated.

2.4   **Meeting an unfamiliar dog** continued

8 Now he is happy to let his father help him reach out to the dog.

9 Having stroked him together, Benjamin's father looks to see how his son is feeling, talking to him about what a nice dog it is, and how much the dog enjoyed Benjamin stroking him.

10 Now Benjamin boldly reaches out to the dog on his own, encouraged by his father and the owner.

11 Supported by his father, Benjamin spends some time stroking the patient dog.

12 Benjamin seems to feel very pleased with what he has done, and he and the dog's owner share warm smiles.

Differences in attachment relationships

Babies almost invariably develop an attachment to their care-givers and it is only in very deprived circumstances, such as very poor-quality residential institutions where babies receive almost no personal care, that attachments are not formed. Nevertheless, the nature of a baby's attachments will vary between his different attachment figures, largely depending on the quality of care that each of them provides. In general, within the group of individuals to whom the baby is attached there is a hierarchy of preference, so that if several of these people are present, one, or perhaps two of them, will be singled out by the baby to comfort them if they are upset or fearful.

Attachment security

The quality of a baby's attachment to their parent that is of most importance for their general development is what is known as their security. Two key features characterize secure attachments:

- First, the baby will develop the sense that their parent, or other person to whom they are securely attached, is emotionally available, and ready to be responsive if the baby needs them. This means that he does not need to anxiously check on his parent's readiness, or willingness to help him.
- Second, the baby who is securely attached feels confident, not just that his parent is available, but that they will comfort and support him when needed, and will be able to relieve his distress.

2.5 A frightening tortoise

When babies are faced with something that alarms them, they will often want to be in close proximity to an attachment figure to feel secure. Once they feel more confident, however, such close contact will not be so important and their urge to explore can come into play.

Ben, aged 17 months, is here visiting a children's farm with his father, where they come across the tortoise enclosure. Ben's keenness to be near the tortoise ebbs and flows with his nervousness, as this unfamiliar creature moves around. As his own feelings shift, so his need for close contact with his father changes too.

1 Ben sits comfortably between his father's knees, as his father talks to him about the tortoises and gently places his arms at Ben's sides. Ben is intrigued by these slow, lumbering creatures.

2 When one of the tortoises starts to come up close, however, Ben isn't sure what might happen, and he turns round quickly to his father, reaching up to him.

3 Once settled safely on his father's lap, Ben feels much more comfortable about the tortoise being so near, and watches happily.

4 After a while, Ben feels bold enough to get up from his father's lap, and shows his father his new active interest in the creature's movements.

5 Soon, his fascination with the tortoise, and his confidence in the situation, mean that he can move away from his father, right up close to the cage, even placing his finger on the tortoise's foot as his father looks on.

In a secure relationship, therefore, the baby's feeling of dependency on the parent is not something that itself makes the baby anxious, and the baby does not need to feel inhibited about showing when he is upset and needy. Rather, the baby can use the parent as a 'safe haven' if he wants comfort and support, freely expressing his feelings of vulnerability and seeking close contact with the parent, in the expectation that his needs will be responded to in a caring and timely manner. Having been given such comfort, securely attached babies will typically recover quickly from any distress and, using their parent as a 'secure base' from which to explore, will settle back easily to enjoy other activities (see picture sequence 2.6).

2.6 Baby's secure attachment pattern

When a baby is secure in their attachment to their parent (or other care-giver), they show this particularly clearly in situations that mildly challenge their attachment needs. This could be, for example, arriving in an unfamiliar place and encountering a new person, and then being briefly separated from their parent. In such a situation, before the separation, secure babies are happy to explore their new environment, and they may be interested in the unfamiliar person. When the parent leaves the room, however, the baby's attachment needs come to the fore. Because the secure baby has been used to receiving sensitive care, he or she can feel free to express any dismay about their parent's departure and their wish to be near them, so a typical response is that they will protest and become upset. When the parent returns, the secure baby can also feel confident that their parent will respond to their distress and comfort them, and the baby will therefore approach the parent and seek close contact. Once the secure baby is reunited with their parent, they will quite easily be reassured by their presence and will become calm relatively quickly, meaning that they can renew their interest and pleasure in exploration.

Here, Iris, aged 18 months, has come with her mother to the university research centre where, in a situation that challenges her attachment needs, she shows all the classic signs of security.

1 Iris and her mother are shown into a waiting room, where there are a number of attractive toys. Iris begins to explore them as her mother sits nearby reading a magazine.

2 Iris settles down to play, aware of her mother's presence, but happy to explore the toys on her own.

3 When an unfamiliar person enters, Iris is quite interested. Iris watches the stranger as she starts talking to her mother, but calmly carries on playing.

4 When the stranger joins Iris on the carpet, Iris is happy to engage with her, while her mother remains seated nearby.

5 However, as soon as her mother walks towards the door, Iris immediately stops playing with the stranger, and turns to watch her mother.

2.6   Baby's secure attachment pattern continued

6 The stranger calls Iris over and tries to engage her in play . . .

7 . . . but Iris resists the idea of playing with her and pulls away.

8 Iris runs over to the door.

9 She cries out for her mother.

10 And then reaches up as her mother comes back into the room.

11 Iris sinks into her mother's arms and snuggles against her with relief.

12 Once Iris has had a good cuddle with her mother, she lifts her head to look around the room again.

13 Noticing that Iris is ready to be interested in the toys again, her mother points to a colourful frog. Iris still holds on to her mother though, and sucks her finger.

14 Her mother stretches across to bring the frog over, so that Iris can stay close to her until she is quite ready to leave her mother's lap.

15 Soon, Iris has slid to the ground and becomes absorbed in play.

2.6   Baby's secure attachment pattern continued

16 And now Iris is ready to go across the room to find something else …

17 … bringing it over to share with her mother.

It is important to note that a baby's sense of security and emotional closeness to their parent does not mean that they will always want to be physically close to them. Indeed, a parent who comforts the baby when he cries is not causing the child to become over-dependent, rather they are giving their baby the reassurance and confidence that will allow him to act independently. In effect, a healthy attachment–exploration balance operates in secure babies and young children, so that on the one hand, when feeling vulnerable (such as when they are ill, frightened, tired or facing some new challenge) attachment needs will increase and can easily be expressed, but on the other hand when attachment needs are met and the baby or young child feels confident and comfortable, the desire to explore and be independent becomes stronger (see picture sequence 2.7).

2.7   Adjusting to a new environment

As a child enters a new and complex environment, the balance between attachment and exploration shifts. Attachment needs are typically strong at first, then lessen, and can re-emerge when the demands on the child change. At such times the child will want to be close to their parent, and might also want to use some kind of transitional or security object to help them manage. As the child becomes more confident, the urge to explore increases. Now, direct contact with the parent is no longer needed, but the parent's presence nevertheless provides a secure base from which the child can wander and return to. This attachment–exploration balance does not end with infancy.

Here we see 3-year-old Isaac showing all the signs of the secure child's adjustment when he has the new experience of attending a parent-child play group, held at a museum.

1 Isaac and his mother arrive at the museum and are directed to the play group.

2.7   Adjusting to a new environment continued

2 All the other children have been before, and are familiar with the routine. Isaac snuggles into his mother's lap as the play-leader, Bekky, brings out some hand puppets. Their soft, cuddly, feel is helpful as the children settle in.

3 Isaac watches with interest as the other children each choose their puppets.

4 But he can't quite bring himself to move away from his mother's lap to get one himself.

5 Bekky understands that he feels a little anxious, and she brings the box of puppets over to him, so that he can remain in contact with his mother.

6 Isaac is thrilled with his duck puppet, and Bekky offers him another one.

7 Isaac is becoming bolder, and having taken his second puppet, he holds it up for Bekky to see, already beginning to make a good connection with her.

8 When Bekky leads the children in singing 'Twinkle, twinkle little star', Isaac holds on to his puppets tightly. He doesn't know this routine and he snuggles back again into his mother's lap.

9 Now Bekky shows the children a book that Isaac knows well, *The Hungry Caterpillar* and he sits forward more confidently, although still holding on to one of his puppets, while the other children have put theirs away.

2.7   **Adjusting to a new environment** continued

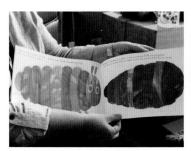

10 Bekky takes time to show the children each page and talk about it.

11 Bekky has noticed Isaac's keen interest and feels he is ready to respond now, so she invites him to join in talking about the picture.

12 Now feeling much more comfortable, Isaac leaves his mother's lap, though he still holds his puppet, and comes forward to show Bekky what has happened to the caterpillar.

13 Now it is play time. Isaac is happy to be away from his mother's lap and has put his puppet away . . .

14 . . . he's ready to explore with the other children.

15 Now, Isaac is feeling so comfortable that he even begins to explore beyond the play area, looking at the farm wagon in the museum section.

16 He comes back after a little while to tell his mother about what he has seen.

17 And then he settles down to play with the other children.

Attachment insecurity

Although most babies do develop secure attachments to their parents, this is not always the case. Research involving close observations of babies' responses to everyday attachment challenges has identified three different insecure patterns, where the baby does not seem to have the same confidence that their parent is willing and able to meet their needs.

Avoidant insecure attachment Babies who have what is called an avoidant insecure attachment to their parent show little, if any, visible distress in situations that should strongly activate a baby's attachment needs, such as their parent leaving them in an unfamiliar environment – something that normally causes secure babies to become upset (see picture sequence 2.6, above). Further, whereas secure babies do not hesitate to seek contact and comfort from the parent when they return, babies who have an avoidant pattern of attachment will largely ignore their parent when they come back and avoid close contact, perhaps occupying themselves with toys and seeming to prefer playing on their own. Although superficially these babies might appear to be unaffected by their parent's absence, because they do not outwardly seem distressed, research has shown that their heart rate and other physiological responses (like levels of the hormone cortisol) increase in such situations, indicating that they do pose a stress for the baby. What might seem, then, to be the response of a baby who is managing well and independently, is actually more likely to reflect the baby experiencing the situation as difficult, but feeling it cannot be resolved by seeking the parent's comfort and support. This avoidant pattern is considered to be insecure, as it suggests that the baby is wary of expressing their needs and not confident of receiving a comforting response from their parent when distressed.

Ambivalent-resistant insecure attachment This pattern refers to babies who seem highly anxious about the availability of their parent and about their attachment needs being met. These babies typically monitor their parent's presence closely, often finding it difficult to settle to play and explore their environment in conditions that would not pose a challenge to secure babies – say, when a friendly but unfamiliar person is also present in the room. Like secure babies, the baby who is insecure in an ambivalent or resistant way will also show distress in the face of attachment challenges such as being separated from the parent in an unfamiliar environment, but in this case their distress is extreme. Furthermore, unlike secure babies, who can be consoled and comforted by their parent's return, these insecure babies remain upset, and sometimes angry, despite the parent's attempts to comfort them, and they are unable to settle back to play and explore. This pattern of response is considered insecure because it seems as though the baby is constantly and overwhelmingly anxious about their parent's availability.

Disorganized attachment Unlike the secure, avoidant or ambivalent-resistant attachment patterns described above, which all appear as organized attempts by the baby to manage challenges to their attachment needs, some babies either have no clear-cut pattern of response or, if one of the other response patterns is present, it is nevertheless dominated by more disorganized behaviour. These babies usually show strange, often contradictory behaviours that seem to have no goal when facing a challenge to their attachment needs. For example, the baby may begin to approach their parent as they come back into the room after a brief absence, but then veer off in the opposite direction; they may make undirected, stereotyped movements (for example, rocking to and fro, banging their head or flapping their hands repeatedly); or they might suddenly freeze or even appear frightened, particularly when the parent is present. This pattern of response is considered insecure because of the baby's apprehension and confusion about expressing attachment needs.

Babies' security and the role of parents

The importance of sensitive responsiveness

In line with John Bowlby's original theory, over 30 years of research has established that a parent's sensitivity to their baby is a key predictor of attachment security. This quality of sensitivity includes the parent being accessible to and accepting of their child, being warmly and cooperatively involved, and being appropriately and promptly responsive to the child's signals and needs. This appears to be especially important at moments of distress, when the need for comfort and support is greatest (see text box D, p.95 for more details on sensitivity).

In very young babies, their ability to control their behaviour, understand what is going on and anticipate what will happen next is limited, and even ordinary everyday experiences such as being bathed, having a nappy change or feeling hungry, can make them feel vulnerable and even quite desperate. Working out the baby's individual cues and ways of responding, and establishing what works best so that sensitive care can be given, can require considerable practice. But over time, as parent and baby become accustomed to each other, situations that previously felt challenging and demanded full concentration can increasingly be dealt with smoothly and with ease, giving parent and baby more freedom to explore and be playful (see picture sequences 2.8–2.11 about early feeding issues and 2.12–2.14 about successful and enjoyable feeding).

2.8 Supporting a baby in distress

Young babies are entirely dependent on the care of others. They need sensitive support to help them manage difficult feelings. Each individual baby's way of signalling their needs will vary, and there are individual variations too in how babies respond to their experiences. Parents, therefore, have to get to know their baby's cues and habits and learn how best to adjust their own behaviour. Particularly when the baby's feelings of distress are intense, this requires patience and sometimes even a strong nerve, in order to negotiate ways of helping the baby effectively. Feeding is often an area where these skills come into play, especially in the first few weeks before routines are smoothly established, and when a hungry baby can quickly become distressed and their behaviour disorganized.

Here Stanley, just a week old, is desperate for a feed and so distressed that he finds it difficult to latch on to the breast, even when his mother positions it ready for him. She has to support Stanley's head patiently and carefully, and help him through his distress and his disorganized attempts to begin feeding.

1 Stanley thrashes around and cries desperately for a feed.

2 His mother has to use both hands to support him, which is not easy when he is upset and agitated.

3 Even when she has helped him into a position to feed, his distress is still overwhelming for him.

2.8   Supporting a baby in distress continued

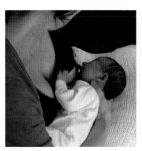   

4 It takes patience to help Stanley latch on.

5 In this situation where Stanley's strong feelings are quite difficult for him to manage, some trial and error is involved.

6 But he is eventually able to take the nipple . . .

7 . . . and now he settles more calmly to feed.

2.9   Working out meanings at two weeks

Even after two weeks feeding can be awkward. Routines for latching on are still being established and the mother is still working out the cues to help understand her baby's behaviour and what might be causing distress.

Here, we see Stanley and his mother again. They are gradually getting used to feeds, but there are moments where his mother has to do some careful adjusting to help him. After his feed, there are more challenges for Stanley and his parents, as he has difficulty settling and it's not clear what the problem is. Importantly, Stanley's parents try hard to understand his experience and find solutions, responsively adjusting their care as they attempt to ease his distress.

1 Stanley has been feeding calmly for a while . . .

2 . . . but then he turns right away from the breast.

3 His mother looks at Stanley uncertainly, not quite sure whether he is signalling that he has had enough.

2.9 **Working out meanings at two weeks** continued

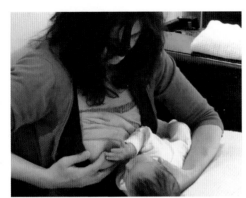

4 After a pause, Stanley's mother positions him to see if he wants more, but the procedure for latching on is still not completely smooth and Stanley's hand gets in the way of the nipple.

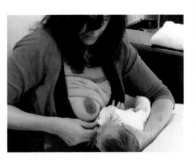

5 His mother has to manoeuvre Stanley's hand out of the way, while still giving his head good support.

6 At last well-positioned, Stanley is ready to latch on.

7 His mother supports him carefully until he is settled.

8 Then they can continue comfortably with his feed.

9 After Stanley has fed, his father holds him, and tries to help him burp.

10 But Stanley starts crying, and his father isn't sure what is the matter.

11 He wonders whether Stanley is still hungry, so takes him back to his mother.

12 Stanley seems to be in pain, so his mother puts him in a position that has worked before, and gently tries to soothe him with her voice. She is doubtful that he can still be hungry.

13 But Stanley doesn't settle, so his mother tries a different position, and rubs his back.

2.9   Working out meanings at two weeks continued

14 The new position hasn't worked either, so she offers him her finger to see if he will suck it, suggesting that he might want more feed.

15 But Stanley rejects her finger.

16 His mother rubs his tummy again, watching and trying to figure out what is troubling him.

17 Eventually, she goes back to the first position and although Stanley is still upset, he does seem to be calming down. So his mother continues to hold him like this, rocking him gently and talking to him softly.

2.10   A change in routine

Stanley is now 6 weeks old, and is just starting to take feeds from a bottle. This is a good opportunity for Stanley's father to become involved in this aspect of his care. But changing the feeding method and getting to know each other's cues requires new coordination and adjustments on both sides, and this first bottle feed with his father is quite tricky.

Not feeling certain yet that he can read his baby's signals accurately, Stanley's father asks his wife for advice, drawing on her greater familiarity with their baby's responses. With her support, Stanley's father can resume the feeding successfully, more confident in his ability to take care of his son.

1 Stanley and his father are enjoying this new experience of a bottle feed.

2 Stanley sucks calmly while his father affectionately strokes his cheek.

3 Stanley feeds contentedly for a while.

2.10   **A change in routine** continued

4 But then he abruptly breaks off, having gulped down too much milk.

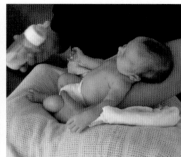

5 Stanley's father removes the bottle …

6 …and pauses the feed to check how Stanley is.

7 Stanley seems calm, so his father offers the bottle again.

8 But Stanley immediately gets upset and jerks his head away.

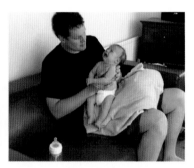

9 Stanley's father really isn't sure what the matter is.

10 He thinks Stanley might need more milk and tries to settle him into position for feeding again.

11 But, as he reaches for the bottle, he's not at all confident, and calls across to Stanley's mother.

12 Stanley's mother comes over and helps settle Stanley into a more comfortable position, where he can start to feed again.

2.11   Trial and error in early feeds

After a few weeks, typically both mother and baby have become much more practised at reading each other's cues about feeding. Iris's mother knows exactly how to position her daughter so that she can feed comfortably. Iris is now very familiar with the routine of how a feed starts and she can anticipate each step of the preparation so that latching on is smooth. Other parts of the feed, though, are still not quite so clear and involve some trial and error – for example, to work out just when Iris has had enough milk. Parents who notice the baby's reactions when their behaviour is misinterpreted can be guided to a better understanding of what responses are needed.

1 Iris looks up expectantly, familiar with this position, and her mother's first moves to prepare for feeding her.

2 She opens her mouth wide, ready to latch on to the nipple ...

3 ... and settles easily to feed.

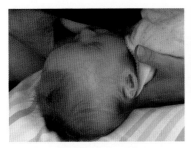

4 Later, having fed for a while on both breasts, Iris begins to slacken off in her sucking.

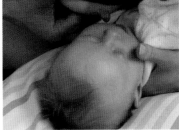

5 She turns away, as though she might have had enough.

6 But then she turns back again ...

7 ... and she sucks some more, so perhaps she is still hungry. Iris's cues are not so easy to understand, and perhaps Iris herself isn't sure whether she wants much more feed.

8 While she is back on the breast, her sucking is more feeble, and she's also taking an interest in looking up at her mother.

2.11 Trial and error in early feeds continued

9 When Iris breaks off again, and seems ready for engaging socially, her mother wonders whether she has come to the end of her feed.

10 She offers the breast one more time, to check, but Iris doesn't seem keen.

11 In fact she begins to get agitated.

12 Her mother also wonders whether Iris might be uncomfortable, so sits her up and pats her to help her burp.

13 Then she offers Iris the breast again.

14 This time Iris makes it very clear that she no longer wants to feed.

15 Her mother responds, acknowledging that Iris really isn't hungry.

16 And she lifts Iris to her shoulder to calm her.

2.12 Play during feeds 1

Astrid, aged 4 months. As feeding becomes established and more routine, less attention is required to negotiate the different steps involved. The task of satisfying the baby's hunger can more easily be taken for granted, and this frees up both parent and baby to enjoy being more playful during feeds.

Here, Astrid, who is beginning to enjoy reaching out towards objects, uses feeding time to playfully explore her mother with her hands and, in turn, there is plenty of scope for her mother to engage socially with her baby in a way that wasn't possible a few weeks before.

1 Astrid is now very comfortable with breastfeeding, and getting into the right position, and feeding well can be managed without the concentration and effort that was required earlier.

2 Once settled into the feed, Astrid starts to explore her mother with her hands.

3 She reaches up to feel her mother's skin, while her mother also enjoys affectionately stroking Astrid's head.

4 She talks to her daughter about what it's like to play like this.

5 Astrid then reaches up, and spends a while playing with her mother's necklace, as she continues to feed.

6 As soon as her feed is finished she is ready to take an interest in what's going on around her.

2.13   Feeding smoothly, with father

Astrid, aged 4.5 months. A few weeks later and bottle feeding is negotiated smoothly and without distress. Astrid's father frequently feeds her the expressed breast milk that her mother has prepared. He has become highly sensitive to her cues, knowing just when she wants to pause and when she wants to be free to break off and look around. Similarly, Astrid now knows the routine well and can anticipate what will happen next, so that she is able to participate actively and enjoy some measure of control.

1 Astrid's father shows her the full bottle, giving her time to signal her readiness to feed.

2 As her father lifts the bottle towards her, Astrid joins him in holding it, and opens her mouth wide in anticipation.

3 Her father delights in Astrid's enthusiasm, as she avidly settles to feeding, and she can enjoy the sense of helping to control the feed as she clasps her hands over his.

4 Astrid's hunger has abated a little, and her hands slacken from the effort of helping to get the bottle to her mouth. Now she can notice what else is around her, and enjoy being more sociable . . .

5 . . . before resuming feeding for a little while longer.

6 Now Astrid has had quite a lot of milk and her attention wanders more widely. Her father is happy to let her break off from feeding and enjoy looking around.

7 When Astrid turns back, he shows her the bottle again and waits to see how she responds, rather than taking it for granted that he should put the bottle to her mouth.

8 Astrid doesn't pick up on the offer, so her father continues to check how she is behaving and accepts that she has probably had enough . . .

9 . . . then he wipes her clean.

2.14   Play during feeds 2

Here we see Saavan, at 6.5 months. His feeding has now become routine, which frees him up to enjoy exploring with his hands. This allows social games to develop around Saavan's gestures, so that mother and baby can take pleasure in each other's company, even in the absence of eye-contact and shared smiles.

1 Saavan loves to wave his hands around while feeding.

2 His mother catches his hand . . .

3 . . . and they enjoy a tactile game together as Saavan continues with his feed.

The importance of thinking about the baby's experience

Recent studies have shown that it is not just what the parent does, in terms of actual behavioural responses, but also the way they think about their baby and his attachment needs that is linked to the baby's sense of security. In particular, when the parent can reflect on the baby's experience and accurately perceive his feelings and intentions, this seems to bring further benefit to the baby. This kind of insightfulness is no doubt partly expressed in the parent's practical care for their child. But it is also possible that the parent's specific signals about the meaning of the baby's experience are an extra help in fostering the sense of security. Thus, research on babies' social and emotional development more generally (see Chapter 3, p. 148,

Regulation of responses through social awareness and referencing) suggests that, along with empathic responses showing that the parent knows how the baby feels, the parent's ability to make sense of the baby's experience, and especially their signalling that difficult feelings can in fact be managed, can help the baby to cope. In the early weeks and months, showing such understanding through facial expression, voice and touch are key, but as the baby's understanding of language develops, talking about difficult experiences becomes more relevant (see picture sequences 2.15–2.19).

2.15   Managing a bad day

It can be difficult for parents to know how to manage a baby who feels tired or unwell. In the early weeks there can be much trial and error involved in trying to support a baby who is distressed for reasons that are not clear.

Here, on a day when Iris, aged 11 weeks, had difficulty in settling, we see her mother expressing some of the core ingredients of sensitive care. First, Iris's mother shows a real attempt to understand her daughter's experience and sympathizes with her; second, she sensitively adjusts her care to respond to Iris's changing states and signals; and finally, Iris's mother is able to tolerate and support her daughter's distress and give comfort without becoming distressed herself. Iris has slept well and has been fed, she just seems rather out of sorts. Her mother initially tries to engage her in face-to-face play in her bouncy chair, but Iris remains unhappy. Her mother communicates her sympathy and concern, marking Iris's expressions with her own clear facial signals, showing that she understands how Iris feels, but also communicating her support and her willingness to try to help Iris recover from her difficult mood.

1 Although Iris had seemed happy to be placed in her bouncy chair, ready for playing with her mother, her mood suddenly changes, and she begins to look upset.

2 Iris's mother mirrors her daughter's expression, signalling that she knows exactly how Iris feels and, as she does so, Iris watches her mother's face intently.

3 Now Iris's mother shifts her emotional expression – she still shows sympathy, but instead of mirroring her daughter's distress, she tries to help Iris recover, wondering if Iris might be coaxed into the mood for play. Iris calms a little, still watching her mother closely, but doesn't quite manage to overcome her difficult mood.

4 As Iris turns away, her mother sympathizes, and acknowledges that she really doesn't seem to be able to settle.

5 She has one more go, as Iris turns back towards her, to help Iris engage . . .

6 . . . but her mother can see that Iris is finding it hard, and again she lets Iris know that she sympathizes . . .

2.15 Managing a bad day continued

7 …and that she will take action to help.

8 She abandons any idea of play, and lifts Iris from her chair.

2.16 Managing a bad day 2

Iris's mother has picked her up and cuddled her, and Iris now appears more settled, so her mother props her up comfortably to see if she will enjoy playing with a colourful soft toy. But Iris becomes upset once more, and her mother again communicates her sympathy and her efforts to understand and help her daughter. She abandons the idea of play with the toy and instead gives Iris physical support and comfort, once more taking her in her arms to soothe her.

1 Iris is settled comfortably, and at first seems to be interested in watching her toy elephant as her mother moves it to and fro.

2 Soon afterwards, however, Iris shows signs of becoming upset, and her mother watches Iris's changing expressions carefully, while trying to make the toy attractive.

3 Now Iris is clearly upset; her mother shows her concern and acknowledges that Iris just isn't in the mood for this kind of play.

4 She abandons the toy and instead tries to soothe Iris with her voice and comforting touch.

5 As Iris's distress mounts, her mother's face reflects her sympathy and the fact that she knows how difficult it is for Iris to be in this state, as she begins to lift Iris from her seat …

6 …and then holds her closely, still using her voice to support her daughter.

2.17   Managing a bad day 3

Iris's mother realizes that Iris is unlikely to settle if she isn't being held, so she keeps her daughter in her arms and tries to see if Iris wants to engage in play from this position. But today only one thing seems to work and Iris is really only happy when her mother holds her close, patting her gently, without any other distractions.

1 Iris's mother holds up another toy to see if Iris might be entertained by it, watching Iris's face to gauge her reaction.

2 Seeing that Iris is not in the mood, she quickly puts the toy down.

3 Iris begins to cry again, so her mother starts to shift her position away from any unwelcome stimulation.

4 And, instead, concentrates on holding Iris close and soothing her …

7 … gradually, with gentle words …

8 … and rhythmic patting.

9 Iris begins to settle …

10 … and relaxes in her mother's arms.

2.18   A painful experience – immunization 1

Iris, aged 4 months. Babies' attachment needs are clearly seen at times when they are vulnerable, for example, if they are in pain. Here, we see Iris having her first immunization jab – her mother soothes and comforts her throughout, helping to reduce the stress of a difficult experience.

1 The nurse explains the procedure to Iris's mother.

2.18   A painful experience – immunization 1 continued

2 Iris's mother holds her daughter securely and talks to her while the nurse gets ready.

3 When the jab is given, Iris screams and clings on tight to her mother's T-shirt, while her mother continues to talk to her soothingly . . .

4 . . . stroking and comforting her.

5 The nurse wants to give the second jab, so they need to turn Iris round, but she's reluctant to let go of her mother's shirt and be moved.

6 Iris's mother is completely focused on trying to support her daughter, continually talking and soothing her through this difficult time.

7 Now the second jab is delivered . . .

8 . . . and Iris's mother lifts her immediately, so that she can put her in the best position to comfort her . . .

9 . . . then spends some time holding Iris close, rocking, patting, and soothing her with her voice until she recovers.

2.19   Immunization 2

Ben, aged 13 months, now needs his second round of immunization. At this stage of his development, it is possible sometimes to distract him from difficult experiences and his mother hopes that showing him his favourite book will help, but the jabs are still painful and upsetting. Ben's mother offers him close physical support and affection, but she also talks to Ben about what is happening, acknowledging that she knows how he feels and giving him simple explanations. In this way, she helps him to cope with his difficult feelings. She sensitively gauges his level of need for contact with her at each stage, and is flexible in her responses, abandoning the idea of Ben being placed in his buggy when he signals that he is not quite ready to be separated from her and needs more close contact.

1 Ben is about to have his jab and his mother hopes the impact might be lessened if Ben is distracted by one of his favourite books.

2.19   **Immunization 2** continued

2 But even *Thomas the Tank Engine* can't totally block out the pain.

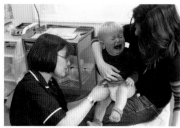

3 Ben's mother quickly puts the book down and turns to comfort him ...

4 ... lifting him and holding him close to reassure him of her support.

5 As Ben begins to recover, his mother talks to him, noting that the jab was sore for him, and that she understands how he felt.

6 When the second jab is due, Ben is very wary of the nurse and cannot be distracted by his book.

7 Once more the jab is painful.

8 Ben's mother picks him up, holds him close and comforts him with a kiss.

9 Again she talks to him, letting him know she understands how sore it was.

10 She explains that the nurse had to give him the jab, but that now it is all over.

11 Ben's mother tells him how well he managed, and suggests that they go home and play Ben's favourite game.

2.19   Immunization 2 continued

14 ....but when it comes to letting go of his mother, Ben finds he still feels vulnerable, and would in fact rather stay in his mother's arms.

12 They get ready to leave the clinic.

13 Ben's mother begins to lower him into his buggy. He seems happy with the idea at first ..

15 His mother sympathizes, and tells him she sees he's not quite ready yet.

16 So she carries Ben until he does feel ready, pushing the empty buggy.

Parenting styles linked to different insecure baby attachment patterns

Just as sensitive parental responsiveness has been shown to accompany a baby's being securely attached, so systematic links have also been found between particular kinds of parenting insensitivity and different kinds of insecure baby attachment. So a baby who develops an avoidant attachment to their parent will be more likely than other babies to have a parent who is uncomfortable with close physical contact, and who has an excessively stimulating, intrusive or over-controlling style. A baby who has an ambivalent-resistant insecure attachment, on the other hand, is more likely to have a parent who is inconsistently sensitive, or under-involved. Finally, babies who show disorganized attachment responses are more likely to have experienced parenting behaviour that has caused them to be frightened. Apart from this last disorganized pattern, babies' different types of response all seem to be adaptive strategies for managing their attachment needs according to the behaviour they have come to expect from their parent. Thus, the secure baby's strategy is to seek support, since they can expect it to be provided; the insecure avoidant baby's strategy is to try to minimize their dependency on the parent, since expressions of such dependency are discouraged or met with difficult, intrusive responses; and the insecure ambivalent/resistant baby's strategy is to emphasize their dependency in order to maximize the chances of obtaining a response.

The associations between a parent's sensitivity and their baby's security of attachment have been found in many different countries and different social groups. The fact that these associations indicate genuinely causal relationships rather than, say, simply the influence of a baby's own characteristics (like their temperament) on their parents' responsiveness, is indicated by three sets of findings:

• The attachments babies have to their different carers can vary, with each one largely depending on the quality of care given by the adult concerned. This applies not only to possible differences between babies' attachments to their mothers and fathers, but babies' security of attachment to professionals is also related to the sensitivity of these carers.

- It is possible to predict a baby's likely pattern of attachment to their parent before the baby is born, on the basis of the way the parent thinks about attachment needs (see more below, this page, under *Parents' attachment patterns*).
- Interventions that improve parents' sensitivity also bring about higher rates of security in babies' attachments.

The role of the baby's own characteristics

In contrast to the research showing the importance of the care they receive in the forming of babies' attachments, there is very little evidence showing any direct effect of a baby's genetic make-up.

Even a baby's individual temperament does not seem to directly influence whether they are securely or insecurely attached, although it may affect the quality and emotional strength of their responses (such as tending to be fearful or negative). Babies' temperaments could, however, be relevant to their attachments in other, more indirect, ways. First, some babies – for example, those who react with strong emotions and who become easily distressed – may be far more affected by their rearing environment than those with more placid, less reactive, temperaments (see also Chapter 3, on babies' self-regulation). These reactive babies may, therefore, be particularly likely to become insecure if the parenting they receive is insensitive. On the positive side, highly reactive babies may also benefit more than other babies if their parent receives support and is then able to give more sensitive care. A second way in which a baby's temperament may be relevant to their attachment security is through the effect on parents. For example, having a reactive, easily distressed baby can place considerable demands on parents and make it harder for them to give sensitive care. These parents may be in particular need of support.

What affects parents' ability to give sensitive care?

Background circumstances

Parenting does not operate in a vacuum, and with accumulating background difficulties (such as lack of money, problems with work, low social or partner support), the risk increases that the baby's attachment to their parent will be insecure. Obviously it is far more difficult for parents to give sensitive care when they are preoccupied with such problems. But some of these background difficulties can themselves have a direct effect on the baby's attachment. For example, not only is a parent's capacity to be sensitive to their baby likely to be undermined if they are in a problematic relationship with their partner, but the security of babies and young children is also likely to suffer if they witness conflict between their parents.

Parents' own characteristics

Parents' attachment patterns Aside from background circumstances, a parent's own resources will also affect their ability to meet the baby's attachment needs. Of particular significance are the attachments that parents had in their own childhood, and the meaning those relationships still have for them. Thus, parents who are secure themselves and who can be emotionally open, balanced and resolved about the care they received (even if their childhood was not ideal), find it easier to understand and sympathize with their baby's emotions and needs, and their babies are more likely to form secure attachments to them. Researchers describe this style of a parent's own attachment as 'autonomous', meaning that the adult can think about their own early relationships in a free and unprejudiced way.

Parents who are insecure, by contrast, may struggle much more with the demands of parenting. Some have learned to manage potentially painful feelings by blocking off memories, and dismissing the value of emotional closeness. This dismissive attachment style is likely to make it hard for the parent to perceive their baby's attachment needs and be accepting of them, and

D The nature of sensitivity

Sensitive parenting, as described by the leading attachment researcher, Mary Ainsworth, has a number of core features:

Awareness Sensitive parents are alert to even small, subtle cues, such as changes in their baby's facial expression or, for example, special movements like pulling an ear – signals that the baby might be becoming tired. Sensitive awareness also involves the parent's accurate reading of signals. This means that their perceptions are not biased or distorted (for example, by imagining that a tired baby is trying to annoy them by crying). Finally, sensitive awareness involves empathy, where the parent not only registers and accurately interprets the baby's cues, but also feels for and sympathizes with the baby.

Responsiveness Not only does sensitive parenting involve accurate and empathic awareness of the baby's experience, but also that responses to the baby are appropriate and well-timed. Exactly what is appropriate, and the proper timing of responses, of course vary with the situation and with the baby's development. For small babies, appropriate response generally means very promptly attending to the baby's cues and wishes. So, they are picked up when they want to be, soothed when distressed, fed when hungry, played with when they are feeling sociable. The nature of appropriate responsiveness, and its timing, changes as the baby's understanding and capacity to tolerate difficult feelings develop. So, sensitive parents of older babies will still acknowledge their wishes, but may at times supportively help the baby to wait for what he wants, rather than providing it right away.

Cooperation Sensitivity includes cooperation and respect for the baby's autonomy and his own separate desires and wishes. In particular, cooperative parenting is non-intrusive – that is, the parent does not impose their own wishes, or interfere with the baby's agenda. As a result, physical contact is neither interfering nor overwhelming, nor does the parent constantly demand and instruct or seek to exert control over the baby, but instead they are responsive to the baby's cues.

Acceptance The notion of acceptance describes the parent's capacity to bear the frustrations of caring for a baby, including times when negative or irritable feelings arise, and to feel overriding love and acceptance of the baby's individuality.

in turn their baby is more likely to develop an avoidant pattern of insecure attachment to them.

Other parents who are insecure may be constantly preoccupied and angry about difficulties arising from their early attachment experiences, and find it hard to make any coherent sense of them. This may lead them to respond inconsistently when their babies show their attachment needs, and their babies are then more likely to become insecurely attached to them in an ambivalent-resistant way.

Finally, if parents have experienced some previous trauma or loss that they have been unable to come to terms with, or if they are overwhelmed by current difficulties in their lives, they may be very preoccupied with those problems. This may cause them to completely blank off from their baby at times, or even lose control of their behaviour. Both kinds of reaction can be frightening for babies, who are then more likely to develop a disorganized attachment to their parent.

In sum, the way in which a parent thinks and feels about their own early attachment experiences is likely to have a profound effect on how they respond to their baby's attachment needs and, in turn, the nature of the baby's attachment to them.

Parents' general adjustment Parents' personality, mental health and general well-being can also all affect their capacity to provide care that fosters secure baby attachment. Studies have consistently shown, for example, that parents who are well-adjusted (that is, self-confident, positive, adaptable) and/or who feel low levels of stress, have babies who are more likely to be secure. By contrast, if parents are highly anxious, or are perhaps depressed, it can be more difficult for them to give sensitive care, and rates of secure baby attachment are accordingly lower.

Early attachment and longer-term development

An important question is whether early attachment relationships show long-term associations with the child's emotional development and well-being. There are several ways in which this could be the case. These include the effects of early attachment on how children come to think about themselves and others, and develop distinctive patterns of social relationships. But it is also the case that the style of parenting that influenced the baby's early attachment pattern is likely to endure and have a continuing influence on the child's longer term development.

Early attachment and later social relationships
Many studies have shown that the pattern of interactions concerning attachment that babies have with their parents gradually becomes a model for the way the child comes to think and feel about themselves and their relationships generally – for good or ill. For example, babies who are used to receiving loving care will develop a model of themselves as being lovable. Such a model then shapes how the baby interprets other people's behaviour, as well as their expectations of how others will respond to them, and this affects the growing child's interactions with others.

The associations between the nature of a baby's attachment to their parent and the child's later perceptions of themselves and others are often

shown in research using play with dolls, drawings, or stories. Commonly, the child is asked to imagine what might happen to a child doll or story character who faces some attachment challenge (for example, the parents are going out for the evening, leaving the child behind), or some other potentially difficult interpersonal situation (such as the child accidentally breaking something belonging to the parent). In these studies, children who were secure as babies are likely to show the parent figures as responsive and caring, and to suggest positive solutions to the situations. Also, compared to children who were insecure as babies, they show a better understanding of others' feelings, especially negative ones. Importantly, these links between early secure attachment and the older child's good social understanding are generally supported by the parent continuing to give sensitive care and, particularly as the child's language develops, by the parent discussing emotions and the reasons behind people's actions in an open way.

As well as the influence of early attachment on how young children grow to *think* about relationships, research also shows consistent associations between babies' early attachments and the quality of their actual relationships with others. These links are particularly strong when it comes to intimate relationships. So in early childhood, and even into adolescence, children who were secure as babies have more harmonious, positive relationships with their close friends and also feel themselves to be better supported in their close relationships. Early attachment appears, however, to be of rather less relevance for the child's looser, more casual relationships, like general interactions with other children, where parents' ongoing support for their child's social relationships appears more important.

Early attachment and later behaviour problems
Aside from children's social understanding and relationships, researchers have often studied whether babies who were secure might be less likely than insecure babies to have behavioural problems in later

childhood. This could be the case because the secure child's greater social and emotional understanding enables them to negotiate challenging interpersonal situations better, and because they have learned how to manage their own difficult emotions well.

Two recent reviews involving almost 6,000 children have clearly shown that those who were securely attached to their mother as babies are indeed less likely to have behaviour problems than those who were insecure. For the kinds of problem known as 'externalizing', like aggressive or oppositional behaviour, the association with early insecurity was particularly marked in children who had shown a disorganized type of attachment as babies, and it was also stronger for boys than girls. Furthermore, although this link was found across social classes, it was particularly strong for children living in very deprived circumstances. For problems known as 'internalizing', like anxiety and social withdrawal, although there was still a significant effect of early insecurity, it was not as marked as for the externalizing problems, and in this case it was an avoidant style of insecure baby attachment that posed a particular risk.

The influence of ongoing circumstances and parenting

While the research shows continuities between babies' early attachments and their later development, it is also important to bear in mind that in general the quality of children's upbringing is usually fairly constant, and the ongoing circumstances and nature of parental care have an important influence on behaviour. If circumstances change, therefore, and the parent's sensitivity alters as a result, the link between the baby's early attachment and later behaviour problems generally becomes weaker. For example, one large-scale study in the US showed that insecure babies had fewer behaviour problems if they later received sensitive care (usually as a result of an improvement in the parents' circumstances). Similarly, where secure babies' parents later experienced difficulties in their lives and found it hard to maintain sensitive parenting, their children's risk of having

behaviour problems increased. Nevertheless, these results should not be taken to mean that the effects of early attachment experiences are entirely open to change. While there is some degree of flexibility in a child's developmental pathway in the early years, as time goes on possibilities for change are more limited. This may be especially the case when it comes to close, intimate, relationships, not least because the behaviour of the individual themselves is likely to contribute to past patterns of interpersonal relationships being perpetuated. For example, children reared in institutions often develop difficult styles of responding to others and in later life they can continue to have relationship difficulties, despite moving into more favourable environments.

Help for parents

Because babies' attachment relationships play such a central role in their development, helping parents to provide care that will foster their children's security has become a priority. In past years, intervention programmes tended to focus mainly on helping parents behave in more sensitive ways towards their baby, but while these were often successful in improving parenting practices, they did not always bring about gains in the babies' secure attachments. Accordingly, more emphasis has lately been placed on helping parents to think about their babies' experience. Sometimes this involves getting parents to consider their current feelings in the context of the care they themselves received in childhood. Another therapeutic approach has been to use video feedback: when parents are able to watch videos of their interactions with their baby, they can take time to observe the baby's responses and see things afresh from their baby's point of view. This is helpful not only in thinking about difficult experiences and behaviour, but video feedback can also help parents become more aware of their babies' affectionate attachment signals. In this way, positive cycles of communication can be improved and parents can be encouraged by seeing strengths in the relationship with their baby that they had not appreciated before.

One conclusion that emerges from considering the range of interventions is that different approaches work for different families. This is unsurprising considering the variety of circumstances parents face, and their differing backgrounds and personal histories (for example, parents may seek support because they are about to become carers of institutionalized babies who are likely to have a history of disturbed attachments, while others may be experiencing difficulties themselves, such as depression). Babies' characteristics, such as their temperament, also appear to influence the effectiveness of interventions, with parents of more emotionally reactive babies finding support particularly helpful. In general, families living in high-risk conditions may require support that is broader based and longer term, whereas those facing fewer background problems may be able to benefit from less intensive, briefer programmes.

Babies and non-parental care: daycare and its effects

Throughout history, parents have sometimes needed to involve others in the care of their babies and young children. Although there have been periods when babies have been cared for more exclusively by their mothers, since the 1980s most children under two years in the US and UK have experienced some kind of formal non-parental care. The question of how such care might affect a child's development is obviously of great importance, not just for the parents and children themselves, but for society as a whole. Accordingly, studies of non-parental care have been carried out with several thousand children across a number of countries.

Strikingly, one of the largest of these studies found that the overall effect of non-parental care was negligible. Nevertheless, the study made it clear that the nature of that care was important. In particular, of all the various types of childcare arrangements studied – grandparents or other relatives, nannies who

came to the family home, childminders who cared for babies in their own homes, and day-centres (including nursery care) – only this last category of daycare showed associations with child development. For this reason, and because daycare is now the fastest growing form of care for babies and toddlers, this section focuses on understanding which aspects of daycare are most important and how babies' experiences and relationships can best be managed in this context.

One of the key themes to emerge from daycare research is the importance of quality. A high staff-to-baby ratio, good staff training and higher rates of pay all contribute to high staff morale, a sense of professionalism and a low staff turnover. These features, in turn, are associated with care that is sensitive to the baby's social, emotional and cognitive developmental needs. This applies to carers' one-to-one relationships with individual babies, but also their ability to manage a group of children well. Regulations about pay and conditions, and financial support for families with babies in daycare, vary greatly between countries and, in general, provision of care is better in those countries where care is more tightly regulated and well-supported by government. This is particularly so in Scandinavian countries, where daycare is almost universally of a very high quality. In the US, by contrast, daycare is often poorly regulated, conditions vary greatly and are on average less satisfactory, and this is likely to be the case in other less well-regulated countries.

Adjustment to daycare

When parents embark on a daycare arrangement for their child, they commonly experience a range of complex feelings and concerns. They may feel there are conflicts between their parenting role and their other commitments, and wonder if they are doing the right thing by leaving their baby in care. They may fear the daily separations, for themselves as well as for their baby, and may worry that the baby will have difficulty in adapting to the daycare setting with its unfamiliar demands. Parents may also worry that their own relationship with their baby will suffer. Despite these fears, research has shown that much can be done to support babies' experiences in daycare and to maintain good parent–baby relationships. It is also the case that although child development has been shown to be affected by daycare, and especially its quality, these effects are in general relatively small and are far outweighed by the effects of background family factors and parents' own relationships with their baby.

Supporting the baby at daycare: settling in

There is no doubt that starting daycare can be stressful for babies. It is common for babies to cry when their parent leaves, and for them to be quite easily upset for several weeks after they begin attending. Some studies have found this is particularly the case if the baby does not begin daycare until around 12–18 months, when they may be more consciously aware of the separation from their parents than younger babies. Upset feelings can recur when the baby may be feeling more vulnerable – say, when coming back to daycare after a holiday break, or after being off sick. Babies show raised levels of the stress hormone, cortisol, when they begin to attend daycare. Notably, this occurs just as frequently in babies who are securely attached to their mother as those who are insecure and suggests that the repeated and prolonged separations experienced at daycare may pose a challenge to the expectations the baby has built up about their parent's availability, until he has had time to adjust and settle in. Daycare staff, no matter how sensitive, may not be able to prevent such distress. In view of this, it is important for parents to be able to support the baby's transition into care since, if they can take the time to settle their baby, staying with them and introducing them gradually, according to how the baby is adapting, any distress is likely to be reduced. Indeed, one study showed that where the mother–baby attachment was secure, and where parents were able to gradually and sensitively settle their baby in, the rise in cortisol levels typically associated with starting daycare did not occur (see picture sequences 2.20–2.24 about starting daycare and picture sequence 2.25 being settled in daycare).

2.20   Starting daycare at 6 months 1

Edmund, aged 6 months, is about to start attending a high quality nursery. He is already very familiar with the place, since his older sibling attended there and he and his mother know the staff well, but this is the first day of his own attendance. Each baby has their own 'Key Person', the carer who will take special responsibility for them.

In this picture sequence, Edmund starts to get to know his Key Person, Kirsty. He seems to settle well and his mother decides to leave him there for just one hour on this first occasion. He spends almost all the time one-to-one with Kirsty, but Kirsty is also able to help Edmund connect with other children. Since this first experience went so well, next time Edmund stays at the nursery for a full day. The second picture sequence traces his day from being left by his mother, through play, mealtime, sleep, bottle and play again, until his mother collects him.

We see how Kirsty very sensitively adjusts her care according to how Edmund is managing, and he responds well to her, though he's very keen to be in contact with his mother when she returns. Having settled so well through the day, Edmund will now start full-time care.

1 At the nursery Edmund watches his mother carefully as she talks to Kirsty, who will be his 'Key Person' carer.

2.20 **Starting daycare at 6 months 1** continued

2 Kirsty leans in to greet Edmund and his mother encourages him with a smile.

3 Soon, Edmund is happy to play with Kirsty, while his mother sits nearby filling in some forms.

4 Once Edmund seems happily settled with Kirsty, his mother leaves them together, but looks through the doorway as she goes to check that her son is still content. Edmund sucks on a wooden spoon as he sits near to Kirsty and looks around.

5 Kirsty concentrates on playing one-to-one with Edmund, and he happily explores different toys with her.

6 When another child comes along, Edmund turns to watch him, looking just a little uncertain.

7 Edmund turns to Kirsty and stretches out to her, and she responds by leaning in close to him.

8 Kirsty feels Edmund might like a bit more close contact with her, now that the play area is busier, and she lifts him up to play on her lap.

9 Another boy comes up to look at Edmund, giving Kirsty a hug from behind. Kirsty holds Edmund up to help him make contact with this new boy.

2.20   Starting daycare at 6 months 1 continued

10 Once Edmund's first hour of play is over, his mother comes back to fetch him. Edmund leans towards her, as she reaches out to take him.

11 She sweeps him up and round for a big hug, while Kirsty enjoys watching Edmund reunite with his mother.

2.21 Starting daycare at 6 months 2

1 The next day, Kirsty talks to Edmund, as his mother gets ready to leave him for his first full day at nursery.

2 She again spends some time playing with him one-to-one, so that he can settle in easily.

3 Edmund is comfortable enough to be able to enjoy his time with Kirsty.

4 Later in the morning, Kirsty sits Edmund in a high chair, ready to give him his lunch – but Edmund becomes quite upset. He might feel this is a big new thing to manage, especially as contact with Kirsty isn't so easy now.

5 Kirsty sees that this is difficult for Edmund, so she prepares to take him out of the chair.

6 She gives him a warm cuddle to reassure him.

2.21   **Starting daycare at 6 months 2** continued

7 Kirsty settles Edmund on her lap to give him his lunch, and he feeds happily.

8 Once Edmund has had quite a bit to eat, Kirsty gives him some finger food to eat by himself …

9 …and now that he's not so hungry and is more settled, she gives him another try in the chair. This time, Edmund can enjoy it, especially with the added interest of being able to feed himself.

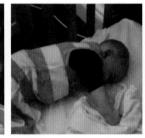

10 Now it's time for Edmund to have a sleep and Kirsty carefully puts him in his cot, placing him the way his mother has told her he likes …

11 …and following his mother's guidelines for settling him, her hands gently but firmly across his back.

12 Edmund soon settles into a sound sleep.

13 When Edmund wakes, he seems pleased to see Kirsty and reaches up to her.

14 Kirsty picks Edmund up and gives him a friendly greeting …

15 … before noting down for his parents the time that he has slept.

16 Kirsty then tells Edmund that she will give him his bottle.

2.21   **Starting daycare at 6 months 2** continued

17 As Edmund sucks, he looks intently up at Kirsty's face and she talks to him warmly through his feed.

18 Now it's time for play again. Still giving Edmund one-to-one attention, Kirsty takes him on her lap to play with dough, and Edmund enjoys exploring the texture with his fingers.

19 Edmund's mother arrives to collect him, and is pleased to see that he seems to be happy and settled with Kirsty.

20 Kirsty picks Edmund up to take him to his mother.

21 He reaches enthusiastically out to join her.

2.22   **Starting daycare at 13 months 1**

Oliver, aged 13 months. The process of settling into daycare will differ between babies according to their age and temperament, and their familiarity with the setting. For Oliver, who has had no experience of daycare before, settling into daycare is managed gradually over a number of days. On the first occasion, Oliver's Key Person, Anna, spends a lot of time talking to his parents about him, finding out as much as possible about his routine, how he responds, his likes and dislikes, and how his parents would like her to care for him. Anna also allows plenty of time to answer their questions and encourages them to talk about any concerns they might have. She knows this can be a challenging experience for parents, as well as for the babies.

The first picture sequence shows the introductory session and Anna's gentle start at making a relationship with Oliver, through picking up sensitively on his cues.

1 Oliver and his parents arrive at the daycare centre, where they meet Anna, who will be Oliver's Key Person.

2.22 Starting daycare at 13 months 1 continued

2 Anna settles everyone into a room with toys, where they can talk together about Oliver and what his parents' views are about his care. Oliver is interested in looking around, though he stays close to his father, and holds onto his shirt.

3 Oliver's father notices that his son is interested in a toy turtle and he shows Oliver how it moves, while Anna talks to his mother.

4 Anna signals to Oliver that she also likes the turtle and he watches her carefully.

5 As Oliver spends more time in the playroom, he becomes bolder and starts to explore, his father watching quietly.

6 Oliver has spotted some very interesting shredded paper across the room and he crawls over to investigate it, while the adults continue their discussion.

8 Anna takes this opportunity to make a connection with Oliver, holding up the paper and scattering it for him – he responds with glee.

9 After a while, and once Anna and Oliver's parents have had a good talk, Anna suggests they show Oliver the main playroom.

7 Oliver is intrigued by the paper and enjoys pulling it apart.

2.22   Starting daycare at 13 months 1 continued

10 Anna holds out her hands to Oliver, offering to take him, but he's not quite sure . . .

11 . . . however, he does let Anna hold him, looking across to his mother to check on what she thinks about this, and she warmly encourages him.

12 Anna leads the way into the playroom.

13 She sits with Oliver, and his mother stays nearby, as he explores more toys and checks out what is happening.

14 A little later, Oliver's parents take him home, first helping Oliver to connect with Anna and say 'goodbye' to her.

2.23   Starting daycare at 13 months 2

Three days later, Oliver's mother leaves him at the daycare centre for just an hour. Because Oliver is new to it, his mother stays with him in the playroom for a while, only leaving once he has settled to play. For parents as well as babies this can be a particularly anxious moment, and daycare staff can play an important role in listening to parents' concerns and supporting them. Like many babies in Oliver's situation, he becomes upset when his mother leaves, and his Key Person's response is crucial in helping him to manage. Here, Anna responds very sensitively to Oliver and when he is distressed she picks him up and seeks to provide comfort, giving him her full attention. She flexibly varies her care according to his cues, supporting him when he can manage without close contact with her.

1 Anna is ready to greet Oliver as he and his mother arrive for his second visit to the daycare centre.

2 Oliver's mother takes her time to settle him in, sitting down to talk to Anna, while Oliver sits nearby. He is rather quiet at first, sucking his thumb, and holding on to a soft toy.

2.23   **Starting daycare at 13 months 2** continued

3 Oliver soon livens up, however, and moves over to explore the playhouse. His mother waits with Anna until he seems settled, then she leaves.

4 Oliver is upset to see his mother go, but Anna holds him and talks to him as his mother leaves the centre, telling him that she will be back soon.

5 Anna decides to have some close time with Oliver. She knows from talking to his parents that he likes books, so she settles Oliver on her lap to look at one and he is able to respond and engage with the pictures.

6 After a little while, however, Oliver becomes upset again and wants his mother. Anna tries to reassure him that she will not be very long.

7 She carries him across the room to find something else he might like to do.

8 Anna finds an attractive car for Oliver to play with and keeps him on her lap as he examines it. She has also helped him by giving him his dummy, and Oliver settles to play.

9 After a while, Anna feels that Oliver is ready to move to where some other children are drawing, but she still supports him closely, keeping him on her lap.

10 As Oliver really seems to be enjoying the drawing, Anna feels that he will be able to manage on his own chair, and she makes him comfortable.

11 She stays nearby, ready to respond if he needs closer contact. In fact, he is getting into his stride and draws busily.

2.23   **Starting daycare at 13 months 2** continued

12 Since Oliver has been managing well and the time is drawing near for his mother to arrive, Anna feels it will be helpful for him to spend a little time playing on the floor where the other babies are. She closely monitors how Oliver is finding it, ready to step in should he need her.

13 When his mother arrives, Oliver takes a ball to her that he has been playing with, making it easy for her to share with him what he has been doing. Anna sits by, delighted to watch them both.

14 Anna tells Oliver's mother about his time with her.

15 Then she gives her Oliver's drawing to take home, praising it warmly, as Oliver looks on happily.

2.24   **Starting daycare at 13 months 3**

Three days later, Oliver spends half a day at the centre. On this occasion, as well as having to cope with the separation from his mother when she leaves, he has a sleep there, an experience that can pose a further attachment challenge for some babies. Both these situations need particularly careful management by the daycare staff. As it is quite common for babies to have moments of distress during this settling-in period, the daycare staff need to be available to spend time one-to-one with them. Oliver's Key Person, Anna, gauges his needs for contact at each point. She is especially aware of the importance of separations and going-to-sleep routines, and supports Oliver through them closely. Knowing that this settling-in period is an anxious time for parents as well, the daycare centre has a policy of routinely phoning parents during the morning, usually once the baby has settled to sleep. This supplements the normal practice of giving feedback to parents about the baby's daily experience and it is important in helping them feel in touch with what is happening. When parents' own anxieties about their child's experience in daycare can be allayed, they are better placed to confidently support their baby's time there.

2.24   **Starting daycare at 13 months 3** continued

1 It's a sunny autumn morning when Oliver and his mother arrive for Oliver's first half-day and everyone is outside. They spend some time with Anna watching the other children playing.

2 After a while, Oliver's mother passes him over to Anna.

3 Oliver's mother prepares to leave. Oliver looks at her intently, sucking on his dummy.

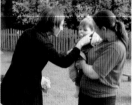

4 Oliver then starts to cry. Anna suggests to him that perhaps they should show his mummy around the garden before she goes.

5 This calms Oliver and they set out, Oliver in Anna's arms, to see what the other children are doing.

6 Oliver's mother spends a little time sharing the play space and the experience of the other babies with Oliver and Anna.

7 Then she explains to Oliver that she now has to go, but will be back later.

9 Anna suggests that she and Oliver find something to play with in the garden and Oliver calms down as he looks at all the activities – but still keeping his arm around Anna's neck and sucking his dummy.

8 Oliver still finds the separation upsetting and Anna tries to reassure him that his mother will be back later. She holds him close.

10 Once Oliver is settled, Anna plays ball with him one-to-one on the ground.

11 Oliver really enjoys this and is also pleased when another baby comes along to watch.

2.24   **Starting daycare at 13 months 3** continued

12 Later in the morning it's time for Oliver to have a sleep. As discussed with his parents, Anna puts him in his cot, with his dummy and his special soft toy. Since he is calm, she leaves after a minute or so …

13 … but when Anna goes, Oliver starts to cry, showing that Anna's presence has become important in helping him manage.

14 Anna immediately returns. She comforts and strokes him and Oliver uses her presence to calm down again.

15 Now Anna places Oliver in position for sleeping, stroking his back in the way that his parents have told her he likes, until he is completely settled. Oliver cuddles his special toy.

16 When Anna stops stroking Oliver, she stays for a while, just to check that he is finally settled and doesn't need her touch any more.

17 She phones Oliver's mother and describes the events of the morning, reassuring her that Oliver has gone to sleep soundly.

18 At the end of the morning, when Oliver's mother returns to fetch him, he is delighted to see her and stretches out to her.

19 His mother moves close, and looks at the toys he has been playing with, helping him make a link between her and his daycare experiences.

20 Before she and Oliver leave, she spends some time talking to Anna, who explains how Oliver has found the morning.

2.25   Settled in daycare

Six weeks later, Oliver, now 15 months, is comfortably settled into daycare, exploring the toys and enjoying his lunch, without needing the one-to-one attention from Anna that he had before. He is also connecting more with the other babies and, in limited ways, is able to respond to their interests too, rather than remaining solely focused on his own experience.

Here, we see Oliver and Edmund together, six weeks after Edmund's start at the centre too.

1 Oliver happily explores the large tunnel, taking his turn to crawl right through.

2 He can also get absorbed for long spells playing with simple Lego blocks.

3 At lunchtime, Oliver joins in with the other babies – he knows the routines well now and is comfortable being part of the daycare community.

4 Oliver's horizons are also expanding to include an interest in other babies' experience. He watches as Edmund crawls towards a frame with a flashing light.

5 Then Oliver leans into the frame to make the light carry on flashing.

6 He watches Edmund to see the effect.

When parents have the opportunity to support their baby and can be confident that he is settled, they are less likely to feel conflicted and anxious about leaving him. This, in turn, helps maintain the security of the parent–baby relationship. This process can be made easier where daycare centres set up routines for parents and staff to communicate with each other concerning the details of the baby's daily experiences and needs (see picture sequences 2.26 and 2.27).

2.26   Attachment needs after a break

Good daycare shows flexibility in adjusting to babies' changing needs for close support and comfort. It is common for babies to feel the need for extra comfort after a holiday or illness break, even if they have attended for some time. Once again, there is a particular need for close liaison between parent and staff concerning the baby's feelings in this situation.

Here Jun, aged 14 months, is coming back after a family holiday and it takes time for him to feel confident again. His Key Person, Kirsty, adapts sensitively and first gives him the extra contact that he needs, then supports him when he feels bolder. This picture sequence shows some of Jun's first two days after the break.

1 Jun's mother brings him into the daycare playroom after a holiday break.

2 Jun clings to her tightly and his mother explains to Jun's Key Person, Kirsty, that she thinks he will need time to settle back in again.

3 Kirsty watches as Jun's mother tells him that he is to stay with Kirsty and play for a while, and she strokes his head.

4 Kirsty holds out her hands in welcome to Jun, but he seems rather uncertain, as he sucks his thumb.

5 Kirsty and Jun watch, as his mother waves goodbye.

6 Kirsty sits Jun on her lap and unzips his jacket. Jun is still looking rather glum and continues his thumbsucking.

7 Kirsty recognizes that it's quite hard for Jun to be apart from his mother again – she warmly cuddles him and Jun nestles into her.

8 After a little while, Kirsty turns the cuddle into a game, to help Jun on his way to enjoying some play. She blows a raspberry into his neck.

2.26   **Attachment needs after a break** continued

9 She checks on Jun's response and he seems to have enjoyed it.

10 So she repeats the raspberry blowing, and Jun chuckles with pleasure.

11 Now Kirsty senses that he is ready to connect with the other children. Still keeping Jun on her lap, she introduces him to the idea of a ball game with one of the other babies.

12 Soon, Jun is engrossed in play and he slides himself to the floor.

13 Since he is now comfortable, Kirsty moves a little away from him, so that there can be a three-part game between her, Jun and the other baby.

14 The next day, Jun settles in much more easily, but Kirsty still feels she needs to spend time being close to him. Jun is happy for quite some while to draw alongside Kirsty.

15 But suddenly, Jun feels the need for closer contact, and he reaches across to her . . .

16 . . . Kirsty warmly responds and picks him up . . .

17 . . . and Jun settles again from the comfort of her knee . . .

18 . . . happily reaching across to start drawing again, once he has experienced a close moment with Kirsty.

2.27   Links to home routines for individualized care

A core part of sensitive caregiving is taking account of the unique characteristics and experiences of each baby. When there is close communication between parents and staff and information is passed on about babies' special routines, their particular ways of being comforted, and their recent experiences, daycare can be made more sensitive to the individual baby. This is especially important in relation to managing a baby's distress and transition to sleep, but knowledge of the baby's family and their daily lives can also play a key role in helping with babies' language and cognitive development, as staff can use the 'inside information' to make links between experiences at daycare and the baby's wider world.

Here we see examples of such individualized care for four babies.

1 The parents of Rosie, 13 months, have asked if she can be rocked to sleep, with her cuddly toys near her.

2 Anna, Rosie's Key Person, soothes and rocks her until she has fallen asleep.

3 Then Anna gently lifts her and places her in her cot, just as happens at home.

4 And Rosie has her special teddy placed next to her as well.

5 Max and Phoebe start to have a tussle over a ball, while Anna watches, ready to step in if needed.

6 In fact, Max quickly signals to her that he wants her support.

7 Anna beckons him to come to her.

8 Max's parents have suggested that he is helped by having his soft monkey when he's upset, as well as when he goes to sleep, and Anna shows it to him.

9 Max cuddles into his monkey and quickly recovers.

10 When he is ready, Anna places Max's monkey nearby while he starts playing with some other toys.

2.27   Links to home routines for individualized care continued

11 Matilda, aged 11 months, comes back to daycare after the weekend and Anna looks through the notebook her parents use to describe any special events. She sees that Matilda has been feeding ducks, and asks her about it.

12 Then Anna finds a toy duck and helps Matilda link it to her weekend experience.

13 Matilda seems really interested and plays with the duck, while Anna continues to talk to her about what she did.

14 Something has happened to upset Sam, aged 14 months.

15 Sam reaches for his special soft cloth which his parents have sent in to daycare with him.

16 Anna brings it over and Sam begins to calm down just at the sight of it.

17 Sam gives his cloth a good suck and holds it close, as Anna watches to makes sure that he's recovered.

Adjustment to daycare: support at home

Parents who place their child in daycare often make a special effort to be more closely involved with them at home. Indeed, some studies have found that mothers who work away from home are generally more intensely and responsively involved with their babies than mothers who are home-based. This added sensitivity is particularly important when the baby is in poorer quality daycare for long periods, in which case the baby may well show increased fussing and crying at home in the evenings. If good support during the day is not available, the baby will particularly need their parents' help in managing these difficult emotions. Unfortunately, when demands on parents necessitate putting their baby in daycare for long hours, managing

to sensitively respond to the baby's needs can be very hard – and when this challenge is combined with poor-quality daycare, the risk of the baby being insecurely attached does increase. Given the importance of sensitive parental support for the baby's development, it is critical that government policy should support both good-quality daycare and the ability of parents with young babies to work fewer and more flexible hours.

Babies' relationships with their daycarers

At daycare the baby is likely to form significant relationships with other adults, and parents often worry that these new attachments might become more important to the baby than their own. In fact, as long as babies enjoy a secure relationship with their parents,

2.28 Signs of attachment to parents in daycare

Babies in daycare do not always show obvious signs of attachment to their parents when collected at the end of the day. This is partly because attachment needs are not strongly activated if the baby is happily settled and feeling secure, so parents should not feel disheartened if their secure baby doesn't show the classic delighted response to reunion in more challenging situations that is described in research literature. It can of course be heart-warming for the parent if their baby does react with delight at seeing them, especially if they know he is closely attached to the daycarer.

Here, we see Alex, now aged 15 months and very close to his Key Person, Kirsty. This is a special day, as the babies have had their Christmas party and on this occasion Alex's father is collecting him.

1 Alex is waiting with Kirsty, as parents begin arriving to take their babies home after the party. He spots his father coming in and grins widely.

2 Now Alex wriggles to the floor, out of Kirsty's grasp.

3 He rushes to greet his father ...

4 ...hugging him closely.

5 Alex's father picks him up and asks him about the party.

6 Kirsty joins them to help tell Alex's father all about it.

7 Then it's home time.

8 Alex's father chats to him about his day as they leave.

there is no evidence to suggest that this happens. On the contrary, several studies have demonstrated that parents typically remain right at the forefront of the baby's attachments, so that if both parent and daycarer are present, most babies will prefer to stay close to and interact with the parent (see picture sequence 2.28).

Parents naturally want their baby to feel secure and comfortable with their daycarer and babies do indeed develop attachments to daycare staff. Just as for attachment to parents, a baby's secure relationship with their daycarer is more likely where the carer is regularly available, able to be highly involved and responds sensitively to the baby. This is far more likely where staff have good working conditions and where they have received training. It is also more likely when the centre offers opportunities for parents and carers to communicate closely with each other about the baby's day-to-day experiences.

Where these conditions apply, babies will show all the usual signs of attachment security that are seen in secure baby–parent relationships, seeking comfort from the carer when they are distressed and being rapidly soothed by them, as well as choosing to spend time with the carer for play and other activities. The daycarer's role is likely to be particularly concerned with comforting the baby while he is first settling into care. After this, they will usually shift to focus more on play, where the carer then offers more support for the baby to explore, and for their relationships with other children. Not surprisingly, where secure attachments to daycarers develop, the quality of the baby's play with that carer is more advanced. But other relationships benefit too – for example, play with other babies becomes more positive. (see picture sequences 2.29–2.32).

2.29   Close relationships with daycare staff

When daycare is going well and staff are sensitive to babies' needs, then the same attachment behaviour found in a secure parent–child relationship can also be seen in babies' relationships with their day-centre carers. These include wanting to be close to them, distress at separation, and the ability to be comforted by them when distressed. Parents sometimes feel anxious that, somehow, their baby is developing an attachment to the carer that could undermine his attachment to them. Research has found this is not the case at all, and daycare relationships can develop perfectly well alongside the baby's attachment to their parents. Also, the baby benefits from feeling close to the person who cares for them during the day.

Callum, aged 13 months, has become very attached to his Key Person, Tanya, and shows his special relationship to her by seeking to be near her when she comes into the room, and when he wants to play.

1 Callum is very aware of his Key Person, Tanya's, presence as she enters the room.

2 He makes a beeline to join her.

3 Callum is delighted when she lifts him up for a cuddle.

2.29 Close relationships with daycare staff continued

4 Later, Callum also seeks Tanya out as a playmate, approaching her as she prepares lunch for some of the other babies. Tanya starts a finger game.

5 She teases Callum, tickling him as she tells him that he's already had his lunch. Callum squirms with pleasure.

6 He then responds with a game using his hands himself.

2.30 Close relationships with daycare staff 2

Another child at the centre, Zak, has become very fond of his carer, Anna. Zak, 13 months, has been enjoying playing with her, but when Anna leaves to get something else for him, Zak is upset to see her go and wants to be held by her when she comes back.

1 Zak looks on as Anna praises him, admiring the way he has made the water change colour by shaking the bottle.

2 Anna passes the bottle back to Zak, and tells him that she is going to find something else for him to see.

3 Zak is upset to see Anna go.

4 So she comes back quickly and holds out her arms to him.

5 Zak reaches up to Anna.

6 She gives him a good cuddle until he feels better.

2.31   Close relationships with daycare staff 3

Babies' needs for closeness with those to whom they are attached increase when they feel tired or ill, and when such relationships are with daycare staff, the staff can help to meet these needs. Alex, aged 13 months, has a strong attachment to his Key Person, Kirsty, and even after a difficult night he is keen to be with her at the daycare centre. Of course, this bond between Alex and Kirsty doesn't in any way diminish Alex's attachment to his father, but it does help Alex manage when his father leaves.

1 Alex's father brings him into the daycare centre.

2 They are greeted by Kirsty, who is Alex's Key Person. Alex's father explains that his son has had a difficult night and might not be quite as cheerful as usual.

3 Kirsty leans forward to Alex and expresses her sympathy for him.

4 She reassures Alex's father that she will keep an especially close eye on him today and they discuss arrangements for Alex's daytime sleep.

5 Alex, in spite of being a little under par, is very happy to go to Kirsty when she reaches for him.

6 He stays comfortably with Kirsty, but watches closely as his father notes down some information about the situation.

7 Before Alex's father leaves, Kirsty wants to make sure that Alex is happy to play, so she takes him over to the table with coloured water bottles, while Alex's father waits nearby. Alex looks at the playthings with interest.

8 Before Alex gets stuck into playing, however, he turns to say goodbye to his father, very much aware that he is going to leave.

9 His father turns to wave from the doorway.

10 Then, comfortable with Kirsty nearby, Alex settles to play in earnest.

2.32   The well-settled child

A baby who is well settled into nursery is less likely to need close comfort from their Key Person, although the relationship can be playful, and of course the Key Person still needs to give caretaking support (for instance, settling the baby to sleep). Play with other children and freedom to explore wider experiences emerge more strongly as the baby's attachment needs recede.

Reeve, aged 15 months, has been at the daycare centre for six months and is well settled. We see him happily playing with other babies, but also enjoying a familiar game with his Key Person, Anna, during a nappy change. The pattern for settling him to sleep was developed in consultation with his parents and is carried out now without Reeve showing any distress. As well as having a close, warm, relationship with Anna, Reeve has also formed attachments to other staff and seeks them out for play too. In line with good daycare practice, the staff take regular notes about the baby's day to share with the parents.

3 Anna keeps a friendly watchful eye on Reeve and Isabelle, as they experiment by wiping the paint on each other's hands.

1 Anna sets up some paints for Reeve and another baby, Isabelle.

2 Soon, both babies are immersed in exploring the paints.

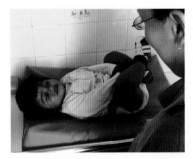

4 When it's time for Reeve to have a nappy change, he knows this is a moment for a game that he and Anna have developed.

5 Reeve initiates playing peek-a-boo, hiding . . .

6 . . . and then uncovering his face to give Anna a surprise.

8 Later, when it's time for Reeve's morning sleep, Anna places him on a mattress on the floor, as requested by his parents, so that he gets a clear sense of the difference between day and night-time routines. He knows this well, positioning himself in readiness to lie down.

7 Now Anna is going to cover her face – it's a routine that Reeve loves.

2.32   **The well-settled child** continued

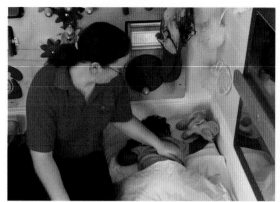

9 Again, following Reeve's parents' guidelines, Anna strokes his back as he goes to sleep. Reeve also has his special soft toy bunny to help him.

10 As agreed with Reeve's parents, Anna checks to see that Reeve is asleep before she leaves him.

11 Although Reeve has a close, warm relationship with Anna, he has also become very fond of Kirsty and often seeks her out for play.

12 Here, Reeve and Kirsty are playing a game of putting leaves in a tub.

13 It's something that takes quite a lot of concentration on a windy day and Kirsty watches patiently as Reeve carefully positions his leaf.

14 She shares his pleasure when it goes in safely.

15 Reeve's mother comes to collect him.

16 Anna takes her through Reeve's day, using the notes that are made daily so that parents are well informed about their baby's experience in daycare.

17 She shows Reeve's mother the painting that he did that morning.

Babies' relationships with each other

One of the key reasons parents choose daycare is to encourage their baby to meet and relate to other children, especially if the baby is an only child or from a small family. Well-supervised groups, not just in daycare but more generally, can provide a secure environment for babies to learn about social cooperation and can offer stimulating play, such as group games or joint musical or art activities. Such groups provide a safe way for small children to explore and deal with a range of emotions, and to practise different methods of social exchange. Although social responses to others are obviously undeveloped in babies, behaviour that is clearly empathic and socially aware, such as kind, helpful acts, can be seen in daycare settings among children of 12 to 18 months of age, and simple social rituals also start to appear. Such positive relations are especially likely to take place when the quality of the baby's relationship with their daycarer is good.

Even the normal conflicts that occur between babies, if well managed by daycare staff, may be useful in giving the baby some awareness of the gap between their own and other children's perceptions (see also Chapter 1, p. 56, and picture sequence 1.35 on the value contained conflicts can have for social understanding). Nevertheless, the skills of the daycare staff in managing small groups are important to prevent these conflicts from escalating, while organized activities and other stimulating interaction can make the risk of serious conflict much smaller (see picture sequence 2.33).

2.33   Daycare's effect on social skills

One of the advantages that parents often feel emerges from their babies' experience in daycare is the development of social skills, including playing with other children and feeling comfortable in a communal environment. This is particularly relevant to older babies. Here, we see some examples of the range of social experiences to be found in good nurseries, including the development of close, affectionate relationships between the babies themselves. Activities range from singing to free play.

1 Callum, Max, Reeve and Isabelle enjoy some joint activities with Anna.

2 Singing together.

3 Reading together.

4 Free play.

5 Structured play.

6 Mealtime.

2.33   **Daycare's effect on social skills** continued

The babies connect with each other in all sorts of ways.

7 Max is amused as James pulls funny faces at his image in the mirror.

8 Isabelle and Jun are getting ready to go outside.

9 First, Isabelle gives Jun a wave…

10 …then Jun leans over to give Isabelle a kiss.

11 Ben is told that it's time to leave daycare now, where he's been playing with his best friend, Remi.

12 Ben gives Remi a warm hug.

13 Ben then turns back to wave to Remi as he leaves.

Family background can play an important role in influencing babies' social responses to each other in daycare. For example, where mothers' interactions with their baby are sensitive, the baby is more likely to be competent in their own interactions with other children. By contrast, babies and young children from difficult backgrounds are more likely than others to respond to other babies' signs of distress by becoming angry, or sometimes anxious. Aside from family factors, the baby's own way of responding is also relevant to how daycare affects their relationships with other children. For example, shy individuals may find it hard to interact with bold babies and toddlers, making daycare more stressful for them than it is for those who are less shy. Daycarers are therefore better placed to understand babies' needs if they are aware of the family circumstances, and of the baby's particular temperament and vulnerabilities.

Effects of daycare on babies' development

Research on the links between daycare and children's wider development has become more sophisticated over the years, and the importance of taking family conditions into account when studying these associations is now well recognized. It is important to bear in mind that the nature of a baby's daycare and how much the parents use it, is likely to depend heavily on factors such as family income and education. This is especially the case in countries where governments provide little or no financial support, and where good-quality daycare may only be possible for higher earners. Unless such factors are taken into account, any associations reported between daycare characteristics and child development may be misleading, because the noted effects might actually be due to the family background, rather than being directly caused by the daycare itself. In fact, the overwhelming weight of evidence where family and parenting are taken into account shows these two factors are by far the most important predictors of a range of children's developmental outcomes.

Aside from the quality of the child's attachment to their parents, areas of child development shown to be affected principally by family and parenting include behaviour problems, social competence, and cognitive and language development. Nevertheless, daycare has been found to have some additional influence, though much smaller, on some of these outcomes, and good quality daycare is recognized to be of benefit for young children's language and cognitive development, as well as for their social maturity and relationships with others. In one area however, behaviour problems, the evidence is more mixed. In the US, where care quality is often not as good as in some other countries, daycare has been associated with a small increase in behaviour problems, but this effect has not been found in recent UK research.

So far as we can tell, the overall effects of daycare on child development are small, vary considerably according to family background, and particularly according to whether families are under stress. Indeed, where parents are stressed, good quality daycare can be of benefit to the child's development. For example, babies whose families are less able to provide good support for their language skills will be very likely to benefit from good-quality daycare. Where the family environment is very difficult, the risk of behaviour problems can also be reduced if the baby or young child attends good-quality daycare. Lastly, it is important to take into account the individual characteristics of the baby when considering the effects of daycare. For example, compared to babies with easy temperaments, babies who are temperamentally emotionally negative or sensitive show an increase in behaviour problems if

they receive poor-quality care, but a decrease if their daycare is of good quality.

To summarize, the sensitive support that babies receive from both their parents and from daycare staff has a critical effect on how well they adjust to daycare and also on the quality of their social experiences and their development. With the number of babies in daycare steadily increasing, it is really important for government regulation to ensure that it delivers a high-quality service and that it is accessible to parents – who should also be supported to work flexibly and use daycare in a way that responds to their baby's needs.

Babies' attachment to objects

Although babies' primary attachments are clearly to the people who care for them, they can also develop clear signs of attachments to objects. Such attachments may seem rather trivial, yet they are worth noting since they can assume great importance in the lives of many babies and small children. This type of attachment typically sets in towards the end of the first year, when a strong preference for a particular object can emerge. The most usual objects are a soft toy, blanket, or cloth, and the baby and his parents often adopt a special name for them, such as 'raggy', 'clothy', or a baby version of some aspect of the object (for instance, 'dirrel' for a cloth with a squirrel picture), and such names are retained long after the baby can talk fluently. These objects are sometimes referred to as 'security blankets' or 'transitional objects', and both the object itself, and its particular qualities, can become intensely important to the baby. If it is lost the baby is likely to become upset and they may also show distress if the object changes in any way – for example, by being washed. Babies often handle their security object in distinctive ways, typically holding it close up to their face, often stroking it, brushing it against their cheek, or fingering a particular part of it, like a ridged edge or a silky label (see Chapter 1, picture sequence 1.26 of Benjamin with his 'clothy'). They may also suck their thumb at the same time, or perhaps pull on their ear lobe or twiddle

2.34 Attachment to objects

Isabel, aged 10 months, always likes to have a 'clothy' with her when going off to sleep. As can be seen in this uncaptioned sequence, she waves it to and fro at first, then brings it close to her face, gently stroking it against her cheek, and almost instantly falls into a deep sleep.

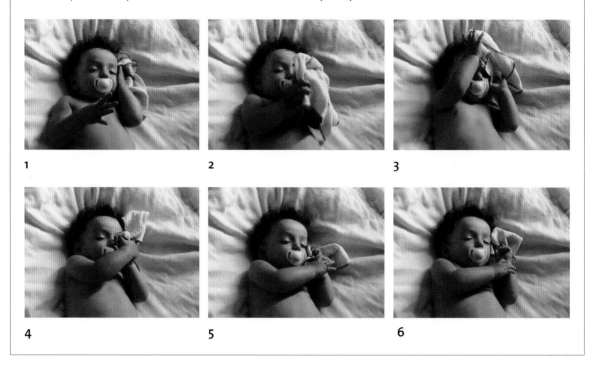

1   2   3

4   5   6

their hair. This is particularly likely to happen as the baby goes off to sleep, but the object can also be used as a general comforter at times of distress. In addition, if their special object is at hand when they are in an unfamiliar environment, then the baby will be more willing to explore and play. So in some respects, the baby's relationship to their special object is rather like an attachment relationship to a caregiver. Indeed, some studies have shown that in conditions of mild stress the baby is just as likely to be calmed by their special object as by their parent – so these security objects can be very useful where the parent is not available to comfort the baby, for example, in daycare (see picture sequence 2.34).

Clinicians and researchers have long speculated on the reasons why some babies develop attachments to special objects while others do not. Some suggest that these objects are substitutes for care that has

been lacking, others that they are used by babies who have had good care and who feel confident enough to start separating from their parent. In fact, no clear relationship has yet been demonstrated between a baby having a special object and their security of attachment to the parent. Nevertheless, certain patterns of child-rearing do seem to make a difference to the chances of special objects being used. In particular, in cultures such as Japan, where children are rarely separated from their parents at night, attachments to special objects are infrequent. In the US, by contrast, where parents are typically not so available to their children at night, these attachments are far more common. Rates of babies' having special objects can also differ very much within countries according to these diverse styles of child-rearing. The findings seem to suggest, then, that developing an attachment to a special object may be a helpful way for babies to adapt to a parenting style that encourages their independence, particularly around sleep routines.

Summary of Chapter 2

Of the diverse aspects of a baby's early development, the nature of their attachments to their parents is of particular importance to later adjustment and well-being. When babies receive care that is sensitive to their attachment needs, including care that communicates the parent's ability to understand their experience, they are likely to grow up to be secure and, in turn, to be at lower risk for developing behaviour problems and difficulties in their close interpersonal relationships. Parents' ability to give sensitive care is related to their own early attachments, to the background stresses that they face, and to their own well-being and mental health. In addition, babies' own characteristics, such as how temperamentally placid or reactive they are, can also have an impact on parents' abilities to respond sensitively to their child. Several interventions have been developed to support parents who are experiencing difficulties, and different kinds of support appear to work best for different parenting situations.

In general, the effects of babies' experiences with their parents far outweigh those of other care experiences, such as that of daycare. Nevertheless, attachment issues are also present in this context and there is much that daycarers, working together with parents, can do to support babies' adjustment to daycare and to help their wider development. If daycare is to provide good support, however, it is essential that governments regulate its quality and help parents use it flexibly. Finally, babies can also develop attachments to special objects. While clearly not as significant for their development as attachments to parents, they can still be important for the babies' feelings of comfort and security, and should therefore be taken seriously.

Ben's sandcastle has collapsed.

3 Self-regulation and control

One of the most challenging tasks a baby faces is that of managing his difficult feelings and states and controlling or regulating his behaviour. Developing good self-regulation is important, because it lays the foundations for a broad range of functions – it helps the child engage well in whatever they are doing, whether this involves cognitive or social activities and helps them adapt positively to new situations and demands. Self-regulation and control skills play a particularly valuable role in containing and reducing aggressive behaviour and increasing social cooperation. Although self-regulation abilities go on developing right through to adulthood, particularly important changes come in the first two years, as advances in babies' cognition and social understanding gradually allow them to take more conscious and deliberate control over their experiences.

Basics of babies' regulation

Even as newborns, babies differ in how they experience and manage what happens to them. One basic aspect of a baby's early regulation is how reactive he is. Thus, some babies have a very low threshold for reacting to even slight stimulation and they respond quickly and strongly, while others are far less reactive. The second basic aspect of early regulation is how well the baby can manage their experience. Again, some babies can do this far more easily than others, perhaps

through being able to find their own fists to suck on to calm themselves, or shut down their reactions to repeated stimulation. The reasons for such differences in reactivity and regulatory capacities are by no means fully understood, although they include both genetic and antenatal factors (for example, at the extremes, excessive intake of alcohol or high levels of maternal stress). Whatever their origin they have a substantial impact on the experience of parents and, in turn, how parents respond to their baby's individual way of behaving plays a crucial role in shaping his future ability to regulate his experience.

Parental support for babies' basic self-regulation abilities

Early caretaking

All babies, whatever their natural capacities, are at first entirely dependent on their caregivers to support them. In the early weeks, their need for support is often particularly clear in relation to hunger (see picture sequences 2.8, 2.9 and 2.11 in Chapter 2 on attachment), or during major changes in handling, such as when the baby is being undressed or lifted out of a bath, or having to undergo unpleasant experiences such as being immunized (see picture sequences 3.1 and also 2.18 and 2.19 in Chapter 2). Although some babies' distress and crying in these caretaking situations cannot easily be reduced in the early weeks, no matter how sensitive the care they receive, parents can generally help their baby recover and become calm by attending to his physical needs, changing or lessening whatever stimulation is causing the problem, or by giving close, comforting contact like holding, stroking, rocking and carrying. But aside from such caretaking activities, and particularly as the baby becomes more socially active, everyday face-to-face interactions can also provide many opportunities for parents to support the development of their baby's self-regulation skills.

3.1   Young babies' distress

Stanley, aged 4 weeks. In the early days and weeks, certain ordinary caretaking routines seem to make some babies feel vulnerable – for example, if removing the baby's clothes for a nappy change, or lifting them from warm water after a bath, they can become rapidly distressed and their behaviour dysregulated. At such times, they may need close, containing contact in order to become calm again.

1 Stanley had a very dirty nappy and his mother wants to give him a good wash. As she undresses him and lifts him up, he becomes very distressed.

2 His arms jerk around in an uncontrollable way as his mother lowers him into the water.

3 Quite soon, Stanley is able to benefit from the feel of the warm water around him, and his mother's secure holding, and he calms down.

4 When Stanley is removed from the bath, however, he becomes agitated, his movements are disorganized …

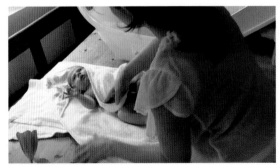

5 … and soon his distress has escalated again.

6 Stanley's mother manages to help a little by starting to make eye-contact and soothing him with her voice.

7 As this works quite well, she takes her time wrapping him in his towel, talking softly to him all the time, and holding his gaze.

3.1   **Young babies' distress** continued

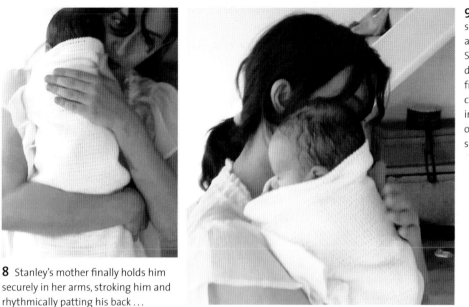

9 ...still talking softly to him as she does so. Stanley settles down and, free from distress, can soon take an interest in looking over his mother's shoulder.

8 Stanley's mother finally holds him securely in her arms, stroking him and rhythmically patting his back ...

Face-to-face engagements

(i) *The 'Still Face'* There is a classic experiment, the 'Still Face', that shows vividly how babies can be greatly affected by their parent's behaviour during face-to-face interactions. But this experiment also shows that babies have a number of strategies to help them cope with mild social challenges, even within the first weeks of life. In the 'Still Face', following a period of normal face-to-face engagement, the parent's responsiveness to the baby is abruptly halted, and for around two minutes the parent adopts a still, expressionless, face whilst still continuing to look at the baby, before resuming normal contact (see picture sequence 3.2 and in Chapter 1, picture sequence 1.6 for another example). Although babies differ in their tolerance of this disruption and in their precise style of reacting, in general when the parent behaves in this way the baby quickly notices and will rapidly attempt to manage the challenge. Often, the baby at first seems to try to influence the parent by making social bids to engage with them, and then will show signs of protest – perhaps grunting, frowning

or thrashing his arms – while he looks at his parent's expressionless face. If these attempts to re-engage their parent are unsuccessful, some babies may become upset or withdrawn. Others seem to cope quite well with this odd situation and the difficult feelings it provokes – they may, for example, turn away from their parent and actively focus their attention on something else, or they may start to self-soothe, possibly sucking on their hand, touching their face or fingering their clothes, as well as perhaps darting an occasional look back, as if checking on their parent's availability. There are also physiological responses that indicate greater arousal and the mobilization of coping mechanisms for stress, that occur in babies during the Still-Face period– for example, changes in heart rate and breathing, as well as elevations in the stress hormone, cortisol. Finally, when the parent resumes normal contact babies typically take a little while before resuming their normal social behaviour, and may continue to show these regulatory adjustments until settling down again.

3.2   The face-to-face Still-Face experiment

Astrid, aged 4.5 months. In the face-to-face Still-Face experiment, the parent engages with the baby normally for a while, before suddenly ceasing to respond and adopting a still, or blank face, while continuing to look at the baby for 1–2 minutes, and then resuming normal contact. This experiment presents the baby with the challenge of an unexpected disruption to the usual pattern of interaction, and of having to regulate their own behaviour without their parent's support. Babies differ in how they respond to this brief challenge, partly because of temperamental characteristics, but also according to their previous experience of interactions with their parent. Babies who are used to sensitive, responsive parenting are likely to have clear expectations that the parent will respond to their social signals, and may therefore tenaciously persist in trying to elicit a response during the Still-Face phase. Furthermore, babies whose self-regulation capacities have been well-supported during previous social interactions are better able to remain well regulated during this challenge.

Here, Astrid quickly reacts to the Still-Face, and cycles repeatedly between trying to engage her father by making social bids to him and then turning her attention to self-soothing and exploring her environment, without becoming dysregulated and distressed. Nevertheless, at the end of the Still-Face phase, when her father makes contact again, she takes a little time to re-engage with him.

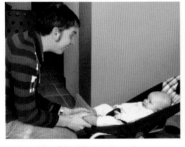

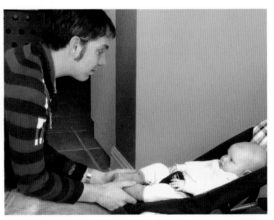

2 When her father abruptly stops engaging with her, Astrid sobers and gazes at his immobile face.

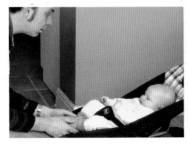

1 Astrid and her father have been enjoying play together.

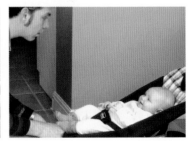

3 She quickly withdraws her gaze, and looks down at her hands.

4 Astrid looks up again at her father, as though checking on whether he is still behaving in this unusual way.

5 Astrid has been used to her father being very responsive to her and she makes a clear bid to him, as though trying to get him to play.

3.2   **The face-to-face Still-Face experiment** continued

6 When he remains blank-faced, she again withdraws her gaze.

7 Astrid occupies herself by examining her hands …

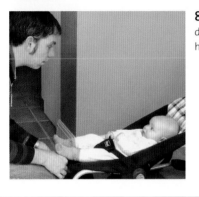

8 … but then quite quickly darts another checking look at her father.

9 Once again, Astrid makes a bid to try to engage him.

(ii) Normal face-to-face engagements The Still Face is of course a very unnatural disruption. But it is also true that far from being perfectly synchronized, normal face-to-face engagements regularly challenge babies as well, though to a very different degree. When these challenges are relatively minor, and are handled well, they can be a useful way for the baby to gain experience of recovering from difficult moments – he can strengthen his capacities to regulate his state, emotions and behaviour and get back on an even keel. These challenges can take a variety of forms: quite often 'mismatches' or 'misattunements' occur in a parent's responses, as when, for example, their excited expression is momentarily too intense for the baby to handle, or when they misinterpret the baby's signal. Episodes like this are an inevitable part of the process of parent and baby becoming used to each other's cues and learning their significance, and they can also be

an important way for parents to convey the particular social meaning that they attach to the baby's behaviour (more on this in Chapter 1). Other potential challenges to the baby's regulated state can occur through interruptions such as sneezes or hiccoughs, unexpected events such as a loud noise nearby, or even when the baby is feeling a pleasurable state that threatens to become too intense.

By and large, with a young baby, the parent manages most of these challenges on the baby's behalf. For example, if the parent has misjudged the baby's signals and the child is startled, or experiences something that makes him briefly uncomfortable, then the parent may actively use their facial expressions and adjust their intonation and tone of voice, first to connect with their baby and empathize with him, and then to support him in making the transition towards a more comfortable state (see picture sequence 3.3).

3.3   Recovering from normal misattunements

Stanley, aged 9 weeks. Face-to-face interactions at 2 months are often rich and complex. There are cycles where each partner takes turns in playing a more active role, while the other is more receptive, and then periods when the two come together to share their experience. As the weeks pass, interactions generally become more playful, with the adult typically introducing surprise elements to entertain the baby. The process for both partners is a creative one and each is continually adjusting to the other. It is common, and a naturally occurring feature of good interaction, for minor misattunements to occur, and these are important opportunities for the baby to experience brief moments of dysregulation that are then repaired, so that he can recover his equilibrium.

1 Stanley has been entertained by his mother making noises with her mouth, puckering her lips tightly and then releasing them in a kissing sound …

2 … or making lip-smacking noises.

3 Stanley seems to be able to handle this stimulating game, and watches his mother with interest.

4 When his mother prepares for the next kissing noise, he follows her movements expectantly.

5 But this time Stanley's mother lowers her head quite fast, and makes a particularly loud kiss, and Stanley is startled, his arm jerking up as he shuts his eyes.

6 Stanley continues the break in contact, looking beyond his mother's face, his expression still a little shocked. His mother notices the change in Stanley's behaviour, and abandons the game. She mirrors his open mouth, looking concerned, and moves her hand closer to give him firmer support.

3.3 **Recovering from normal misattunements** continued

7 Stanley reconnects with his mother, now making eye-contact again. His mother, still supporting him firmly, gently reduces the intensity of her mirroring response, and Stanley calms …

8 … as Stanley relaxes, his mother seems to signal to him, in her smile and raised brows, that something notable and interesting occurred, and that it has been manageable.

9 Stanley, now recovered, initiates another cycle of play, as his mother watches and strokes him.

At other times, a rather different kind of active support may be appropriate, as when the parent helps the baby manage some new experience, like an unfamiliar person joining them. Here, the parent may be supportive by signalling their own positive feelings to the baby and warmly encouraging him to engage with the stranger (see picture sequence 3.4 and, for older babies, Chapter 2, picture sequence 2.3). Alternatively, if the baby seems to be managing a difficult moment by himself, the parent may best support the development of his regulatory skills, not by being very active but instead holding back for a few moments. So for example, if the baby begins to look unsettled, but then turns away and sucks on his fingers or looks around the room, or even if he breaks gaze because his pleasure and excitement in a game has become too intense, it can be most helpful for the parent to pause and give the baby a chance to readjust and become calm by himself, before inviting him to play again.

Such sensitive parental responsiveness during early social engagements appears to be important in helping the baby to develop good self-regulation skills. If the parent responds supportively during normal face-to-face interactions and helps the baby's self-regulation, the baby is able to cope better with the Still-Face disruption, making more active bids to re-engage, remaining more positive and showing better physiological recovery. Other benefits of sensitive support show up in the longer term, so babies' well-regulated behaviour in their early social interaction is predictive of better capacity for emotional and behavioural regulation in later infancy and lower rates of problematic behaviour in the early school years.

3.4   Support for a new experience

Katie, aged 10 weeks. Even in the first 3 months, babies are sensitive to their partner's facial signals and emotional expressiveness, and can benefit from them in managing their engagements with the wider environment. Typically, when something potentially enjoyable is going on the parent will first engage the baby directly, then mark out the event in question, perhaps flashing their brows to suggest that something special is about to happen, while also conveying their enthusiasm and encouragement vocally.

Here, Katie's mother has been chatting to her daughter, when a friendly but unfamiliar lady comes into the room, greets them and then begins to play with Katie. Katie's mother uses her face and voice to indicate that meeting this new person could be enjoyable, and the encouragement helps Katie to respond to the lady.

1 Katie's mother hears the door being opened. She can see in the mirror the reflection of a researcher entering the room, and smiles in response to her greeting.

2 Katie looks up at her mother, who meets her gaze with a smile and raised brows, saying 'Who's this?' with interest, as the researcher leans over to play with Katie.

3 As the researcher begins to pick Katie up, her mother monitors her daughter's expression, and signals her own positive feelings about Katie meeting this new person, repeating 'Who's this?' with a widening smile, encouraging her daughter to engage.

4 As the researcher plays with Katie, her mother sits back, available to catch her daughter's gaze should she look across.

5 When the researcher hands Katie back, her mother greets her and also comments warmly on Katie's experience of playing with someone else.

Physical play

Beyond the first few months of face-to-face social engagements and alongside the baby's growing capacity to handle more intense feelings, the kind of play that parents and their baby enjoy together develops in new ways. Apart from the changes that support the baby's cognitive development and social understanding, such as exploring toys, or practising routinized games (see Chapters 1 and 4), playing often becomes more physically boisterous. At these times, the baby's level of excitement is likely to become very intense, and managing to enjoy the game and not become distressed can exercise both his own and his parent's regulation skills. On the baby's part, just as during early face-to-face interactions, he might need to shift his gaze and turn away from the game for a while in order to reduce the extremes of emotion and arousal, before he is ready for the next round. On the parent's part, the timing and intensity of their participation need to be adjusted to the baby's state so that they are not overwhelming, and to this end the parent will keep a check on the baby's expression (see picture sequence 3.5).

3.5   Regulating excitement in body games

Lottie, aged 5 months. As the baby develops physically, cognitively and socially, the earlier attractions of pure face-to-face engagement can wane a little, and the baby will need more varied kinds of engagement to keep their interest and enjoyment. Parents naturally adjust to these developments by changing the style of their play and one key change is for it to become organized around more vigorous body games. These typically involve the parent monitoring the baby's state and adjusting the tempo and intensity of their play during repeated sequences that end in a shared climax. The games can challenge the baby's regulation skills in quite complex ways and at moments of peak excitement the baby will often regulate their own state by breaking gaze and turning away from the game until their feelings are under control.

Here, Lottie's mother first plays 'peek-a-boo', using Lottie's hands to cover her face, and this then merges into a 'gobbling-up game'.

1 Lottie's mother establishes eye-contact with her daughter and invites her to play.

2 She looms over Lottie, moving her daughter's hands up to cover her face.

3 Her mother throws Lottie's arms wide, greets her with a 'Boo!' and Lottie smiles.

4 Lottie's excitement grows and, as is typical when excitement becomes intense, she briefly turns her eyes away – this helps her regulate her state so that she is not overwhelmed.

5 When Lottie is ready, her mother repeats the hiding ...

3.5   **Regulating excitement in body games** continued

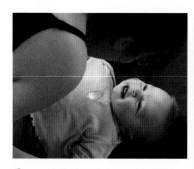

6 …and the 'Boo!' This time, while Lottie still enjoys it, it doesn't seem to enthuse her quite as much as before …

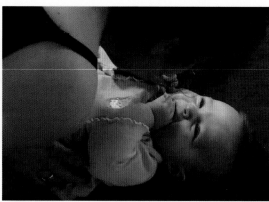

7 …and she begins to suck her fingers so her mother alters the game a little, while keeping the basic structure. Again she establishes eye-contact and invites Lottie to join in the game.

8 But now it has become another favourite, called 'Gobble, gobble'.

9 As Lottie's mother couldn't see her daughter's face during the 'gobble', she raises her head to check that Lottie has enjoyed it, and shares in Lottie's pleasure.

10 Since this game is successful, Lottie's mother repeats the 'gobble' …

11 …and the two of them then laugh together.

While mothers often initiate this pattern of play in, for example, tickling games, or in displays of mock aggression, it is common for fathers to become more involved as the baby's coordination develops. Even though these games are usually physical in nature, as for earlier social contacts the parent and baby use shared looks and expressions to negotiate the different phases of their play (see Isabel, 9 months, with her father in the picture right, and picture sequence 3.6).

3.6   Rough and tumble play 1

Stanley, aged 12 months. Rough and tumble games, mostly between fathers and sons, increase in frequency from around the end of the first year, and are a key way for babies to practise tolerating and managing extremes of emotion, often bordering on fearfulness as well as excitement.

In this sequence, which needs no commentary, Stanley's father takes his son towards the limits of what he can comfortably manage, constantly checking on Stanley's state in between the more vigorous phases of their play, and sharing looks with him throughout, so that the extent and limits of the game are negotiated together.

1

2

3

4

5

6

7

8

3.6 Rough and tumble play 1 continued

9

10

11

12

13

14

Rough and tumble play

Later on, alongside the development in social understanding and the normal increase in aggressive behaviour that takes place between 18 months and 2 years, physical, or 'rough and tumble' play becomes more sophisticated. This kind of play again typically involves fathers with, increasingly, their sons rather than their daughters. The games are often characterized by dramatic play-fighting or fear-provoking episodes, accompanied by chasing, wrestling, tumbling and grappling, where the baby can practise handling extreme, potentially difficult, emotions in a secure context. Studies suggest that two features of this kind of play are particularly helpful to the baby in learning to regulate his aggression and in helping to achieve the normal decline in its expression that takes place after the first two years. First, the fact that the play is

happening in the context of a close relationship means that the baby will not want to give way to any truly hurtful behaviour that could be counter-productive and threaten both the game and the feeling of affectionate involvement – and in this context he learns the limits of what behaviour will be tolerated. Second, the studies suggest that although fathers typically push their baby to take risks and explore their emotional limits, allowing them brief moments of dominance, it is most useful for the development of the baby's self-regulatory abilities if the father does not allow the baby to be too dominant in the game. Ideally, he moderates his own behaviour in response to his baby's signals, so that confrontations are managed and the baby's emotions are prevented from spilling out of control (see picture sequences 3.7 and 3.8).

3.7   **Rough and tumble play 2**

Ben, aged 17 months. As the baby develops, he can take a more active role in negotiating the details of rough and tumble play and, with sensitive support, will often like to experiment with risky feelings and explore the limits of what both he and his partner can tolerate.

Here, Ben and his father play a chasing game that has the potential to be quite scary for him, and he needs his father to step out of his frightening role at intervals to reassure him, until his feelings are back under control. The nature and the intensity of the emotions involved constantly shift and change, and the game requires careful monitoring by Ben's father to keep it from spilling unpleasantly out of control. Babies who are temperamentally inhibited may need particularly sensitive, flexible, support to help them through such play and give them practice in regulating their difficult emotions.

1 Ben's father pretends to be a wild growling animal, and advances across the floor to catch his son.

2 Ben is finding this just a bit difficult to manage . . .

3 . . . and soon turns to his father for a reassuring cuddle.

4 His father gives Ben plenty of time to settle down . . .

5 . . . and then talks to him about how it felt. Then when Ben seems ready, his father asks him if he wants to play the game again.

6 Ben eagerly wriggles down from his father's lap, to position himself for another go.

7 As his father becomes a growling animal again, Ben seems a little more able to cope with the scary feeling, though he sucks on his fingers to help him manage.

8 Ben's father is aware that his son isn't altogether sure about the game, so he holds back a little . . .

9 . . . and lets Ben have control and escape easily.

3.7   **Rough and tumble play 2** continued

10 Ben comes back for another cuddle ...

11 ...and again his father checks on how Ben is feeling.

12 Now Ben initiates a new phase of the game, grabbing his father's cheeks and shouting with glee ...

13 ...and his father follows on with a different kind of physical play that involves nuzzling into his son with pretend eating, rather than chasing.

14 Ben can manage this without the fearfulness of the chasing game, and the two of them enjoy a tussle ...

15 ...his father still checking, though, to make sure that Ben is coping well.

16 This phase ends on an intimate, affectionate note ...

17 ...and then Ben wriggles down again and seems ready for another round of chasing.

3.8   Play fighting

Ben, aged 24 months. Fathers' play, especially with boys, often helps babies learn to manage potentially risky experiences, like feeling frightened or aggressive. In rough and tumble play in particular, so long as the father sensitively modulates what happens, babies can gain experience of being boisterous and expressive, and of feeling powerful, within safe limits. In addition, when this play occurs in a close, warm relationship, where the father has ultimate control over what happens, the baby will also naturally want to hold back on actions that might be seriously hurtful, and in this way he can learn a great deal about regulating his impulses.

1 Ben's father exerts affectionate control through the start of the game . . .

2 . . . with a mixture of hugging and growling . . .

3 . . . but he also lets Ben break off and have his turn.

4 As Ben launches himself in a tackle, his father's expression of mock shock signals that this is something he is willing to let happen . . .

5 . . . as does his exaggerated display of being at Ben's mercy.

6 The game continues in this way for some time . . .

7

8

9

3.8 Play fighting continued

10 And now the balance shifts again …

11 … and Ben's father takes over.

13 … before ending on a note of exhausted and affectionate shared relief.

12 At this point he creatively allows Ben to have some of the action too, but still signals through his exaggerated displays that any pain he feels is just 'pretend'…

The development of babies' deliberate self-control

The baby's ability to inhibit his intense emotions and any harmful aggressive behaviour during rough and tumble play reflects a more general feature of the regulation skills that develop from the second half of a child's first year onwards – what is known as deliberate or 'effortful' control. Unlike earlier signs of regulation, such as self-soothing or breaking eye-contact, effortful control refers to the baby being able to deliberately override his natural, impulsive, way of responding, and instead behave in ways that are less immediately desirable. For example, the baby needs to make an active effort in both 'Don't' conditions (for example, 'Don't touch the toys'), and in 'Do' conditions (such as, 'Do tidy the toys away'). (In general, babies' compliance with 'Don't' requests comes earlier than with 'Do' ones, possibly because actively doing something often

involves rather more complex behaviour than simply not doing something.) The onset of this deliberate control over behaviour and feelings coincides with the development of the brain region (the pre-frontal cortex) involved in decision making and planning or what is known to specialists as 'executive function', where being able to selectively attend to and focus on a task in the face of competing demands is key. This is, then, a more conscious or 'cognitive' kind of control. However, well before these brain regions start to show this surge in connectivity and development, the foundations of these more sophisticated executive function abilities can be seen in the way babies regulate their attention. For example, 6-month-old babies whose attention remains highly focused when they are presented with an array of toys, or who can anticipate what will appear next when shown repeated series of images, go on to show particularly good effortful control, especially in 'Do' conditions, in their second year.

Aside from simply measuring whether or not the baby is able to regulate his behaviour and comply in 'Do' and 'Don't' situations, psychologists have found it important to take note of the quality of the baby's response and, in particular, to distinguish between what is called cooperative or 'committed' compliance, where the baby takes requests on board very willingly and with enthusiasm (see picture sequence 3.9), as opposed to 'situational' compliance, where the baby may do as he is asked but appears just to go through the motions, without any positive motivation.

This distinction is critical, because it is only 'committed' compliance that is associated with the further key developmental step where the baby internalizes the rules of behaviour, so that he can begin to act them out on his own without needing to be monitored (see picture sequence 3.10) – and it is 'committed' compliance that is associated with good behavioural adjustment in later childhood.

3.9   Cooperative and willing behaviour

Ben, aged 15 months. Being able to adjust to someone else's agenda, and follow or comply with their requests, is a key aspect of babies' self-regulation skills. But it is not only whether the baby complies, but how he does so, and specifically whether he complies cooperatively and willingly, that is important – this predicts whether he can master the next step and pick up the rules of behaviour so that he can follow them without someone else monitoring him. When parents are warm and accepting of their baby and can establish a shared agenda, the baby is likely to be keen to join in and cooperate with the appropriate behaviour.

Here, Ben has spilt some of his milk and it's made a mess on the table – he already has some sense that spilt milk should be cleared up and his mother builds on this and encourages him to become enthusiastically involved in helping.

1 Ben and his mother are enjoying a drink together at the kitchen table.

2 Ben's cup of milk is almost empty and he throws his head back to finish it off …

3 … then he and his mother share a smile as he shakes his cup around to show her how much he's drunk.

4 Ben's vigorous shaking has splashed some of the remaining milk on the table and his mother points it out to Ben.

5 She has moved the cup away and gives Ben a chance to explore the spilt milk. As well as enjoying the feel of it, Ben seems to be trying to wipe it away.

3.9   Cooperative and willing behaviour continued

6 His mother picks up on his interest and brings a cloth over, suggesting that he might like to try using it to help clear up.

7 Ben has great fun wiping, and enjoys the satisfaction of seeing the milk disappear, and his mother shares in his pleasure.

8 When the milk is all cleaned up, Ben's mother congratulates him, and they both laugh together to mark out what fun it has been to do a good job.

3.10   Resisting temptation

Iris, aged 12 months. Our ability to override desires and resist acting on them takes deliberate effort and control. For a baby it is particularly taxing when no one is actively supporting and monitoring them, as then they need to have already taken on board ('internalized') the rules of behaviour in order to manage the task of regulation on their own. Babies can more often manage this challenge when their previous experiences of adjusting to requests or demands have been in the context of warm, responsive relationships, where the baby has enjoyed cooperating with others.

Here, Iris faces the challenge of not touching the cat food – something that she has previously been very keen to do, but which her parents have tried to prevent by actively keeping an eye on her and gently supporting her to help her resist while their cat eats its meal. This time, her mother leaves Iris near the cat food unattended. Iris clearly experiences some internal conflict, but she is able to use a number of strategies to overcome the temptation, including looking to her mother, soothing herself, and becoming absorbed in play.

1 Iris watches as her mother puts out fresh food in the cat's bowl.

2 She follows her mother's movements as she walks across to the other side of the kitchen to do some chores.

3 Iris keeps a keen eye on her mother.

3.10   **Resisting temptation** continued

4 She looks with considerable interest at the forbidden cat food …

5 … and turns again to her mother, as though checking on whether she will make the usual signals that Iris shouldn't touch the food, or perhaps she is puzzled that it has been left near her.

6 Iris's gaze is drawn back to the cat food, and she sucks on her toy, possibly to help her manage not going near the bowl.

7 Iris checks back to her mother again; possibly looking to her mother for guidance, or perhaps it is easier for her to comply when she is actively aware of her mother's presence.

8 Iris absorbs herself in play, turning her back on the cat food …

9 … but then she checks back once more in her mother's direction, again sucking on her toy.

11 … and back to where her mother is busy cleaning.

10 Once more she looks with great interest at the cat food …

3.10 **Resisting temptation** continued

12 Now Iris gives another long stare at the cat food, this time doing so without sucking on her toy, possibly not needing it so much.

13 As Iris turns away from the cat food one final time, she screws up her face in an expression she often uses when she seems self-conscious, as though tussling with her conflicting feelings and perhaps telling herself not to do the forbidden thing.

14 At last Iris seems resolved and she plays happily with her toys, without being distracted again by the temptation of touching the cat's bowl.

As well as the natural differences in temperament that contribute to the baby's ability to exert this new, more conscious control over his behaviour, the quality of support the baby receives, together with developments in social understanding, are of great importance.

How parents can support babies' deliberate self-control

Support for the baby's early focused attention and ability to anticipate events

As described in detail in Chapter 4, Cognitive Development, social interactions that are positive and well-attuned to the baby's behaviour help to attract and maintain his attention. In turn and as also described earlier, this ability to maintain attention is important for the development of self-control. Particularly useful techniques for helping babies focus their attention in the first few months are for the parent to follow the baby's cues and modulate their tone as they talk to him, often using rising intonation to express their interest and enthusiasm, or using a pattern of 'theme and variation' in which repeated phrases are slightly varied

according to the baby's level of engagement. In later social interactions, following the baby's cues is again important, but as he becomes able to handle objects his parent can also help him maintain his attention by giving practical support for his activity, as well as through facial and vocal expressions of interest in the baby's experience (see section on facilitation in Chapter 4, p. 199). The baby's ability to register sequences of events and anticipate what will happen next is also a key predictor of the older child's capacity for effortful control, and this ability too can be supported through his social relationships. So if the baby's environment is regular and predictable – for example, if he becomes accustomed to the routine of his meal being prepared or the procedure for getting ready to leave the house – then his familiarity with each step of these routines can help him have some sense of control. Thus, even if parents have to provide additional support, such as temporary distractions or filler activities to help the baby cope, the routine itself can still be useful in helping to tide babies over and tolerate possible frustrations (see picture sequence 3.11).

3.11   Routines, distractions and managing frustration

Ben, aged 10 months. Ben has become very familiar with the routine of meals, from the broad context of being placed in his chair and wearing his bib, to the fine detail of his parent's actions, so he has a clear sense of the sequence of events. This can help him to tolerate the delay in getting his food, but at times having something small to chew on, or a few sips of water, can also help distract him from the urgency of wanting his meal.

1 Ben is really hungry and as he has been placed in his chair he knows that he will soon get his meal, but he watches each step of his mother's preparations attentively.

2 It's quite hard for him to wait and he starts to get a little agitated.

3 His mother realizes his food won't be quite ready for a minute or two, so she brings him a piece of crust to chew on to help him wait, and Ben eagerly seizes it.

4 He still watches every move his mother makes, but is calmed by having his crust.

5 Once the crust is eaten, his sense of urgency builds up again.

6 This time his mother helps him wait by bringing him some water …

7 …and this gives Ben something else to do to distract him from his hunger.

8 Now Ben can see that his meal is finally coming.

9 He knows exactly what his mother's routine is – first stirring the food and then putting a little on the spoon …

10 …before she checks that the temperature is right for him – and Ben is able to wait through each step.

3.11   Routines, distractions and managing frustration continued

11 At the final point in the sequence when his mother places food on the spoon ready to give him, his arms rise up in excited anticipation …

12 …and he begins to open his mouth …

13 …and then really enjoys the first mouthful.

Regulation of responses through social awareness and 'referencing'

From around 10 months, babies become much more consciously aware of other people's responses, including their emotional reactions (see also Chapter 1 on 'connected-up relatedness' in the development of social understanding), and they begin to use this more advanced awareness in a very deliberate way to guide their own behaviour. This is particularly likely in situations that are uncertain, where babies of this age will often turn to their parent to check out their response before taking action. This behaviour is known by specialists as 'social referencing'. In one of the first experiments to show how the baby's behaviour is guided and regulated in line with his parent's response, known as the 'Visual Cliff', a baby who is able to crawl is placed on a strong Perspex floor stretched across a visible drop, with the baby's mother looking across to him from the other side. For one part of the experiment, the mother is asked to display an anxious, worried expression, whereas in the other she is asked to look confident and cheerful. Babies regularly look over to their mother before deciding whether to crawl across the Perspex to reach her, and whether or not they will cross is directly related to the emotional expression their mother displays – they are far more likely to crawl across the visual cliff when she appears positive. Babies also actively use others' emotional responses to guide their behaviour with other people and, again, experimental manipulations of how the mother reacts show that the baby's response to an unfamiliar, but friendly, adult is strongly influenced by what he sees his mother do (see picture sequence 3.12).

3.12   Social referencing

Iris, aged 14 months. From around 10 months, babies will often actively check to see their parent's expression before responding to new experiences, behaviour called 'social referencing'. This applies in non-social situations where, for example, there might be some potential danger, as well as in social situations like meeting someone new.

In this sequence, Iris has come to the university research unit, and she is filmed during a standard 'Stranger Approach' procedure in which she uses her mother as a reference point to help manage her reactions to an unfamiliar person.

3.12   **Social referencing** continued

1 Iris watches with a sober expression as the stranger enters the room, while her mother sits back.

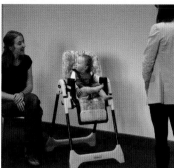

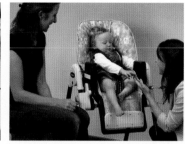

2 Iris's active use of her mother's reaction to help her respond is clearly shown as she turns right round to see her mother's face, and her mother smiles and talks to her encouragingly about the stranger.

3 Having registered her mother's positive response, Iris gives the stranger a smile.

4 As the stranger comes closer, Iris turns again to check on what her mother is doing and her mother continues to encourage her.

5 Now the stranger comes right up close and shows Iris her necklace. Iris is more confident now and reaches out to touch it.

6 Now, as Iris's mother continues to help her make contact with the stranger, Iris can begin to really enjoy the game.

7 She wants to share her experience with her mother and looks across to her …

8 … before turning back to carry on playing with this new acquaintance.

As well as in ambiguous or uncertain situations, babies are also likely to deliberately reference their parent when facing more obvious challenges or frustrations (see picture sequences 3.13 and 3.14). In these more extreme situations, however, the looks the baby directs towards the parent often function as bids for more active intervention, rather than just to gain information. These active looks show that the baby is aware his own capacities are limited, and they can be effective strategies for harnessing a parent's support in regulating difficult situations and feelings.

3.13   Parental support and distraction from frustration

Iris, aged 14 months. In situations where babies are prevented from doing what they want, it can be difficult for them to regulate their emotions unless they receive support from someone else.

Here, Iris twice faces the challenge of the 'Barrier Task', where an attractive toy she has been playing with is removed, but remains in view. On the first occasion, her mother has been asked by the researcher not to react, whereas in the second she is free to intervene and help Iris.

1 Iris plays happily with the musical toy.

2 After a minute or so, the researcher removes the toy from Iris and places it behind a Perspex barrier, while Iris's mother is unresponsive.

3 Iris stretches out towards the toy and becomes agitated when she can't get it.

4 Iris looks appealingly to the person who took it away from her …

5 … but as there is no response, she becomes increasingly frustrated.

6 Now, she looks across to her mother, who still remains immobile.

7 With Iris being left to handle this situation on her own, she is unable to settle, and her distress and frustration continue.

3.13   **Parental support and distraction from frustration** continued

8 Iris is given the toy again and once more happily plays with it.

9 Now it is removed for a second time.

10 This time, however, Iris's mother immediately signals her sympathy for Iris's plight and Iris turns to her.

11 Iris still reaches for the toy, but her mood is calmer than before, as her mother talks to her, suggesting that they might do something else.

12 Her mother has no props, so she invents a game using just her hands, curling them up and inviting Iris to peep inside. Iris is quickly absorbed by the game, and the frustration of the removed toy is forgotten.

13 Iris's mother manages to entertain her daughter with different permutations of the game, and Iris remains captivated throughout the remaining time that the toy is unavailable.

14 When the toy is returned to her, Iris is perfectly calm ...

15 ... and then she enjoys playing with it again.

3.14   Appeals versus self-regulation

Ben, aged 18 months. When babies face difficult challenges, they are aware that others might be able to help them out and that appealing to them and securing their help can be a positive strategy for resolving difficulties that might otherwise spill over into unmanageable feelings or conflicts. At other times, however, when the baby can make some progress by using his own regulatory skills, parental intervention might need just the lightest touch, so that the baby's sense of control is also fostered.

Here, Ben has to cope with teasing from his older brother and he appeals to his mother. She judges that only a mild intervention is required and Ben will be able to sort out the problem with his brother by himself.

1 Ben looks warily on as his brother Joe begins to move towards his bowl.

2 He was right to be apprehensive, since Joe starts to lick Ben's food up.

3 Joe thinks it's a good joke, but Ben objects and makes his feelings clear to his mother. She issues a mild cautionary warning to Joe.

4 Joe uses another approach and this time takes Ben's bowl away . . .

5 . . . . to have a really good lick at it.

6 Again, Ben appeals to his mother.

7 Ben doesn't seem too perturbed as he watches his food disappear, so his mother only intervenes to issue another warning to Joe.

8 Possibly sensing his mother's availability and support, Ben steps in himself, and he reaches over to appeal directly to his brother, managing to stay in control of his feelings.

9 It works – Joe gives Ben his bowl back, and a potentially difficult situation is resolved.

Encouraging enjoyable joint play and cooperation

One of the most striking findings from research on babies' ability to regulate their behaviour and cooperate with others is that these skills are significantly related to the quality of the parent's general interactions with the baby. From around 9 to 10 months, as well as seeking out others' responses for guidance, the baby shows a more obvious awareness of other people's actions and intentions and he is typically keen to join in whatever is going on and share his experience with others (see Chapter 1, p. 20). When the parent can engage the baby warmly in joint activity, in such a way that doing things together is fun, he is far more likely to become cooperative and show 'committed' compliance in general, taking on board his parent's agenda (see picture sequences 3.15 and 3.16). Key ways of achieving this

3.15   Cooperation and sharing

Isabel, aged 9 months. From around 9 to 10 months, babies become particularly keen to join in with what other people are doing, and start to share in a cooperative way. Their ability to do this is very much linked to the quality of their parents' interactions with them.

Here, Isabel's mother is sorting out clothes for washing and finds a way of making it enjoyable for Isabel to have a helping role.

1 Isabel's mother holds up a sock and asks Isabel if they should put it into the machine for washing.

2 Next there is a blanket, and again Isabel's mother includes her daughter in what is happening . . .

3 . . . showing her how it goes into the machine, while Isabel watches, fascinated.

4 Isabel quickly decides she wants to be in on the action . . .

5 . . . and makes a bee line for the machine, looking into it to see where the clothes have gone.

6 Isabel turns to take another item for washing that her mother passes over . . .

3.15   Cooperation and sharing continued

7 …and she pulls herself up so that she can place it right inside.

8 Then Isabel turns again, ready to take something else …

9 …and again busily puts it into the machine for her mother, and enjoys taking an active role.

3.16   Cooperation and helpfulness

Max, aged 19 months. From at least one year, babies not only enjoy sharing activities with other people, but they also have some awareness of others' possible needs and are motivated to help them. Max is on holiday with his family and has the chance to spend a lot of time with his father. He is very keen to join his father in projects they can do together and wants to be helpful.

Here, Max's father sets up simple gardening tasks for his son and supports him to take on an active role, explaining each step in the process clearly so that Max can understand the connections between them and how they fit in with the bigger picture of growing food.

1 Max's father explains that the plants are dry and that they need to fill the watering can up so that they can give them a good drink.

2 Max wants to see how much water is in the can now, and stretches out.

3 His father picks him up to look – the can is almost full.

4 Next Max wants to help his father carry the heavy can over to the vegetable plot.

3.16   **Cooperation and helpfulness** continued

5 His father tilts the can into the right position ...

6 ...and Max is keen to take a role in pouring the water onto the base of the plant, concentrating carefully as his father supports him.

7 The pair go round each plant in turn, Max thoroughly enjoying doing something that is helpful and that has a clear purpose.

are giving the baby small jobs to do that he can manage, and praising and thanking him.

Strikingly, even when the baby faces the challenge of having to do something he would far rather not do, parental warmth and flexibility, as well as humour, can help turn a difficult situation round and capitalize on the baby's natural inclination to cooperate (see picture sequence 3.17). This finding is very much in line with research with older children, showing that if parents behave in warm and responsive ways, avoiding forceful, power-assertive methods of control, children are far more likely to be positive and cooperative.

3.17   **Turning opposition into cooperation**

Iris, aged 14 months. In their second year, it is common for babies to be wilful and assertive, and it can be a real challenge for parents to get the baby to do something they are set against doing. While it is a good idea, in terms of preventing the development of behaviour problems, for parents to follow through with their original plans rather than capitulating in the face of child anger or distress, exactly how this is done is important. If the parent can manage to respond flexibly, perhaps using playful techniques to entice the baby into cooperating, the baby is more likely to be keen to cooperate generally with their parents' agenda and to take on board their rules and values.

Here we see Iris and her mother in an episode where Iris is initially very resistant to her mother's efforts to brush her teeth. Through skilful adjustments and use of play and humour, Iris's mother manages to gain her daughter's willing cooperation and compliance.

1 Iris plays contentedly in her bath and is happy to let her mother wash her.

3.17   **Turning opposition into cooperation** continued

2 When she sees the toothbrush, however, she immediately resists and turns away . . .

3 . . . and this rapidly escalates into angry crying. Her mother pauses, and rather than forcefully pursuing the tooth-brushing agenda . . .

4 . . . she uses one of the bath toys to squirt water playfully on the net that Iris is holding, so building bridges with her tearful daughter.

5 Iris responds well to this and follows through by using her net to hide her face, whilst still being able to see her mother.

6 As Iris lowers the net to reveal herself, she and her mother share smiles – good relations have been restored.

7 Iris's mother capitalizes on this more positive note and on Iris's next hide she reintroduces the toothbrush – knowing that her daughter is watching and not wanting to confront her directly with a further request, she acts out brushing her own teeth with enthusiasm.

8 Iris is intrigued and lowers the net to have a better look.

9 As her mother continues miming, Iris begins to find it fun.

10 Now she's very happy to let her mother bring the brush up to her; the two keep in eye-contact throughout the subsequent negotiation of how the brushing is done.

11 And Iris cooperates well as her teeth are brushed.

12 Soon she wants to take control of the brushing herself and her mother is happy to let her have a go.

13 Iris takes the brushing very seriously and shows her mother how she rinses her mouth.

3.17   Turning opposition into cooperation continued

14 Now what was originally so fiercely resisted has turned into an enjoyable game...

15 ...and when her mother suggests that she might have another turn, Iris is ready to actively cooperate, handing the brush over willingly.

16 Iris sits patiently and quietly as her mother brushes away.

17 And now the job is done, the two can revert to the hiding game again.

Reasoning and talking

As the baby develops an understanding of language, so the parent is increasingly able to help him regulate his behaviour and feelings through conversation, and in particular by talking about why certain behaviours are desirable or undesirable (see picture sequence 3.18) and about the feelings involved in challenging situations.

3.18   Use of reason and limit-setting to discourage 'naughtiness'

Ben, aged 17 months. Ben is intrigued by his older brother's antics at breakfast, but doesn't yet have a firm sense of which kinds of play are acceptable and which are not. When he attempts an entertaining performance of his own he oversteps the mark, but he can be brought into line with gentle but firm handling and a clear explanation from his father.

1 Ben's brother, Joe, has been entertaining their father at breakfast, and Ben looks on with considerable interest.

2 Perhaps Ben wants to be entertaining too – for whatever reason, he swings his cup up to take a large mouthful of juice...

3 ...and then shows his father just how far he can squirt it out.

4 This kind of behaviour is generally discouraged, and Ben's father lets his son know that he's not very impressed, particularly as Ben's jersey is now quite wet.

3.18   **Use of reason and limit-setting to discourage 'naughtiness'** continued

5 Ben looks down at his wet clothes, and seems very interested in what has happened …

6 …so much so that he tilts his cup right over to pour more juice down. His father stretches out to take control of the spillage, explaining that if this is the way Ben is going to behave, he will not be able to have his cup.

7 Ben's father talks to him some more, and explains that it's not a good idea to make your clothes all wet and sticky, and Ben listens with a sober face.

8 Ben asks for his cup back, and his father reasons with him, explaining that if Ben has his cup, he must be sensible and use it properly.

9 Ben seems to understand, and the cup is handed back.

10 Ben looks up to check on his father, as he drinks his juice properly.

11 His father notes how he is drinking and praises him for being so good …

12 …and Ben moves his cup away to show his father how he is keeping his mouth tight shut and isn't squirting at all, and his father continues to praise him warmly.

As can be seen in the last part of Chapter 4 (see Iris and the book of faces, picture sequence 4.35), this kind of talk can happen particularly easily when the baby and his parent can share in thinking about the feelings and motivations of characters in picture books, but general talk about emotions and about why people do the things they do also results in children having a better understanding of others' experience and a tendency to be mindful of others' feelings during play. Indeed, both ordinary, spontaneous conversations, and specific kinds of conversation called 'narratives' (where a kind of story is told with a beginning, middle and end, and where clear links are made between events and experiences), are key ways in which parents can socialize their young child's emotions and behaviour, and convey the values of the family and the wider community. Reasoning with babies and young children who can understand language can also be effective when used pre-emptively – that is, before asking the baby to do something they may not be keen to do (such as clear up toys/get dressed), and it reduces the risk of parents' requests provoking defiance and conflict.

Babies' self-regulation in going to sleep

One area where the baby is frequently challenged in terms of managing their state and difficult feelings is in relation to sleep. Sleep 'problems' are among the commonest reasons for parents to consult professionals, typically because their baby finds it difficult to settle to sleep, both when they are first put to bed and following the normal periodic surfacing from sleep that babies experience during the night. Babies' difficulties in settling to sleep in the first few months are quite common, and in themselves they do not appear to be an indicator for subsequent problems. Marked sleep problems that persist into late infancy are, however, potentially important, not only because they can be stressful for parents, but also because they can be associated with a range of difficulties in later childhood, including poorer cognitive functioning and behavioural problems.

Although individual babies obviously differ in their capacity to shut out stimulation and make the transition from one state of arousal to another, the way that parents manage their baby's settling to sleep is a major influence on his sleep patterns. In the first few weeks, babies have commonly already fallen asleep by the time they are put to bed after a feed. This means that scope for parents to support the baby's self-regulation while they settle him may be limited. But as the baby's periods of wakefulness following daytime feeds gradually grow longer, more opportunities present themselves. There are a number of related strategies that are effective in helping the baby to develop good self-regulation abilities around sleep, and they all involve helping him to form associations between his experience of going off to sleep and the circumstances in which he is settled.

First, it is useful when establishing settling-to-sleep habits if the parent starts to settle the baby only when he shows signs of beginning to tire. Second, it is helpful if a set, quiet, routine can be developed that the baby enjoys, before the settling itself begins. Finally, and of particular importance, the baby's ability to manage falling asleep himself is best promoted when parents are not actively involved – for example, by feeding the baby, or by holding and rocking him to sleep. This last point applies because the baby quickly learns to associate the act of falling asleep with what is happening at the time, so if he becomes used to his parent holding him, then he will need that to be the case in order to fall asleep in the future. Thus, rather than getting actively involved, the parent can help best by observing, and then supporting, any signs of the baby's own capacity to self-regulate. So if the baby has a tendency to become calm while looking at visual patterns they could provide something for him to watch while in his cot, or if the baby is soothed by sucking on his fist, they can ensure that he can easily do this by the way they position him to sleep (see *The Social Baby* for more on this). While the details of day-to-day interactions around sleep settling are likely to vary somewhat according to the baby's state at the time (for example, the baby may require more support when feeling ill), when parents can establish these general patterns of managing their baby's sleep in the first six months, the development of sleep problems is unlikely (see picture sequences 3.19–3.22 showing the development of one baby's pattern from 2 to 14 months).

3.19   Settling to sleep 1

Iris, aged 8 weeks. Establishing a quiet routine for settling the baby to sleep when they are becoming tired, providing opportunities for the baby to use their own regulation abilities, and avoiding more active involvement than is required (such as holding or rocking the baby) are all helpful in promoting the baby's own ability to settle, both in the evening when first put down to sleep, and during the night when the baby surfaces from sleep. On this occasion, Iris manages to settle quite easily within just a few minutes.

1 Iris has been fed and changed, and she is becoming tired, so her mother starts her routine for settling Iris in her crib, loosely wrapping a thin sheet around her, with her hands tucked up near her chin.

2 She sings to Iris and pats her to comfort and calm her ...

3 ... and places her gently on her back in her crib, putting the baby alarm in position.

4 Iris starts to whimper, and her mother tucks a cotton cover securely at her side and briefly talks soothingly to her. She thinks Iris might manage to settle herself, and so doesn't intervene any more.

5 As her mother leaves, Iris cries some more, but her distress is not extreme, nor does it continue for long.

6 Her crying peters out, her movements calm, and she begins to look around.

7 Now Iris has found her thumb and she sucks on it and soothes herself.

8 Quite soon she has fallen asleep.

3.20   **Settling to sleep 2**

Iris, aged 14 weeks. Helping babies develop good self-regulation around sleep does not always go like clockwork and parents will need to respond flexibly to variations in the baby's state and mood. Although Iris has been managing to settle herself quite well by sucking on her thumb over the past few weeks, not every evening is easy. On this occasion, Iris is fractious at the start, and her mother needs to come back to reassure her and give her more support in settling than has been needed in the last week or so.

1 Iris hasn't had an easy evening, and is agitated and upset as her mother gets her ready for bed.

2 Her mother spends time soothing and rocking Iris until she calms down.

3 When Iris is placed in her crib, however, she starts to become unsettled again.

4 Her mother tucks her in securely . . .

5 . . . and rubs her tummy for a little while.

6 At this point Iris is crying, but her mother knows from experience that she can sometimes recover by herself, so she steps away to see what happens.

7 But Iris continues to be distressed and doesn't show any signs of calming over the next minute or so . . .

8 . . . so her mother returns. Without lifting Iris from her crib, she gives her daughter the reassurance of gently stroking her.

9 Iris begins to pull her hand towards her mouth, as her mother keeps providing gentle comfort.

10 Quite soon, Iris manages to suck on her thumbs.

11 Since Iris was showing signs of starting to calm herself, her mother steps away again, but then Iris loses her fists and resumes crying.

3.20   Settling to sleep 2 *continued*

12 This bout of distress is short-lived, however, and then Iris briefly looks around . . .

13 . . . rubs her eyes . . .

14 . . . and looks around again, now with her hand up to her mouth.

15 Iris has one last whimper . . .

16 . . . before calming again . . .

17 . . . and she finally settles down to sleep.

3.21   Settling to sleep 3

Iris, aged 12 months. In societies where parents sleep separately from their children, it is quite common for babies to develop attachments to soft toys or blankets, and to use them as comforters (see Chapter 2, attachment to objects, p.123). Here, Iris has moved on from a crib in her parent's room to a cot in her own bedroom, and she is also now being settled to sleep in very dim lighting (this sequence and the following one are filmed using an infra-red camera setting). Iris's mother has been putting a favourite soft toy into Iris's cot with her for some months now, and Iris uses it very actively to help her make the transition to sleep.

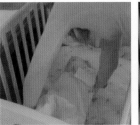

1 Following the routine of a picture book and then milk bottle, Iris's mother places Iris on her back, ready for sleep.

2 She gives Iris her soft toy to hold . . .

3.21   **Settling to sleep 3** continued

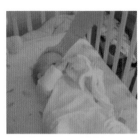 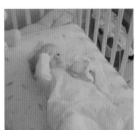  

3 ...strokes her head for a little while, and says 'Good night'.

4 Iris rubs her eyes and pouts as her mother leaves.

5 Whimpering a little, she brings her toy up close to her face ...

6 ...then she whimpers a little more, clutching her toy as she does so.

7 Iris quickly calms as she looks intently at her toy ...

8 ...and becomes drowsy as she holds it close.

9 She is soon fast asleep.

3.22   **Settling to sleep 4**

Iris, aged 14 months. By now, Iris is completely used to the routine of bedtime and can be put to bed when still wide awake – she will amuse herself for a while, then go off to sleep using her special soft toy without any difficulty.

1 Iris has shared some picture books with her mother and now enjoys the next step in the bedtime routine of a drink of milk.

2 Her mother puts her in her cot and strokes her, saying 'Good night'.

3 Iris sits up within seconds, to watch her mother leave.

3.24   **Managing defiant behaviour 2** continued

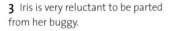

3 Iris is very reluctant to be parted from her buggy.

4 Her mother gently lowers her into the car seat, and tells her that she will be able to have her buggy again when they arrive at their next destination.

5 Iris looks longingly after the buggy, but seems to calm down as her mother straps her into her seat.

6 Once securely fastened in, Iris looks very thoughtful as she grips her soft toy.

7 Now the buggy has been put away, Iris's mother leans across to stroke her daughter's head and praises her for sitting so sensibly.

8 She passes Iris's teddy across and Iris looks very pleased to see him.

9 She holds both her soft toy and teddy close, and seems to have completely recovered from her earlier angry feelings.

A second, somewhat less common cycle where parental inconsistency is a problem is where the baby initiates the process by requesting or demanding something, the parent refuses, the baby repeats his demand, and the parent then gives in, a pattern that again serves to reinforce negative behaviour. As in the first pattern, head-on confrontations where the parent enforces their wishes are unlikely to be productive in the long term. Rather, as with the parent-initiated conflicts, a flexible but authoritative approach to arriving at solutions, involving negotiation and compromise, is more helpful.

Although avoiding the sort of inconsistencies described here is important when resolving conflict, it is worth noting that parents are generally not always consistent with regard to all aspects of the baby's behaviour. When and how parents respond partly depends on the circumstances. In fact, babies become increasingly able to take on board the particular context of their experience, and if bending rules makes good sense (so for example, a high level of riotous mucking about can be appropriate at a birthday party, but not just before bedtime), it will help the baby to gain a better sense of the reasoning behind behaviour.

3.21   **Settling to sleep 3** continued

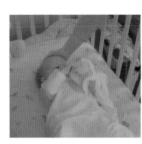   

3 …strokes her head for a little while, and says 'Good night'.

4 Iris rubs her eyes and pouts as her mother leaves.

5 Whimpering a little, she brings her toy up close to her face …

6 …then she whimpers a little more, clutching her toy as she does so.

7 Iris quickly calms as she looks intently at her toy …

8 …and becomes drowsy as she holds it close.

9 She is soon fast asleep.

3.22   **Settling to sleep 4**

Iris, aged 14 months. By now, Iris is completely used to the routine of bedtime and can be put to bed when still wide awake – she will amuse herself for a while, then go off to sleep using her special soft toy without any difficulty.

1 Iris has shared some picture books with her mother and now enjoys the next step in the bedtime routine of a drink of milk.

2 Her mother puts her in her cot and strokes her, saying 'Good night'.

3 Iris sits up within seconds, to watch her mother leave.

3.22 **Settling to sleep 4** continued

4 She is still very alert and turns over to get some toys.

5 She happily plays with them ...

6 ...giving special attention to her favourite soft toy.

7 She enjoys exploring it, waving it up and down ...

8 ...and using it to cover her face.

9 After a while playing, Iris lies down with her toys all around her, and goes easily off to sleep.

It is worth noting that when these principles are adopted before the onset of sleeping difficulties, the baby is unlikely to have more than brief periods of occasional distress. By contrast, if problems have already developed, and the baby then needs to give up an established habit of falling asleep with their parent's active involvement, considerably more distress is likely to be involved. Thus, while methods to wean babies off their parent's involvement can be effective (for example, through 'extinction', which refers to the practice of not responding to the baby's cries in order to 'extinguish' this behaviour, or through 'graduated extinction' – in which the time the baby is left to cry without the parent responding is steadily lengthened, or by building up alternatives to the existing practices), these can be emotionally taxing for both the parents and the baby, and they are generally quite difficult to carry out without considerable support. Some of these approaches also raise ethical questions of whether it is acceptable to leave babies to cry for any length of time, and of whether such experience may raise the risk of the baby developing an insecure attachment (see Chapter 2, p. 77 for patterns of attachment insecurity).

Overall, considering that educational programmes delivered during the pregnancy, or in the course of early routine baby check-ups, are both effective and inexpensive, approaches that focus on prevention of problems are certainly to be preferred.

Factors that may cause difficulties for babies' regulation

Difficulties in parenting

In situations where – often for reasons beyond their control – the parent is unable to be supportive, it can be harder for the baby to build up good self-regulation capacities. Two kinds of difficult parental interaction in the early months, one a withdrawn and the other an intrusive style, have been extensively studied. These are often found in the context of adverse circumstances that can make parents preoccupied with their troubles, or in cases where the parent is quite severely or chronically depressed and finds it hard to notice and respond to the baby's signals. A third, rather less well-studied form of difficulty is an over-protective and unencouraging (rather than actually discouraging) style, which can occur where a parent is extremely anxious, and again their fears and worries can interfere with normal patterns of responsiveness.

i) The withdrawn pattern   Here, the parent behaves routinely in the manner briefly adopted during the Still-Face experiment described earlier (see p. 129 above) when interacting with their baby – that is, they may fail to respond to, or even notice the baby's cues, and instead remain self-absorbed and withdrawn. In the face of this ongoing lack of contact, it becomes hard for the baby to sustain efforts to engage his parent or to regulate his own state and behaviour, and he may himself become distressed and withdraw from social contact. When this pattern continues over months, it may become harder to re-engage the baby, and baby and parent can spend little, if any time in the kind of pleasurable joint activity that fosters the baby's cooperation and self-regulation.

ii) The intrusive pattern   When parents find themselves in very adverse circumstances, or are depressed, it is not uncommon for them to experience feelings of irritability, and this, together with the sense of not being fully in control, can contribute to an intrusive type of interaction. So, for example, when the adult does not realize the significance of the baby turning away from them in order to regulate his state (see p. 133 above), they may attempt to force the baby to re-engage before he is ready; or if the adult is not aware of the baby's social signals they may override them with intense stimulation. In these kinds of forceful engagements, the baby can be tipped into an even more dysregulated state, as the adult's behaviour overwhelms and disrupts him. When this is a frequent, repeated pattern of engagement, the baby's ability to manage his difficult emotions and experiences may be reduced, his dysregulated responses become increasingly challenging for the parent to handle, and conflicts may become regular occurrences.

iii) The anxious, over-protective pattern   When parents experience high levels of anxiety, apart from sometimes missing the baby's signals because they are preoccupied with their worries, they may focus their anxiety on the baby himself. They might worry about his ability to cope with ordinary challenges and perceive him as more vulnerable than he really is. In such circumstances, the parent may find it to hard to give the baby opportunities to self-regulate, instead feeling that they need to protect him or encourage him to avoid difficult experiences. In these cases, and especially if the baby has a natural tendency to be highly reactive and inhibited, these well-meaning parents may actually prevent the baby from learning to manage potential challenges. Also, as the baby's social understanding grows and he becomes more conscious of others' emotional reactions to events, displays of parental anxiety can influence his own response to the environment, so that he too becomes fearful (as described above, p. 148, in the Visual Cliff experiment). Unfortunately, the cycle doesn't stop there, because the baby's increasing tendency to be fearful and avoid challenges can further reinforce the anxious parent's perception of his vulnerability and they may try even harder to protect him.

Individual differences and potentially vulnerable babies

Although developing the ability to regulate feelings, states and behaviour is a task for all children, some seem to find it harder than others. So while the great majority of babies can overcome the normal hurdles involved without great difficulty, others show early patterns of responsiveness that make them vulnerable to longer-term problems in self-regulation. These babies are in particular need of their parents' support. Two such patterns, evident in the first few months, have been given a good deal of research attention. On the one hand, a minority of babies (generally estimated at around 15 per cent) are described as 'irritable', having a 'difficult temperament' or as 'emotionally negative'. These babies seem to be highly sensitive to even small alterations in stimulation and react quickly and strongly to changes in their surroundings. In the early weeks, for example, such babies may cry each time they are undressed to be changed or bathed, or they may start and become distressed at a sudden noise; they often find it hard to make transitions between states, perhaps crying as they wake or finding it difficult to go off to sleep. They may cry rather more than other babies during the early weeks and it may be hard for them either to soothe themselves, for example, by sucking on their fist, or to be soothed by their carer. In sum, these babies seem to be particularly sensitive – easily distressed and with rather poor ability to regulate themselves.

A second, similarly small group of babies shows a pattern of behaviour that is generally referred to as 'behaviourally inhibited'. Early on, in their first 3 to 4 months, these babies are also more than usually sensitive to their surroundings, and if faced with an increased level of stimulation they become highly reactive, rapidly moving their limbs in an agitated way and even showing distress, as if they are uncomfortable and find it difficult to tolerate. This can be seen, for example, when a simple mobile the baby has enjoyed watching is gradually altered by having several other shapes added to it, or when a repeated sound becomes louder, or a smell more intense. At 12 to 14 months, babies who are behaviourally inhibited are vigilant and wary of new experiences, especially social ones – they will typically withdraw from them or avoid them altogether. In an unfamiliar playroom, for example, these babies are likely to stay close to their parent, are reluctant to explore attractive toys nearby, and show clear signs of apprehension and avoidance if someone they do not know comes in and attempts to engage them in play.

Each of these early patterns of baby behaviour may in part reflect the influence of antenatal or genetic factors. However, two lines of research indicate that unless there are fundamental physical problems (for instance, babies suffering from foetal alcohol syndrome), it is by no means inevitable that the

behaviour will persist and develop into longer-term child problems. First, with regard to the pattern of 'irritable' or 'emotionally negative' behaviour, when this is seen in newborns and babies under 3 months the difficulties quite often resolve themselves naturally over time, so that, for example, if some babies cry much more than usual in this early period, it does not mean that they will still do so at the end of their first year. Second, even if some babies do remain highly emotionally reactive right through the first year or so, whether or not this leads on to behaviour problems (such as aggressive, oppositional or attention-deficit-hyperactive behaviour), appears to be strongly related to the baby's rearing environment. Recent research shows that while it is true that babies and young children who are 'emotionally negative' are at greatly increased risk for developing such behaviour problems when they receive insensitive parenting, if parenting is sensitive, this group of children is actually likely to become well adjusted – better adjusted, even, than children of sensitive parents who were not highly emotionally reactive in their early development. It has also been found that if parents are having difficulty and they then receive good support and become more sensitive, where their baby or young child is emotionally negative, he is especially likely to show clear benefits and develop well. For these reasons, rather than viewing such babies as vulnerable and focusing exclusively on the possible adverse outcomes, it may be more appropriate to think of them as 'sensitive', with all that that implies about their potential to benefit greatly from positive experiences.

Interestingly, exactly the same pattern of results described above for human babies has emerged from research with monkeys (rhesus macaques), where similar profiles of high emotional and behavioural responsiveness can also be seen from a young age. When baby monkeys of this kind of temperament are brought up without good parenting, raised only with other young monkeys present or by mothers who are neglectful, they are at greatly increased risk of behaviour problems that resemble human children's problem behaviour. Yet, if these same baby monkeys are reared by a sensitive mother they generally do even better than other monkeys (for example, in terms of their place as adults in the social hierarchy).

With regard to the second group, behaviourally inhibited babies, who are generally considered to be at high risk of developing anxiety, particularly social anxiety, there is a very similar pattern of findings. First, behavioural inhibition is not always stable over the first year. So although babies who are highly reactive and distressed when faced with complex stimulation at 3–4 months are more likely than other babies to withdraw and avoid novelty at 12–14 months, by no means all babies show this continuity – clearly fearful and withdrawn behaviour only really settles into a stable pattern from the end of the first year onwards. Second, whether or not this behaviour becomes really problematic (that is, the child's fearfulness and avoidance becomes so extreme that it affects normal life and they are considered to have an anxiety disorder) is again highly dependent on the parenting they receive, and where parents are able to adjust sensitively to the baby's style of responsiveness, the child may develop particularly well.

Tackling babies' difficult behaviour

It's clear that certain patterns of parenting, and certain baby characteristics, especially in combination, can increase the risk that the baby will develop problems in self-regulation. If, by the end of the second year, these have become marked, persistent and pervasive (that is, they occur in different contexts and with different people), they could develop into more serious, long-term problems, so it becomes important to tackle them. (Do note that such marked and pervasive problems are distinct from a baby's normal expressions of assertiveness, limit-testing, or occasionally fearful behaviour – which are almost inevitable in early development, but generally diminish as the child acquires more positive self-regulation strategies.) A first principle is that, even though difficult patterns have

already become quite established, it is still worthwhile trying to put in place the kind of parenting support discussed above, that may have been absent earlier in the baby's development. With babies who have become unresponsive, dysregulated, or fearful, this is not always easy; nevertheless, taking time to watch what the baby is attending to and doing, following his cues and supporting and praising his efforts, warmly responding to even small social signals, can gradually help build up rewarding contacts, and strengthen the baby's abilities. As well as these positive steps, it is also worth attempting to break unhelpful patterns of interaction, and here it is useful to consider babies' self-regulation difficulties in two groups – 'externalizing' problems, such as aggressive/angry, defiant behaviour, and 'internalizing' problems, such as general fearfulness or extreme shyness.

'Externalizing' problems, including aggressive/angry, defiant behaviour

In this case parents should try to minimize the following habits: harsh parenting, physical punishment, lax supervision and inconsistent discipline. When a toddler is habitually aggressive and defiant, it is often the case that parents have become locked in conflictual cycles with him that risk perpetuating, or even escalating, the problem behaviour. Breaking these negative cycles and establishing positive ones is the key target. One common negative cycle is where the parent repeatedly asks the toddler to do something, the toddler repeatedly refuses and becomes aggressive and the parent eventually capitulates. This pattern perpetuates the toddler's aggressive and defiant behaviour because, from his point of view, it has been successful in causing the parent's demands to stop. As one eminent researcher, G. R. Patterson, puts it, if parents must get involved in conflict, then 'they must win each time they do so'. This does not mean that the parent should enforce their will on the child through power-assertive tactics, since harsh discipline, or the use of physical punishment, is itself likely to provoke further anger and distress in the toddler. Rather, the parent needs to find other means to get around the baby's opposition, while still achieving the desired end. This style of parenting is often referred to as being 'authoritative' rather than the harsher 'authoritarian', and it involves a combination of warmth and firm handling. Useful techniques can be to help prepare the baby in advance, through pre-emptive reasoning (see above, p. 159), as well as finding some temporary diversion from the confrontation itself,

possibly through play, entertainment or comfort, or just changing the setting, until the baby is in a better state to manage what is being asked of him (see previous picture sequence 3.17 and new sequences 3.23 and 3.24 below). Above all, maintaining parental warmth towards the baby himself, if not his present behaviour, is likely to help diffuse his anger.

3.23   Managing defiant behaviour 1

Ben, aged 17 months. The way parent–child conflicts are habitually resolved is an important predictor of children's future ability to self-regulate. If conflicts escalate and parents enforce harsh or physical punishment, or if they behave inconsistently and give in, child behaviour problems are more likely to develop. By contrast, use of reasoning and finding flexible solutions or distractions, while still behaving warmly towards the child, can be effective in diffusing their anger and antagonistic behaviour.

1 Ben has a very sore bottom and he badly needs to have his nappy changed, but he really doesn't want to let his mother change him.

2 Ben's mother takes him over to the changing mat, and explains to him that she has to change him to help him feel better.

3 Talking to him seems to have helped a little . . .

4 . . . so she lowers him onto his mat.

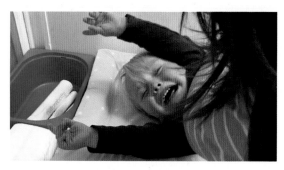

5 But Ben screams anew . . .

6 . . . so his mother finds a different way to do the change, picking him up and slipping his trousers down while she holds him.

3.23   **Managing defiant behaviour 1** continued

7 She manages to get Ben's trousers off, and gives him a good cuddle.

8 Then Ben's mother turns back towards his mat, and as she does so, she draws his attention to the animals on his mobile.

9 She holds Ben securely as he reaches across to grab one of the figures – he has stopped crying and becomes absorbed in making the mobile move around.

10 Once he is thoroughly settled, Ben's mother lowers him onto his mat again, from where he continues to enjoy watching the moving figures.

11 Ben points up to one of them, and his mother follows his cue, catches it …

12 …and brings it within Ben's reach.

13 Now he is happily playing with his toy, so his mother can proceed with the nappy change and Ben barely seems to notice it.

3.24   **Managing defiant behaviour 2**

Iris, aged 18 months. Sometimes, children's behaviour is difficult in circumstances where the possibilities for flexible, creative and distracting techniques to resolve conflict are limited. Nevertheless, if the parent can remain affectionate as well as firm, and offer other sources of comfort, they can help the baby overcome frustration and anger, and cooperate more willingly.

1 Iris and her mother have finished their session at the university, and they need to leave quickly for an appointment across town. Iris wants to continue pushing her teddy's buggy around the car park, and resists her mother's explanations and efforts to steer her towards the car.

2 Her mother picks Iris up, talking to her firmly but affectionately, and making sure that she has her special soft toy.

3.24   **Managing defiant behaviour 2** continued

3 Iris is very reluctant to be parted from her buggy.

4 Her mother gently lowers her into the car seat, and tells her that she will be able to have her buggy again when they arrive at their next destination.

5 Iris looks longingly after the buggy, but seems to calm down as her mother straps her into her seat.

6 Once securely fastened in, Iris looks very thoughtful as she grips her soft toy.

7 Now the buggy has been put away, Iris's mother leans across to stroke her daughter's head and praises her for sitting so sensibly.

8 She passes Iris's teddy across and Iris looks very pleased to see him.

9 She holds both her soft toy and teddy close, and seems to have completely recovered from her earlier angry feelings.

A second, somewhat less common cycle where parental inconsistency is a problem is where the baby initiates the process by requesting or demanding something, the parent refuses, the baby repeats his demand, and the parent then gives in, a pattern that again serves to reinforce negative behaviour. As in the first pattern, head-on confrontations where the parent enforces their wishes are unlikely to be productive in the long term. Rather, as with the parent-initiated conflicts, a flexible but authoritative approach to arriving at solutions, involving negotiation and compromise, is more helpful.

Although avoiding the sort of inconsistencies described here is important when resolving conflict, it is worth noting that parents are generally not always consistent with regard to all aspects of the baby's behaviour. When and how parents respond partly depends on the circumstances. In fact, babies become increasingly able to take on board the particular context of their experience, and if bending rules makes good sense (so for example, a high level of riotous mucking about can be appropriate at a birthday party, but not just before bedtime), it will help the baby to gain a better sense of the reasoning behind behaviour.

'Internalizing' problems, including general fearfulness and extreme shyness

In the case of babies with internalizing problems, the habits parents should try to minimize are over-protection, lack of encouragement, and showing obvious anxiety themselves. When babies have developed significant fears or worries, or markedly inhibited or shy behaviour, it is understandable for parents to want to lessen their distress, and as a consequence parents can become over-protective. Parents of babies and children with such problems may also find it hard to remain positive and warmly encouraging when their baby faces some challenge. These difficulties are especially likely when the parents are anxious themselves, something that is common in parents of anxious children. It seems that anxious parents are particularly sensitive to the slightest indication of distress in their baby – they may believe that challenges are more threatening than they really are, and that their child is experiencing more of a struggle than is actually the case. Together, these different processes can become fixed in vicious cycles, as in the case of externalizing problems. In this case, a parent's worry that their child will not be able to cope leads them to step in to manage on their baby's behalf whatever difficulty may be present, thereby preventing the baby from gaining the experience of managing for himself, and reinforcing any sense of his own vulnerability. Any absence of warmth or positive encouragement, and any display of anxiety by the parent, can also contribute to the baby's lack of confidence and willingness to engage with potential challenges. Parents who are not anxious themselves may find it relatively simple to break such cycles if these are explained to them. They will discover that their child has greater potential to manage than they imagined if, rather than stepping in, they watch and provide encouragement. (Parental use of self-help manuals to adopt such practices, backed up by guidance from healthcare professionals, has been found very effective in reducing anxiety in 7- to 12-year-old children.) In cases where parents are anxious, however, more support to break such cycles may be needed, including receiving help for their own anxiety as well as for the parenting difficulties.

Summary of Chapter 3

Babies make huge strides in being able to regulate their emotions and behaviour through their first two years, and at each point parents can play a vital role. This typically involves supporting the baby's own natural tendencies to regulate their experiences, and providing a secure and affectionate context where he can have the experience of successfully managing mild challenges. In early development, support for the baby's regulation abilities is often through their physical contacts, and the provision of predictable routines and consistency in how things are done can always be helpful; but as the baby develops cognitively and in social understanding, parents can increasingly support the baby through reasoning and negotiation. Babies are naturally inclined to want to share their experiences, and a key way for parents to strengthen their baby's longer-term tendency to be cooperative and well-regulated is by supporting his participation in shared activities in a way that he enjoys.

Although babies differ from one another in how easily they can manage and regulate their experiences, it is not inevitable that early difficulties will persist and become problematic behaviour. Indeed, supportive parenting can help more sensitive babies develop particularly well. And even if difficult patterns of behaviour do develop, whether of the externalizing (for example, aggression) or internalizing kind (for example, anxious behaviour), there is much that can be done in these early years to help a baby manage their experiences better.

Isabel says her first word, 'doh' (dog).

4 Cognitive development

The term 'cognitive' covers all the different skills relevant to general intelligence, and includes attending, perceiving, reasoning, learning, and language skills. In young babies, even actions and motor skills are key components of their cognitive development. Psychologists studying cognitive functions are often interested in the associated brain processes and how they are influenced by experience, including social interactions. Although the experiences that babies provide for themselves help develop their cognitive skills, those that happen during social interactions support and enrich babies' cognitive development in unique ways.

The developing brain

By the time a baby is born their brain is already well developed, with almost all the cells, or neurons, it will ever have – some 100 billion of them – in place. The main changes that occur after birth are not therefore in the numbers of nerve cells, but are to do with the 'wiring', the network of connections that develops between them. This growth in connections happens very fast, more than 80 per cent of it taking place within the first two years of life. Much of the brain's developing structure and the way in which the branches and connection points (the connections are called synapses) grow between the cells, depends on genetic processes. For example, cells at the back of the eye, the retina, are preset to send out connections to the visual areas at the back of the brain. But the activation of cells and their connections also has a major influence on the developing brain: cells and their connections which are frequently activated become stronger and survive, whereas those that are not used are pruned away. Indeed, just as the rapid growth of nerve connections is a key part of early brain development, so is the fact that as many as 50–70 per cent of the brain cells that were first produced wither away in the postnatal period. This sculpting process, in which brain cells and their connections are generated and eliminated according to their activation, means that the nature of the baby's experience is of great importance for the shaping and fine-tuning of the brain and, consequently, the related cognitive processes.

Effects of experience

Many of the key studies showing how experience affects brain development have involved studying animals which have the same genetic background but are reared in different conditions. Some studies have looked at the effects of very general features of the animal's environment, such as the level of stimulation. For example, rats reared in settings providing similar stimulation to their natural environment are not only more cognitively efficient, being better at finding their way through mazes to get food, but they also have more developed brains than rats reared in an environment with minimal stimulation. Research with rats has also shown how parenting affects brain and cognitive development. For example, the pups of mother rats that frequently lick and groom their young have more synapses in the brain area that is involved in spatial memory (the hippocampus), and are better at learning to negotiate mazes than other rat pups. Strikingly, this does not just reflect an inherited difference between the two groups of pups, because the brain growth and behaviour of rats born to low stimulation mothers is significantly better if they are removed from their own mothers and are fostered and cared for by mothers which lick and groom their young frequently.

The timing of experience and environmental stimulation also seems to matter for some aspects of brain development. If a kitten is prevented from using one of its eyes while young, then the normal connections between the cells in that eye and those in the visual area of the kitten's brain do not develop, so the eye is effectively blind. Importantly, the kitten's brain development adjusts to this situation and actually compensates, with all the wiring of cells between eye and brain shifting to the eye that does receive visual stimulation, so that the kitten is still able to see. Such

---

E How the baby's detection and 'computing' abilities work with language

Some of a baby's learning skills have been likened to a computational process that detects the regularities and patterns in the stimulation around him, as well as their relation to his own activity. Much research into these skills comes from studying babies' language development and one of the main findings is the rapid fine-tuning of the baby's sensitivities, as they are adjusted to his own particular language environment. In the first few months of life babies are able to detect the separate speech elements (known as phonemes) that occur across all languages, picking up on distinctions that are often signalled by tiny sound changes only a few milliseconds long. But by the end of the first year, the baby stops being able to detect elements that are absent from the language he normally hears and becomes more sensitive than ever to those that are present in that language. This change is to do with the strengthening of neural networks that code the patterns of speech the baby hears, a process sometimes called 'native language neural commitment'. A classic example of this is the finding that, in the first few months, babies across the world can hear the distinction between 'ra' and 'la', but whereas babies in the US who are regularly exposed to this distinction become more sensitized to the sound difference, Japanese babies, whose native language does not have the distinction, lose the ability to detect it.

Aside from babies becoming sensitized to such very fine differences, these computer-like skills also help them pick up on more general aspects of the speech they hear most, such as the way in which larger sound elements are typically combined, and which part of words are stressed. These detection abilities are very helpful in chunking up the flow of sounds the baby hears into separate words. For example, although the elements of 'pret-ty-ba-by' are equally spaced, the probability in English of 'ty' following on 'pret' is far higher than it is of before 'ba', and detecting this likelihood allows the baby to correctly chunk the sounds as the two words, 'pretty baby'. Then in English words, stress usually occurs on the first of two syllables – as in 'apple' or 'orange' – and learning this general pattern is again helpful to the baby in chunking up a flow of sounds he hears into separate words. (There are, of course, exceptions. For example, if an English-exposed baby hears the words 'guitar is' as part of a string of words, the usual stress rule can lead him, mistakenly, to hear the elements as 'gui' and 'taris'. In fact, by studying babies' mistakes, psychologists are able to learn a lot about the way in which they process the sounds they hear.) What is striking is that babies detect and use these probabilities in speech sounds so rapidly that after just a few minutes' experience of hearing repetitions of certain combinations, eight-month-olds can treat them as whole words.

findings have proved very important for understanding human babies' eyesight. For example, babies born with cataracts need to have the experience of seeing patterns soon after surgery if any improvements are to occur in their ability to see clearly. If this kind of stimulation can be given, neural activity is triggered within hours and, for some aspects of vision, the result can be near-normal levels of functioning.

To sum up, the findings from animal studies and research into particular clinical problems tell us that the brain and cognitive development of normal babies is also likely to be profoundly influenced by the nature of their experience and its timing, rather than simply being a matter of natural growth. Key questions are, therefore, what kinds of experiences are important, how they influence the baby's development and learning, and how babies' carers can best support such experiences.

The building blocks of cognitive development

The baby's own activity and detection abilities

The environment of the baby, particularly his social relationships, is of major importance in his cognitive development, but the baby himself also plays a very active role in pushing his development forward. Indeed, his constant motivation to develop further is such that he will often abandon a skill once he has mastered it, in favour of new challenges, even if these are quite costly at first in terms of efficiency and effort – one example would be when the baby gives up crawling in favour of learning to walk. Particularly in the early weeks as parents get to know their baby, understanding more about his activity and perceptions and the positive contribution these make to his cognitive development can be helpful for parents when they start to support him.

Certain features of the baby's activity and perceptions are particularly relevant to his cognitive development. First, and from the start, many of the baby's most important actions are purposeful and

flexibly sensitive to his surroundings, rather than being simple, automatic reflexes. One recent study using ultrasound even reported purposeful actions by foetuses directed towards a co-twin between the 14th and 18th week of gestation. Further, in the newborn period, the baby quickly adjusts his behaviour to circumstances – changing his sucking, for example, as he learns to anticipate the flow of milk, or directing his arm movements towards objects that catch his interest, even if he is unable to make contact with them. Second, babies are fascinated by discovering the connections between what they do and what happens around them. Even very young babies can pick up on such connections and adapt their behaviour to control events, as we see from experiments showing that the newborn will learn to suck more on a dummy if it is fitted up so that his sucking triggers the sound of his mother's voice, or the two-month-old will learn how to kick to make a mobile move. This impulse becomes particularly clear in the second half of the first year, when the baby will endlessly practise and become completely caught up with the success or failure of his actions, repeatedly testing them and actively experimenting to find out what effects he can have on his environment. The third key aspect of babies' early activity is that they seem to want to find out more about their own behaviour and the connections between their different senses. For example, the baby seems keen to discover the relationship between what it feels like to move his hands, and the sight of them moving, so that in a darkened room he will change the position of his hand to keep it in the path of a moving beam of light. Two- to three-month-olds, in particular, spend a lot of time intently watching their own hand movements, activity that has been called 'body babbling'. Finally, babies have extremely impressive computational abilities. These are especially clear when they detect connections and regularities in the speech they hear around them, so that the baby becomes sensitized within a just a few months to the particular patterns, sounds and stresses of their own language (see box E).

How activity helps the baby's cognitive development

Gaining control The baby's natural curiosity and active engagement with his environment help his cognitive development in many ways. For example, as he constantly practises his movements and adjusts them repeatedly to his surroundings, the baby's initially awkward and piecemeal actions become smoother and more precise, the scope of what he can do is widened and he gains much more control. 'Body babbling' (as explained earlier, this is the baby practising and watching his own movements) is particularly useful now, strengthening the brain's connections between vision and touch, so that the baby gradually learns to guide actions precisely according to what he sees. Indeed, if animals (such as rhesus macaques) do not have the experience of being able to link what they see and do in their first few weeks, their ability to visually control their hand movements is very impaired. Research also suggests that the baby's repeated experience of coupling the sight and the feeling of his own hands moving may support the development of mirror neuron systems that are important in helping him understand, and therefore learn from, the actions carried out by others (see Chapter 1 for more on mirror neurons). The baby's progress in motor skill and control takes place across the whole range of activities, but feeding patterns, being very regularly repeated, show this learning curve particularly clearly (see picture sequences 4.1–4.4, and box F on p. 180 on feeding for more detail).

4.1   Development of motor skills in feeding 1

Even within a single feeding session, a baby's motor skills can become better organized.

Here we see Lottie, aged 5 months, being fed with a spoon for the first time. At the beginning of the feed she shows no inclination to open her mouth as the spoon approaches, but within just a short time, and with Lottie's mother encouraging her, she quickly gets the hang of it.

1 When Lottie's mother lifts her first ever spoonful of food towards her, Lottie shows no anticipation. She seems interested, but doesn't open her mouth in readiness.

2 Her mother brings the spoon to Lottie's lips, and as Lottie feels it make contact, she lifts her own spoon up to her mouth as well.

3 Lottie pushes some of the food out of her mouth with her tongue, not yet able to control holding it in her mouth. She seems fully concentrated on the new taste. Her mother gives her plenty of time to explore this new sensation.

4 Lottie's mother signals that another spoonful is coming.

4.1   Development of motor skills in feeding 1 continued

5 Lottie wants to control this one herself, pulling hard on the spoon to bring it to her mouth.

6 She concentrates on having a good chew on it while her mother helps by steadying it for her, letting Lottie have control of this new experience.

7 Now the next spoonful is on its way and Lottie begins to open her mouth in readiness.

8 Again, Lottie is keen to take control, and her mother watches as Lottie attempts to place the spoon in her mouth herself – getting it in place though is quite difficult, and the spoon pushes into the side of Lottie's mouth.

9 It seems to have caused her some discomfort, so Lottie's mother helps her manoeuvre it into her mouth more gently.

10 Just a few spoonfuls later, Lottie is coordinating her actions smoothly with her mother, watching closely as the spoon arrives and opening her mouth in anticipation.

11 Lottie still wants to take part, holding on to the spoon with her mother, and now shaping her mouth in a better way to accommodate it.

4.2   Development of motor skills in feeding 2

Ben, aged 10 months, is now very familiar with the feeding routine, but he still enjoys experimenting with the textures of different foods. As he does so, he gains increasing control over his movements and they become more precise.

1 Ben is now enjoying finger foods, and his mother gives him a piece of banana.

4.2 Development of motor skills in feeding 2 continued

2 Before eating the banana, Ben examines it. His mother sits by, happy to let him find out about his food.

3 Ben picks up the piece of banana, curling his fingers around this slippery thing.

4 He then eats some.

5 Ben squidges the banana left in his hand, fascinated by its feel; his mother supports his experience, squeezing her own fingers in sympathy.

6 A little piece of banana has dropped onto the table and Ben carefully tries to pick it up, using a fine pincer movement.

7 Then he enjoys eating this tiny scrap.

4.3 Development of motor skills in feeding 3

While feeding, babies can encounter a wide range of experiences that are helpful to their cognitive development. As well as developing more precise control over their hand movements, they can enjoy exploring the great variety of different textures, whether hard or soft, liquid or solid, smooth or rough, dense or feather-light.

Here Ben, aged 11 months, delights in playing around with the remains of his yoghurt.

1 Ben is absorbed in running his hands around the base of the bowl.

2 Looking at the traces of his finger movements . . .

3 . . . before having a final lick.

4.4   Development of motor skills in feeding 4

Daily experiences of feeding help the baby refine his skills. Ben, now 14 months, has become accustomed to using a spoon to feed himself, and the sequence of his actions shows flexible adjustment to the different foods, as well as good anticipation. Nevertheless, it's tiring work and reverting to finger feeding can be a relief at times!

2 Ben changes the angle of his spoon and also pushes its base up against his plate, so that the pea falls nicely into the bowl of the spoon.

1 Ben is trying to get a pea on his spoon, but holding the spoon quite flat makes it difficult.

3 As he lifts his spoon, his mouth opening is perfectly timed …

4 …as are his lip movements to take the pea into his mouth.

5 When getting the next spoonful, Ben uses the same technique of having a steep angle, and aiming for the side of his bowl.

6 The macaroni is successfully put in place and Ben concentrates on keeping it on his spoon.

7 Now he realizes that he will need to open his mouth much wider than he did for the pea, and again his anticipation is very accurate.

8 But all this spoon work is quite taxing, especially when Ben is still keen to get food inside him, so he happily reverts to using his fingers …

9 …and then he can be sure of having a large mouthful.

F **Developing control through action: feeding**

Over time, the baby moves on from his first fumbling attempts to latch on and adjust to the flow of milk during his earliest feeds, to the confident control of breast and bottle (see picture sequences 2.9 and 2.11 in Chapter 2), and the later management of spoon feeding, where a particularly complex set of skills develops. In the first spoon feeds, the baby can't anticipate when, or exactly where, the spoon will arrive at his mouth, nor which mouth movements will be needed to take the food off the spoon and keep it from spilling down his chin – with the consequence that initial attempts are inefficient and, above all, messy! Over the following weeks and months, however, the baby is likely to become intently interested in the nature of his food and what he can do with it and, if given the opportunity, he will endlessly investigate it, enjoying the feel of it and how it can be handled. He will work hard, if his carer lets him, to master feeding himself. With practice, the baby's spoon feeding eventually shows impressive skills of organized planning, anticipation and fine motor control (see picture sequences 4.1–4.4). What might appear to parents, then, as random behaviour, or simply 'messing about' as the baby explores his food, is likely to be part of an important process of gaining skill and control (while at the same time giving the baby much satisfaction and pleasure).

4.5   Object concept 1

Where babies search for things that have been hidden shows how they understand the nature of objects. The 'object concept' task is a classic test, when the baby is presented with objects that are hidden in increasingly complex ways. Some illustrations of this task are shown in the sequences below with Iris, who is 14 months old.

In the first stage, the researcher hides a small object under an opaque cup. When babies are 5 months old they will usually succeed in searching under the cup, as though they understand that the object is hidden there.

1 The researcher covers the object with the cup, as Iris watches.

2 Iris reaches over and removes the cup . . .

3 . . . and finds the object there.

Understanding the physical world Just as the baby's activity advances his motor skills and gives him more control, so play and exploration help him understand the nature of his environment and the laws that govern it (see picture sequences 4.5–4.7). Through infancy, the baby is constantly updating and revising ideas about his physical world, seeming to experiment and test out ever more sophisticated rules. He may endlessly throw things from his high chair, for example, and watch in fascination as they fall to the ground. As he does so, he learns about the effects of gravity. He may enjoy

stacking games with bricks, and as he does so he learns about what is needed for one object to support another. Similarly, as the baby updates his understanding of the continuing existence of objects when they disappear under different conditions (say, behind screens, under cloths, or inside containers), so his play with them changes, and he may start to experiment with hiding things himself – perhaps placing toys repeatedly in a box, closing it and then opening it, to 'discover' his toys again (see picture sequences 4.8 and 4.9).

4.6   Object concept 2

In this more advanced task, the researcher uses two cups: she hides the object twice under one of them, and each time the baby will find it. Then on the third hide, she switches to hide the object under the other cup. At 10 months, babies will usually use a search strategy in line with the researcher's hides, swapping over to look under the second cup on this third occasion. Before this age, however, babies will often persevere with their original strategy and

continue to lift the first cup where they found the object successfully before, even though they have just watched the object being placed somewhere else. This has been thought to reflect the use of a rule that normally works well, namely, 'look for something where you are used to finding it'. It might also reflect the baby's difficulty in stopping themselves from repeating a pattern of behaviour that has been in full swing for a while.

1 The researcher uses two cups, and hides an object under the cup to Iris's right.

2 Iris reaches across …

3 … and removes the cup without hesitation.

4 The researcher repeats hiding the object under the same cup …

5 … and again Iris reaches straight for it.

4.6 Object concept 2 continued

7 Iris changes her search too, and finds the object easily.

6 On the next occasion, the researcher changes to hide the object under the other cup.

4.7 Object concept 3

In this further test of the baby's understanding of objects, the baby has to make an inference: 'If the object is not in the place where I last saw it [in this case, the researcher's hand], then it must be in the place where her hand disappeared.' On average, babies succeed in finding the object when they are around 14–15 months.

1 The researcher shows Iris the object in the palm of her hand.

2 While Iris is watching, the researcher puts her hand into the cup and lets the object drop silently inside it. Iris watches carefully.

3 The researcher then proffers her closed hand, and Iris opens it to find the object – this is where she saw the object before.

4 But Iris sees that the researcher's hand is empty . . .

5 . . . so she reaches over to search in the place where the researcher's hand disappeared with the object.

6 And there it is.

4.8   Experimenting with objects 1

Ben, aged 14 months, enjoys watching what happens as he repeatedly hurls objects down from his high chair. Here, he is lucky to have a brother who is patient enough to keep retrieving them.

1 Ben lifts his cup high, to throw it to the floor.

2 He stares down at it.

3 His brother, Joe, kindly picks up Ben's cup for him.

4 Ben repeats his action . . .

5 . . . and again seems to find the effect fascinating.

6 Patient Joe gives Ben back his cup yet again.

4.9   **Experimenting with objects 2**

Isabel and her twin brother, Benjamin, aged 15 months, have become intrigued by opening and closing containers and placing small objects inside them. It is something both of them like to do time and again. It is at this age that babies begin to develop more adult-like concepts of the persistence of objects.

1 Isabel carefully picks up a small toy...

2 ...and drops it with interest into her tin...

3 ...then she very deliberately puts the lid on.

4 Benjamin reaches behind the tin to retrieve a small toy.

5 He drops it into his tin...

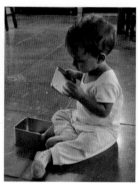

6 ...then takes the lid to cover it up.

7 Now he removes the lid...

8 ...drops another toy inside and is ready to put the lid on again.

9 Having hidden the toys, Ben then peers at the tin, as though thinking about the hidden toys inside.

Making sense of others' actions Aside from learning more about the physical world, developments in the baby's own activity help him make sense of others' behaviour, understand what their goals are, and thereby learn from them more effectively. For example, at the age when the baby starts to like putting things inside containers (around 10–12 months) – but not before – he becomes able to understand someone else performing a similar action and his gaze will dart ahead as he watches them, in anticipation of where they will place the object. Similarly, at around 6 months, when the baby normally has experience of spoon-feeding, he will look ahead to someone's mouth as he watches them lift a spoonful of food. The same understanding is not shown, by contrast, if the baby watches someone lift an object towards their head in a similar way, but to do something that the baby has not yet done himself, like combing his hair. The conclusion that babies' own activity affects their perception of others' behaviour has been neatly shown by studies in which babies are given unusual experiences. In one, 3-month-olds (an age when babies can't yet reach out and successfully grab hold of things) who were given Velcro mittens that enabled them to hold on to Velcro-covered toys when they touched them, became better at anticipating how someone else would reach out to handle the toys than babies without this extra experience. Similarly, 14- to 18-month-olds who were given the unusual experience of having their eyes covered by a blindfold, afterwards behaved as though they understood what wearing one would mean for someone else – that is, they did not change their gaze to follow a blindfolded person's head-turn towards a nearby object. Without this experience, by contrast, the babies behaved as though the blindfolded person could see, and turned their own head accordingly. Memorizing others' actions is also supported by the baby performing similar actions himself: for example, if the baby watches someone playing with toys in a particular way and is then given a chance to play with them briefly himself, he will remember what was done with the toys one day later better than a baby who had only watched the other person.

All these studies show the advantages of the baby being free to experiment and explore his environment, and they have direct implications for his carers – for it is through social relationships that the baby's own potential to master his world can be fully developed.

The role of social relationships 1: the baby's contribution

First connections with other people

While the baby's own activity and detection skills are important in supporting his cognitive development, their benefits are greatly enriched by, or even dependent on, his interactions with other people. Right from the start, babies' key behaviours involve seeking engagement with others, as in the newborn's attraction for faces and for eye-contact, or the way they will turn towards the sound of a human voice in preference to a non-human sound with similar characteristics. The baby rapidly identifies particular features of the people who care for him, showing preferences for his mother's face, voice and smell over those of other women. All these preferences, some of which develop even before birth, help forge close relationships and ensure that the baby and their carers are in active contact with each other. This means that the parent is perfectly placed to give support that helps the baby's cognitive development, as well as providing social and emotional care.

Communicating interests and intentions

The fact that many important baby behaviours, even in the newborn period, have the qualities of intentional actions, rather than being formless and random, can help parents understand what the baby wants and needs, putting them in a much better position to support him appropriately. Their ability to read the baby's intentions and cues is very important for helping to foster his cognitive abilities throughout infancy, of course, but being sensitive to the baby in the newborn period, or in the early weeks before his capacities to control his environment are well developed, may be particularly helpful. It is a shame, then, that some conventional wisdoms (or 'old wives' tales') still deny the extent of a baby's early awareness and the meaningful nature of his responses (for example, claiming that babies cannot see or hear until they are at least a few weeks old, or that if they smile it is only in response to 'wind'). Regrettably, such beliefs can carry considerable force and parents' intuitive sense of their baby's experience can be all too easily undermined. Realizing, however, that the baby really is interested in something that catches his eye and really is reaching out towards it, can cue parents to help their baby experience the world as he wants. Later on, when the baby can act more independently, if the parents know that the baby 'playing with' his food, or throwing things from his high chair, is not just for fun but is also helping him discover more about his senses and the way the world works, they may be encouraged to support his efforts and help him transform his impulse to engage with the world into action that achieves a goal.

Imitating others

Although babies learn a great deal through their own activity, such learning involves much trial and error and can be a slow process. But by watching what others do and imitating them, the learning can be speeded up and made more efficient. Imitating others can also expand the scope of what the baby learns, from how to use tools to understanding complex cause-and-effect relationships, or picking up the particular social habits and customs of family and background culture. Certainly, before babies understand speech well or can use language themselves, imitating those around them is one of the main ways they learn, with 12- to 18-month-olds acquiring one or two new behaviours every day through imitation.

Early imitation In general, babies like to imitate the actions that they frequently perform themselves. In the first few weeks, these may be mouth movements like sticking out the tongue (see Chapter 1), expressions of emotion, and even eye-blinks and finger movements. As the baby often practises such behaviours in the womb,

he usually has considerable control over them by the time he is born. Indeed, when the newborn imitates, his behaviour generally appears very deliberate, often occurring after a few seconds delay and becoming more accurate with every repeat performance, even involving 'creative errors' if his partner's behaviour is unusual. However, babies will not always imitate what someone else does and whether they do depends partly on the surroundings (for instance, how much background noise or activity there is, or the lighting), and on whether they are alert and interested in being socially engaged. There are also important individual differences, such as in motor control, which influence the baby's tendency to imitate, something that has even been noted in monkeys. So, while early imitation is remarkable, parents need not feel distressed if their baby does not seem keen on doing this when they interact with him, nor feel they should make strenuous efforts to coax their newborn baby into imitating if he seems reluctant.

Developments in imitation Beyond the first few weeks, as babies develop more skills like reaching out and grasping, or vocalizing, they usually start to imitate these new behaviours more than the ones they copied before. This happens not so much because their ability or desire to imitate the previous actions 'dies out', but because the baby's new skills, and his increasingly active role in social interactions, are becoming more dominant – in fact, the baby may imitate 'old' behaviours if his partner emphasizes and highlights them as part of a social game (see picture sequence 4.10). And as the baby's skills multiply, he can also begin to imitate actions that he hasn't done before, by combining the ones he can already manage into new arrangements.

While young babies will imitate their partner's exact movements, as their communication and social understanding develop and they become more aware of other people's intentions, so they begin to imitate the goals of other people's actions, rather than the precise behaviour itself. By 15 months, the baby does

4.10   Imitating 1

Imitation occurs from the baby's earliest days and is one of the clearest signs of their social nature and sense of connection with other people. It is also an effective way for babies to learn from others. What actions babies will imitate change as they develop, from simple movements over which they have good control, to complex sequences they see performed by others, as well as others' intentions.

Here William, aged 9 weeks, is enjoying a social game, playing face-to-face with his mother. Their game is in the form of a 'conversation' in which they each take turns to play the prominent, active part, while the other is more receptive. Although William is past the stage of the more serious, studied imitations of tongue protrusion that can be seen in newborns, he and his mother do poke their tongues out at each other as part of this game.

1 William is actively mouthing as his mother looks on, encouraging him to be social.

2 He sobers a little and watches intently as his mother takes the initiative, poking out her tongue very clearly.

3 Now William does the same, as his mother watches him and enjoys his efforts.

4 They finish this conversational sequence with a shared smile.

not necessarily even need to see someone successfully achieve their final goal – just watching a failed, but clearly goal-directed effort, is enough for him to perform the intended action correctly (see picture sequence 4.11).

What the baby increasingly focuses on then, when he imitates at this age, is the meaning of what people do, and he begins to make quite complex judgements about others' intentions, using such reasoning to guide his imitation. For example, if the 14- to18-month-old

4.11 Imitating 2

As babies become better able to understand what motivates other people's actions, when they witness an act that looks as though it has not gone as intended they will imitate the intended act, rather than what actually took place.

Here Iris, at 18 months old, takes part in an experiment (first carried out by Andrew Meltzoff and colleagues) in which a researcher makes a mistake while performing an action – in this case, dropping beads outside rather than inside the cup. Iris watches carefully and then imitates the intended action, not the one she saw.

1 Iris watches carefully, as the researcher holds the beads directly above the cup.

2 When she releases them, they fall slightly to one side . . .

3 . . . and they end up on the table.

4 The same action is repeated . . .

5 . . . with the same result.

6 Now the researcher offers Iris a turn.

7 Iris takes the beads.

8 Straight away she holds them over the cup . . .

9 . . . making sure they drop inside it.

baby sees someone performing a deliberate behaviour and emphatically saying 'There!' after its completion, he will be likely to imitate it, but if exactly the same behaviour is shown as an accident, accompanied by an exclamation of 'Whoops!', then he will not (see Chapter 1 for more on the topic of how babies' imitation reflects their social understanding). Exceptions to this general rule of the older baby imitating goals, rather than precise behaviours, occur either when the purpose of the other person's action is unclear, or when the baby gets involved in a social exchange with someone who deliberately shows them exactly how to do something (see picture sequences 4.12 and 4.13). Such exact copying is common between babies and their older siblings, where the desire to be 'just like' their big brother or sister is powerful and can dominate play (see picture sequence 4.14), as well as between pairs of babies from around 18 months.

4.12   Imitating 3

Ben, aged 17 months, has found his father's drums. He's fascinated by them, but is uncertain about how they might be used, turning them this way and that as though trying to figure out the best thing to do.

1   2   3   4

4.13   Imitating 4

Ben's father comes over with some drumsticks, and shows Ben what to do. Ben is very keen to watch his father, and picks up the idea very quickly.

1 Ben's father gives Ben a pair of drumsticks, sets the drums in position and shows Ben what to do.

2 Ben watches his father with rapt attention.

4.13   **Imitating 4** continued

3 Ben is very keen to have a go himself, as his father pushes the drums towards him.

4 He immediately gets the right action.

5 Ben looks up as his father praises him.

6 Now Ben's father shows him very clearly again.

7 Ben concentrates hard to bring his drumstick down in the same place.

8 He is soon freely drumming away.

9 He seems very proud, and excited by what he has achieved, keen to share his triumph with his father.

4.14   **Imitating 5**

One of the most striking arenas for imitation is in play between toddlers and their older siblings, where the impulse to be just like their brother or sister is strong. Here we see Ben, now just aged 2, with his 6-year-old brother Joe, playing soldiers. Joe is a keen teacher and Ben faithfully copies each of his brother's postures and actions throughout the game, and when they have their soldier snacks.

1 Joe helps Ben get into his soldier kit.

2 Ben looks up, putting his hat on as his brother does the same.

4.14   **Imitating 5** continued

3 Ben pays careful attention as Joe prepares to demonstrate an important move.

4 Joe falls to the ground with arms outstretched.

5 Ben does the same and looks at Joe to check he has got it right.

6 Now Joe is demonstrating another manoeuvre, and Ben pays attention to the positioning of his feet, making sure they are just like his brother's.

7 Both boys stand with arms out and Joe bends at the knee, preparing to launch himself down . . .

8 . . . which ends with a dramatic legs-in-air display.

9 Joe sets Ben up to copy him, explaining how you start.

10 Then Ben launches himself . . .

11 . . . managing to get his legs up in the air too.

12 Almost inevitably, it seems, the boys end up in a wriggling heap.

4.14 Imitating 5 continued

13 Now it's time for soldier snacks, and Ben looks on as his brother sorts the food out.

14 Joe takes a share for Ben from his bowl . . .

15 . . . so that they both have the same.

16 Ben holds one of his hands round his bowl, just like Joe.

17 They both snack in unison.

Other developments concern how much of someone's behaviour will be copied, and babies increase the number of separate elements they can imitate in one action sequence as they get older. The length of delay they can tolerate between what they originally saw and their imitation also increases (for example, where 6- to 9-month-olds can manage a 24-hour delay, 14-month-olds can perform their imitation after a week, even for new actions). Similarly, the baby increases his ability to ignore a particular context (like the room where the original action took place) and the specific objects involved, especially when the action to be imitated is familiar and well organized.

Capitalizing on babies' imitation The fact that babies have a natural tendency to imitate is often, and quite unconsciously, exploited by adults who want to encourage the baby to do something, and this can often be seen during mealtimes when whoever is spoon-feeding the baby will open their own mouth at the point when the baby should open his to receive the food. Strikingly, this impulse to encourage feeding by trying to prompt imitative mouth opening is also performed by babies themselves, not just older partners, reflecting the fact that imitation is a really fundamental way of transferring skills and knowledge (see five examples in picture sequence 4.15).

4.15   Imitating 6

The fact that babies will imitate is often used by other people, quite unconsciously, as they open their own mouths when encouraging a baby to eat.
    Here we see this happening across the age span, from a 90-year-old great-granny, to a mother, an adolescent uncle and even babies themselves, with another baby or even when pretending to feed a doll.

1 Isabel, aged 10 months, and her great-granny.

2 Summer, aged 9 months, and her mother.

3 Isabel, aged 9 months, and her uncle.

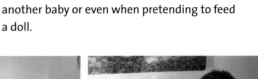

4 Benjamin, aged 11 months, and Max, aged 19 months.

5 Isabel, aged 15 months, with her father, brother and a doll.

The role of social relationships 2: the parent's contribution

The overwhelming importance of parents' social interaction with their baby for the baby's cognitive development has been shown in many studies. However, the particular form of social responsiveness that will be most helpful alters with each developmental stage and, while the baby's changing behaviour can often provide clear cues, what parents need to do in order to support them best is not always immediately obvious. Understanding more about the baby's signals, the nature of his development, and how advances in his behaviour are linked with his cognitive progress, can help parents provide the right kind of support. And although much of that helpful parental response takes place quite intuitively, it can still increase parents' satisfaction with their role if they understand how what comes naturally to them is supporting their baby's development. Such knowledge can give them more confidence in their parenting. And at times when they find it more difficult, knowing something about the nature of babies' development can give carers a better framework for providing helpful care.

Contingent responsiveness

One very general feature of parental responsiveness that is important for babies' cognitive development is what is called its contingent nature – the close association in time between what the baby does and the response he gets from his parent. When showing contingent responsiveness, the parent closely monitors the baby's behaviour and what he is attending to, ready to pick up on his signals and respond quickly enough for the baby to be able to notice the connection. Although this kind of responsiveness is a very general feature of parents' interactions with their baby – it takes place when meeting the baby's attachment needs as well as when helping him to manage difficult emotions (see Chapters 2 and 3) – it is perhaps even more relevant to the baby's cognitive development. First, as the baby notices consistent links between what he does himself and someone else's response, he gains a sense of reward and control, and of there being cause and effect, both of which are core aspects of learning skills. Furthermore, when the baby experiences this sense of contingency, his positive interest in his surroundings increases and he is likely to attend for longer periods, and again these are key aspects of behaviour linked to better cognitive functioning.

Although research has shown that the baby can become very engaged with *objects* that react contingently, increasing his kicking, for example, to make a mobile move, *social* contingency is much more effective in attracting his positive interest and involvement, especially when provided by someone who is emotionally close to the baby. This probably reflects a natural human tendency to want to engage with other people, but it is also undoubtedly because other people can be so much more finely tuned and modulated in responding to what the baby does than can any mechanical device, and their emotional responsiveness also provides support for the baby's engagement in a way that cannot be offered by machines. The most helpful contingent responsiveness is, then, not only a matter of timing, but is also dependent on the appropriateness of the response – that is, how well attuned it is to the baby's behaviour. Babies quickly become used to the contingently responsive nature of their partners' interactions, and studies show that by 2–3 months, if this quality is disrupted, even if the form of the partner's behaviour is just the same, the baby's positive interest and involvement is reduced (see picture sequence 4.16 and the accompanying charts showing the baby's measured responses of gazing and smiling).

Lastly, and again importantly for the baby's cognitive development, experiments also show that if the baby interacts with someone who does not behave in a

4.16   Double video experiment

Contingency: One way to see whether babies are sensitive to the contingent nature of their partner's behaviour is to disrupt it and see if the baby notices. In this 'double video experiment', baby and mother interact with each other in different rooms, via a closed circuit TV system. When the baby watches the screen in 'live' time, their mother's behaviour is 'contingent' on what they do, and the baby shows all the normal social responses of interest, positive mood and active communication. But if the baby watches the same sequence of their mother again in a replay version, even though her behaviour is exactly the same, it is no longer responsive, or contingent. In this situation, 2-month-olds reduce the amount of gaze and smiling to their mother, and appear puzzled and confused, showing that it is not just what the mother does that matters to them, but also its responsive nature. Seeing a final 'live' display of their mother restores the baby's positive mood and behaviour.

4.16   **Double video experiment** continued

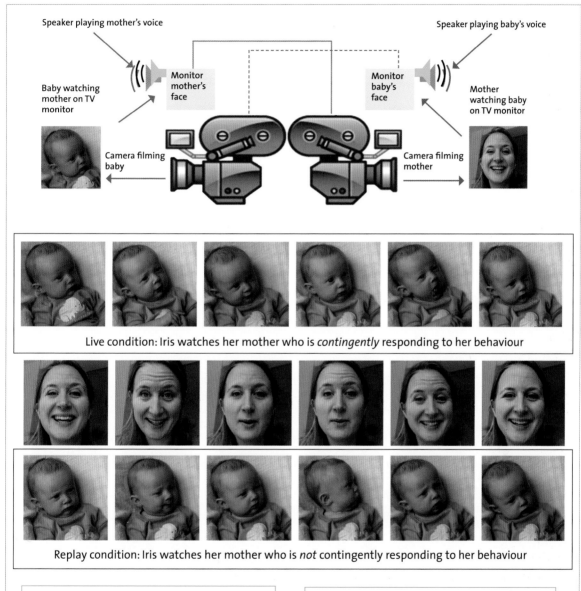

Live condition: Iris watches her mother who is *contingently* responding to her behaviour

Replay condition: Iris watches her mother who is *not* contingently responding to her behaviour

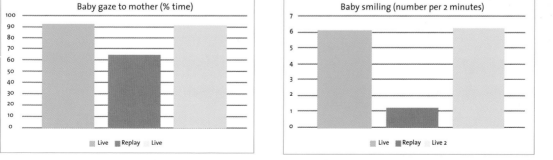

contingently responsive fashion, then the negative reaction to this disruption carries over more generally, so the baby will subsequently show less positive attention to stimulating displays and be slower in learning tasks. These findings from experiments are echoed by many naturalistic studies showing that where parents are contingently responsive to their baby, the baby has better attention and learning abilities, as well as doing better on broader measures of intelligence. Some studies even suggest that cognitive benefits arising from such responsive interaction early in development may continue right through childhood.

Contingent responsiveness in early interactions

While the baby's experience of general parental responsiveness is relevant to their cognitive progress throughout infancy, the nature of responsive behaviour changes as the baby grows and develops. In the first few weeks, much contingent responsiveness takes place during face-to-face interaction. In this context, the baby's interest in engaging socially, their varied facial expressiveness, and their signals of active communication mean that the parent is likely to find many opportunities for contingently responding moment-by-moment to the baby's cues. Most of this responsiveness happens completely naturally, without any conscious awareness – for example, if the baby makes active mouthing movements, if his emotional expression changes or if he yawns or sneezes, parents will often pick up on the baby's behaviour, typically repeating and gently emphasizing their response with clear, slightly exaggerated facial expressions, perhaps also remarking on what the baby has done to highlight its significance and give it social meaning.

Much responsiveness in early interactions involves

4.17   Encouraging interest and attention

Before babies are old enough to reach out and grab objects for themselves, they can still enjoy the experience of engaging with the physical world, especially when an adult takes note of the baby's interest and attention, and presents toys or objects in an interesting and engaging way.

Here, Iris, aged 9 weeks, enjoys looking at a colourful toy. Her mother holds it at just the right distance for Iris to see it clearly and monitors her daughter's level of interest, making small adjustments to the toy's position and manipulating it to help Iris get full enjoyment from watching it, as well as signalling her own enthusiasm and support with her smiles and changing expressive comments.

1 Iris's mother brings the cloth figure, its face forward, within Iris's visual range, and watches her response.

2 Iris raises her brows, and looks intently interested, pursing her mouth; her mother affirms Iris's interest, pursing her own mouth and saying 'Oooh'.

3 Iris smiles as she looks at the face and her mother encourages her pleasure, smiling broadly herself.

4 Iris's mother tilts the toy a little and looks enquiringly at Iris to gauge her response – Iris concentrates hard.

the parent imitating the baby in more than one way. So they may use their voice and even touch, as well as their facial expression, to signal the connection to what the baby is doing (see also Chapter 1, picture sequence 1.2). As well as giving the baby feedback that is contingent in time, these multi-modal imitations of his behaviour can help the baby to link up different sensory experiences, which in turn supports him in developing greater control over his actions. In addition, these imitations can be particularly effective in engaging the baby socially and in encouraging him to become more attentive and positive in the interaction. Finally, it is also possible that parents' imitation of babies' facial expressions may help activate and strengthen those parts of the mirror neuron system involved in understanding other people's intentions (see more on this in Chapter 1).

Although babies often enjoy face-to-face engagement in their early weeks, they are by no means always keen and may sometimes show signs of tiring of social play. It is sometimes possible to capture the baby's interest again if the parent slightly adjusts how they are playing, so that it includes some fresh element, but this is not invariably the case and the baby may signal that he has simply had enough by turning away or becoming unsettled. At this point, he may just enjoy being quiet for a while or might become absorbed in looking at something attractive nearby. Rather than trying to stimulate the baby to engage further, an appropriate, contingent, parental response could be to follow his line of interest and, for example, bring whatever has caught the baby's attention nearer, so he can enjoy a closer look. Then, if his attention to starts to flag, moving the object slightly can help the baby pick up interest (see picture sequence 4.17), as can a change in tone of voice and intonation as the object is shifted around.

4.17   Encouraging interest and attention continued

5 Her mother shifts her attention back to the toy and now Iris has had a good look, she moves one of the figure's limbs, commenting to Iris on what is happening.

6 Iris's mother's gaze darts back to monitor her daughter's interest, and Iris seems intrigued for a good few moments longer.

7 Iris's attention had started to flag, so her mother repositions the toy, turning the stripy fabric to face Iris.

8 Her mother looks to check on how Iris is finding it – she looks very engaged, her brows furrowed in concentration.

9 Iris's mother watches as her daughter responds with real interest in the new pattern.

10 She turns the toy again just slightly, to help maintain Iris's interest, and watches quietly as Iris enjoys her visual exploration.

Contingent responsiveness after three months

During face-to-face interactions in the first few weeks, the baby seems to be most attracted to highly contingent responses by his partner, but as he develops this preference changes. This may reflect the baby's natural impulse to broaden his horizons, the kind of interaction that he has already mastered perhaps no longer being sufficiently novel and stimulating to hold his interest. In line with this development, the kind of responsiveness that parents need to use to secure their baby's attention also shifts, and from 3 to 4 months it is typical for the style of social play to change. Now the baby enjoys responses that are less perfectly contingent, ones that introduce elements of surprise and humour or play around with the timing, with well-paced pauses and end points. Body games, too, become common, and they move the focus of the interaction on from pure face-to-face engagement, as does play with toys (see picture sequence 4.18 and Chapter 1 sequences 1.8 and 1.14). Such games can include many elements that exercise the baby's cognitive skills. These include helping him remember more complex sequences of actions, anticipate events, understand how individual elements of his experience are organized together, and experiment with different possible endings and alternative ways of achieving the same goal.

4.18   Body games

By 3 months, when babies have become very familiar with face-to-face 'conversation-like' interactions with their parents, they may begin to respond more to different kinds of play that bring fresh stimulation. This change often involves body games, where a routine is repeated over and over, like 'Pat-a-cake', 'Round and round the garden' or, as shown here with Iris, aged 4 months, 'Row-row-row the boat'. As well as being fun, such games can be helpful for the baby's cognitive development, since they allow the baby to remember and predict each step of the game, and to develop a sense of connected elements in a series, with a clear structure of beginning, middle and end. Both the cognitive benefit and the pleasure can be greatly enhanced by the parents as they monitor the baby's interest and enjoyment and, in response, play around with the timing and expressiveness of each step they make in the game, perhaps prolonging a pause and emotionally highlighting an approaching climax, so that the baby is helped to register the sequence and anticipate what's coming next.

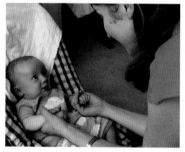

1 'Row the boat' is one of Iris's favourite games. As her mother takes Iris's hands and expressively signals its start, Iris smiles as though she knows the game will begin.

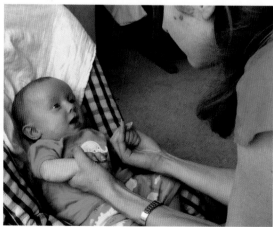

2 Iris's neck and shoulder muscles already adjust in readiness as her mother raises her arms to start lifting her, and she starts to open her mouth wide . . .

4.18 Body games *continued*

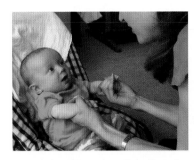

3 …and continues in anticipation of the climax.

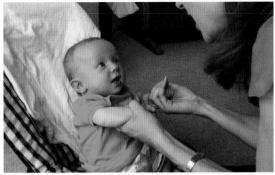

4 Iris watches as her mother uses her face and voice to support each step of the game.

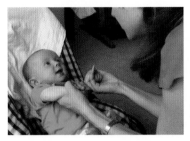

5 Now, Iris controls her head as she is lowered back onto her chair.

6 Then she enjoys being pulled up again.

7 Her mother's look and voice match Iris's experience of being lowered, then starting to be lifted again …

8 …and then change in intensity to mark the next climax …

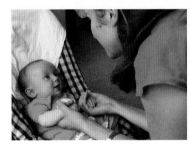

9 …before subsiding as Iris relaxes happily back into her chair.

Facilitation

As babies begin to be more independently active, a way of responding that can be particularly helpful for their cognitive development is 'facilitation'. This still involves contingent responses, in that the parent monitors the baby's focus of attention and behaviour and responds in a timely way, but it is a different way of responding. Facilitation is often focused on guiding and helping the baby to perform actions on things in his environment which he might not be able to manage on his own. For example, around 4 months when babies begin to want to reach out and grab things, but their control over their movements is still too limited to be really effective, the parent can facilitate their baby's efforts by holding the toy steady and within reach, so that he can enjoy swiping at it and, with such support, may even be able to hold onto it. This gives the baby practice in using his emerging skill and also helps him gain greater control over his experience (see picture sequence 4.19).

4.19   Reaching out

Naomi, aged 4 months, is becoming more able to reach out and grab things, but she still benefits from her mother's aid in positioning objects for her and helping her to enjoy them in different ways. Naomi's mother carefully adjusts what she does – she facilitates Naomi's sense of control by placing the toy where her daughter will be able to reach out for it herself, and she takes account of Naomi's level of interest, pacing her actions so that Naomi has time to enjoy each step of her play before introducing some new aspect.

1 Naomi is keen to engage with this interesting toy and she waves her arms in its direction.

2 Naomi's mother brings the toy nearer so that it is easier for Naomi to reach, but she still lets her daughter try to grab it herself, rather than putting the toy directly into her hand.

3 Naomi manages to grab hold of the toy successfully, and begins to tug at it as her mother watches.

4 Naomi is delighted at what she can do and her mother lets her enjoy her success.

5 Once Naomi has had time to pull repeatedly on the toy, her mother helps her enjoy it in a slightly different way by releasing a small bell so that it rings when Naomi next gives a tug, enriching her daughter's experience further.

Then, as the baby begins to master reaching and grabbing, he will need less direct facilitation for this behaviour. At some point, the baby will only need his parent to set the situation up, so that he can enjoy practising and experimenting for himself. He can be encouraged by his parent's enthusiasm as they watch, and may only need them to more actively assist his efforts if he runs into difficulty. Indeed, allowing the baby to try out his skills himself at this stage, even if not immediately successful, can be more helpful in the long term for his fully mastering them, than stepping in to do it for him (see picture sequence 4.20).

Scaffolding

While facilitating the baby's activity is very useful in relation to things that he clearly aims to do, there

4.20   Facilitating baby's own efforts

Ben, aged 10 months. Allowing the baby to try to do things himself for a while, and only stepping in to support him if he runs into difficulties, can help him learn and develop. Here, Ben's mother is available to help, but she takes a back seat while Ben tussles with a book he wants to share with her. After a slightly tricky start, Ben manages to sort it out for himself and then his mother becomes more actively involved.

1 Ben signals to his mother that he's keen to share his book with her.

2 She joins him on the floor, where he is trying to figure out how to get the book ready himself.

3 As he is making progress and trying out different strategies, his mother lets him continue on his own, supporting his efforts with her interest and in her comments to him.

4 Once Ben has reached a point where he has managed to do what he wanted, his mother becomes more actively involved, helping to get the book into a good position.

5 She starts to share the dinosaur pictures with Ben.

are often times when he is developmentally ready to tackle something in a more complex way but doesn't quite know what the possibilities are. In these circumstances, the parent can be helpful in a different way by 'scaffolding' the baby's experience. This kind of support is pitched so as to respond to the baby's current ability, while also helping him progress fractionally, but steadily, beyond it. It might involve, for example, introducing the baby to a new, just slightly more complex shape to post through a shape sorter. Or, as the baby begins to be aware of colours as features of objects, the parent might name the colour of the shape for him as he posts it through the correct hole, so helping him to become more aware of the concept of colour. Scaffolding like this is still contingently responding to the baby's current interests and activity, but differs from simple responsiveness and facilitation because it also involves the parent initiating and encouraging the development of new skills, and it helps the baby organize his mental experience in new ways.

Giving scaffolding support becomes particularly relevant from around 9–10 months, when the baby makes another important developmental advance to 'connected-up relating' (see also Chapter 1). A key element of this is that the baby becomes more interested in what other people are attending to and wants to take part in doing things with them. Now, he will more readily follow someone else's line of gaze, or their pointing finger, as well as watching the actions they perform on objects, when he will often attempt to join in. Strikingly, the way babies pay attention to things seems to benefit from such sharing – when this happens

their brain activity is significantly different compared to responses recorded when the baby is looking at something on his own. Given the baby's developing ability to register the focus of other people's attention, and his motivation to act on things together with others, parents can use this development in the way they scaffold, to help structure and enrich their baby's experience accordingly. So, once they are sure their baby is ready they can more easily draw his attention to interesting objects and events, they can even guide his behaviour in simple ways, in an elementary form of 'teaching' that means the baby's imitative abilities come more fully into play (see picture sequences 4.21–4.24). Importantly, where parents have been sensitive to their baby in social interactions in his early months, the baby seems to do better at responding to such guidance.

4.21 Scaffolding a new experience 1

Isabel, aged 10 months, now readily attends to what someone else is interested in, and when her carers monitor her attention and give support and encouragement, she will join in doing something with them and can follow simple suggestions. Her new abilities make it much easier for her carers to teach her.

Here, Isabel's uncle finds a beautiful bug. He attracts Isabel's attention to it and then shows her what can be done. He sensitively notes her level of interest, and how confident she seems, and he helps her to explore the creature with him.

1 Isabel's uncle exclaims, as he spots a brightly coloured bug when he is rearranging the rug where they have been playing.

2 Isabel immediately shows an interest in what her uncle has found.

3 She moves over to be close to the action, and gazes, fascinated, as her uncle gently strokes the bug.

4.21   **Scaffolding a new experience 1** continued

4 Isabel's uncle talks to her about the bug and she concentrates hard.

5 She looks a little apprehensive as her uncle asks her if she would like to touch it too.

6 Her uncle shows Isabel how to stroke the bug again, and Isabel tentatively leans forward, with her finger pointing at the ready...

7 ...just before she finally reaches across, Isabel looks up to her uncle's face, and he warmly encourages her to join him in stroking the bug.

8 Reassured, Isabel reaches over and starts to stroke the bug too, widening her experience of the world.

4.22   **Scaffolding 2**

Iris, now aged 12 months, has not had much experience with this shape-sorting toy, so her mother scaffolds her play, and gives her considerable support and guidance. This involves her attending to what Iris is interested in, and then gently setting up each step of the task for her, drawing on what Iris can already do, to help her achieve as much as possible herself. She paces her actions, not rushing Iris, so that each step is clear to her daughter. Iris is able to follow her mother's pointing and her suggestions, and has the satisfaction of success with the game.

1 Iris chooses the yellow cube.

2 As she inspects it, her mother moves the hole for the cube into place for Iris ...

4.22   **Scaffolding 2** continued

3 …and she steadies the box, as Iris places her cube on it.

4 Iris's mother clearly shows her where to place her cube …

5 …and Iris responds by pushing her shape further forward.

6 Iris's mother guides the cube into position …

7 …and holds it in place while Iris begins to push it down.

8 Iris manages to get the shape through the hole.

9 Now Iris's mother sets her up with a second brick, and this time she holds it in position above its hole for Iris to see, while Iris watches intently.

10 When her mother places the brick alongside the hole, Iris reaches out to grab it herself …

11 …and tries to push it through.

12 It's not at quite the right angle, so her mother lines the brick up ready for Iris to slip it in.

13 When Iris succeeds in pushing it through, her mother gives her a clap, and Iris looks quietly pleased.

4.23   Scaffolding 3

A few weeks later, at 14 months, Iris still loves playing with her shape sorter, but now she is very proficient and her mother needs to give her far less support to manage it.

1 Iris has chosen the red brick, and turns the box so that it is well positioned for her to post her shape. All her mother does is steady the box to prevent it rocking.

2 Iris confidently lines her brick up, her mother still gently holding the box in place ...

3 ... and Iris deftly pops the brick into its hole.

4 She gives it a satisfied pat, as though to mark what she's done, 'There!'

5 And Iris straightaway looks to share her pleasure in mastering the game with her mother.

4.24   Scaffolding 4

Ben, at 14 months, is very familiar with his shape-sorter truck. As he can now do quite a lot for himself in this game, his mother does not need to give the close, direct support that he needed before. Still, it's not always easy for Ben to post the bricks through their holes, so his mother sits by, available to help. She watches how he is managing and lets him try on his own before stepping in to guide him at times when he gets stuck. Her strategy means that Ben can achieve as much as possible for himself and despite the game being challenging it is also satisfying for him. This spurs Ben on to repeat it again and again until he has completely mastered it.

1 Ben is trying to put a brick into the wrong-shaped hole. His mother watches for a few moments to see if he will realize he needs to place it elsewhere.

4.24 **Scaffolding 4** continued

2 But Ben persists, so his mother points out the correct hole, and suggests he try that one.

3 Ben is able to follow her suggestion and moves his brick across, but then finds it difficult to push through the hole, so his mother gently helps to turn the brick, so that it's positioned in the right way.

4 Then she takes her hand away, allowing Ben to push the brick through on his own …

5 …and he has the satisfaction of seeing it drop down.

6 Ben's mother finds the same kind of brick for him, so that he can practise again.

7 But he goes for the wrong hole again. His mother watches …

8 …and after Ben has had a good try, she again shows him where to place it.

9 Ben moves his brick to where he mother is pointing, and succeeds in posting it.

10 All the bricks are in the truck now, but Ben is very keen to have another go, so he points to the back of the truck to signal that his mother should open it.

11 His mother responds to his request, as Ben waits eagerly.

12 Ben seizes one of the bricks he's been trying so hard to post.

4.24   Scaffolding 4 continued

13 This time, with the truck turned round, the hole he needs is right in front of him. This might make it easier for him to choose the correct one, or he may now realize which shaped hole he needs for this brick.

14 In any event he is immediately successful, pushing it through himself without any help. His mother begins to clap . . .

15 . . . and Ben looks up proudly at her to share his achievement.

Vocal and verbal support

Although the practical 'scaffolding' described above often supports babies in learning new motor skills by, say, encouraging them to imitate actions that the parent, or an older brother or sister, demonstrates (see again picture sequences 4.12–4.14 above), verbal scaffolding is a fundamental way of helping babies'

language and concept development. As illustrated later in this chapter, one context where parental scaffolding is particularly effective in promoting language and thinking skills is book-sharing, but in fact the scaffolding process that helps these developments happens all the time, in the natural flow of all kinds of social interaction (see picture sequences 4.25–4.29)

4.25   Talking about dogs 1

The neighbour's dog, Ballina, has wandered over, and Isabel, 10 months, is delighted that she will sit still long enough to be stroked. Once Ballina moves away, Isabel's granny can talk to her and help her carry on thinking about the dog, even though

Ballina is no longer in view. Topics include how nice it was to stroke her, her comings and goings, and what she is now doing, marking out the experience Isabel has had with gestures and shared looks, as well as words.

1 Isabel is thrilled to have the chance of stroking Ballina with her granny.

2 Isabel changes hands, and Ballina stirs as her owner calls her.

4.25 **Talking about dogs 1** continued

3 Isabel looks rather crestfallen as Ballina moves away and her granny reassures her, explaining that Ballina needs to go for her dinner.

4 Granny marks Ballina's disappearance inside with a wave goodbye.

5 Isabel points happily to where Ballina has gone …

6 . …and her granny acknowledges Isabel's point, by turning to look.

7 When Isabel points again, her granny responds – yes, the dog's gone to eat her dinner.

8 They spend a few more moments talking about how Isabel stroked Ballina, and what Ballina is doing now.

4.26 **Talking about dogs 2**

The next day, Isabel and her granny settle down to share a picture book with photographs of dogs. Now that Isabel is so familiar with the basic idea of dogs, she can enjoy focusing on the details of what they are like and what they do. Isabel's granny points to, and names, the things that catch Isabel's attention and she also enacts the links to both Isabel and herself. When Isabel is diverted by finding a stick of lavender on the floor, her granny follows her lead, and then incorporates this too into the talk about dogs. This use of the picture book picks up on and reinforces many of their observations of dogs over the previous days – their soft fur, their wet tongues and noses, their habits of panting and sniffing – so Isabel is very ready to engage in this sharing of something that has become important to her.

1 Isabel leans in enthusiastically to start turning the pages of the book about dogs.

4.26   **Talking about dogs 2** continued

2 The picture she and her granny are looking at shows a dog with its long tongue hanging down – Isabel seems quite intrigued.

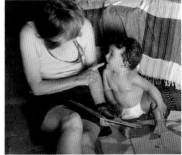

3 Her granny raises her finger to Isabel's tongue, naming it for her.

4 Then she touches her own tongue, while Isabel watches intently.

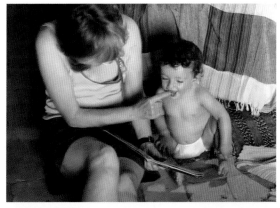

5 Now Isabel enjoys having her tongue touched and named again, while looking at the dog's tongue in the picture.

6 Next they look at another picture of a dog with its mouth open – this one seems to be panting.

7 And so while Isabel copies the dog's open mouth, granny makes a panting noise, to help Isabel understand what the picture shows.

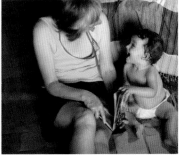

8 Then Isabel herself tries panting – she's very good at it, and she and her granny enjoy panting together.

9 Just as Isabel's granny is about to move on to the next picture, Isabel spots a stick of lavender on the floor and picks it up.

4.26   **Talking about dogs 2** continued

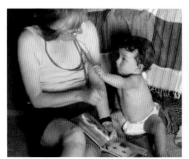

10 She holds it up, keen for granny to see it too.

11 And granny shows Isabel that lavender is something that has a lovely smell, placing it beneath her nose, and making an enthusiastic sniffing sound.

12 Isabel has a good sniff of the lavender herself, acting out the gesture earnestly.

13 Then granny suggests that the dog in the book might sniff the lavender, and holds the stick under the picture dog's nose.

14 Isabel makes her sniffing gesture again, as her granny talks to her about dogs liking to sniff things too.

4.27   **Talking about dogs 3**

Isabel's uncle has found one of his old toys – a dog with a wind-up, waggy tail. As they explore it together, there is more talk about dogs and what they do.

1 Isabel looks on intently as her uncle shows her how the toy dog's tail wags.

2 As Isabel touches it, the movement is blocked and she looks up at her uncle, as though to check out what is happening.

3 Her uncle explains and encourages Isabel to move her hand away, and as she does so the dog's tail starts wagging again.

4 Isabel puts her hand on the tail again, experimenting with how it works – she wants to share what she has done and looks up to her uncle again, and he registers her discovery with a 'Wow!'

4.28   Talking about dogs 4

Dogs can be heard barking in the fields around the house, and as the sound of them comes and goes it gives Isabel and her granny a chance to think together about the idea of dogs being somewhere near, even when they can't be seen or heard.

1 Isabel and her granny have found a shady spot, from where they can look across the fields.

2 Isabel has heard a dog barking and immediately becomes alert, pointing in the direction of the sound. She makes the beginnings of her own 'dog' word and granny agrees that, yes, they can hear a dog, there must be one nearby.

3 As the barking stops, Isabel's pointing begins to change into a gesture more like a wave – granny takes notice of this.

4 Her granny follows Isabel's line of gaze, joining her in wondering where the dog has gone.

5 Granny supports Isabel's gesture of waving goodbye to the dog, and again joins in with her own wave.

6 Now Isabel hears barking from the farm across the next field, and she points to this new place.

7 Her granny agrees that there's another dog and, following on Isabel's pointing, says she thinks they might see it rounding up the sheep.

8 The two of them point together, as the dog continues to bark.

9 But then the dog stops and disappears from view, so Isabel and her granny make their waving gestures again, and think together about what this dog might be doing.

Supporting cognitive and language development by talking to the baby in particular ways becomes even more important towards the end of the first year, when the quality of verbal interaction from the parents can be a better predictor of general infant intelligence than just behavioural responsiveness. Still, these verbal exchanges between parent and baby have a long developmental history, and vocal communication is a part of social engagement long before babies utter their first words. Babies themselves regularly make 'cooing' and other melodic sounds from around 3 months (in fact, 'cooing' sequences have even been recorded between premature babies and their parents), and by around 6–7 months, these early sounds have usually become quite systematic. By then different kinds of baby vocalizing are treated by parents as having distinct meanings: for example, those that are high pitched, with a rising intonation pattern, are typically taken as invitations to play, while vocalizations with a vibrating quality and no changes in intonation are generally perceived as 'nagging' requests. Around the same age, vocalizing also starts to take on characteristics of the parents' speech, so that cross-cultural differences can be heard in babies' babbling. Now, sounds combining consonants with vowels – 'ba' or 'ma', for instance – are added to the baby's previous repertoire of simple vowel sounds like 'ooh'. In line with this development, parents begin to treat their baby's vocalizations differently, starting to respond to the simple vowels as mere playful noises. They now only treat the baby's vocalization as meaningful 'speech' when it contains the new consonant-vowel combinations, and then will often make encouraging comments or questions, such as 'Oh, really?' or 'Is that right?', as though the baby were an active conversational partner.

When adults, and indeed children, talk to babies, regardless of their native language, they intuitively use a particular kind of speech or 'baby talk', which specialists refer to as Infant Directed Speech or IDS, as opposed to Adult Directed Speech (ADS). IDS has a number of special features – utterances are typically short, often repeated, and are delivered in a higher pitch than ADS, with exaggerated, often melodic, contours, and more rising intonation patterns. Studies show that not only is IDS preferred by babies, it actually appears to be very helpful to the baby in processing the language he hears. For example, one experiment in which babies' listening responses were recorded showed that if 6- to 8-month-olds heard speech in IDS they could recognize the words, even a day later, better than if they had heard the same speech presented in ADS (in fact, the babies showed no recognition at all for words they had heard in ADS). Similarly, hearing normal IDS helps babies at this age to distinguish separate words in the flow of speech sound, as well as to learn pairings between speech sounds and other kinds of stimulation (see more on this below). It is likely that these benefits of IDS come about because its special musical, or prosodic, features help direct the baby's attention to important cues: thus, parents typically use a rising intonation to attract the baby's attention, whereas an intonation pattern with rising and falling contrasts helps maintain their interest.

A particularly important conclusion from research into babies' language learning is, unsurprisingly, that

Figure **4.1**

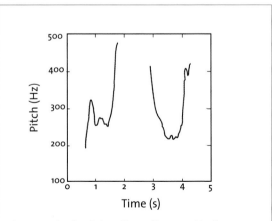

An example of an intonation pattern used by the mother of a 10-week-old baby, showing the variation in rising and falling contours that helps the baby maintain attention and learn associations between speech and other kinds of stimulation.

input from others of a socially responsive kind is vital, and that children who are very deprived socially may possibly never be able to learn normal language skills. Therefore, although the sheer volume of words that babies and young children hear their parents use does have a strong association with the child's own language development (a finding that is especially true for boys), its interactive, responsive nature is also fundamental. Some key experiments illustrating this involve babies learning foreign languages: in one study, 9-month-old US babies spent time with a Mandarin Chinese speaker who, over twelve sessions, read books to the babies and talked to them about some toys which she showed them. Afterwards, these babies could distinguish contrasting speech elements (phonemes) that occur in Mandarin but are absent from English, whereas babies who had not attended the sessions could not detect the distinctions. Even more strikingly, however, if babies were given exactly the same amount of exposure to the Mandarin Chinese language as the first group, but in this case only by letting them watch the material on TV or hear it broadcast over a loud-speaker, rather than in sessions with someone the babies could interact with, then no such learning took place.

Aside from parents being generally responsive to their babies, certain kinds of verbal responsiveness seem to be particularly helpful for the baby's language, as well as for their all-round cognitive development. What is most helpful at any one time depends on the baby's abilities and developmental stage. So, as noted earlier, towards the end of the first year when verbal rather than behavioural sensitivity becomes more important, the most effective way of talking to the baby to help his language development is when the parent follows the baby's line of interest and encourages him by describing and commenting on his actions, clearly labelling what the baby himself is focused on. By contrast, more forcefully attempting to direct the baby's attention to another focus when he is already absorbed in something is a parenting style that can be disruptive and may even have negative effects on the baby's vocabulary.

The language development of babies who are already starting to use sounds that stand for words, or even actual words themselves, can benefit from slightly different input. For example, the parent may expand on the baby's efforts to speak, imitating words that are correct or saying the word correctly if the baby's effort is incomplete or different from the word the parent uses when talking to him – so the baby might point and say 'bi', and the parent might respond, 'Oh yes, you want a biscuit.' Here, the parent does not tell the baby he is mistaken, but simply slips in the correct version of the word in a natural way that supports the baby's efforts and extends them in the right direction. This kind of support, with its low-key, corrective elaboration of the baby's efforts to speak, is helpful right through language learning in the first two years – it works, for example, for encouraging correct grammatical forms, responding to the baby's, 'We goed to the park' with, 'Yes, that's right we went to the big park this morning.'

At the stage where the baby is more ready to be interested in what someone else is attending to, parents may also find that it is easier to engage him in a new topic. This is especially so when they use both gestures and language to help capture the baby's attention, and when it is done supportively, not in an intrusive, forceful manner, the baby's own vocabulary is likely to improve. The extent to which parents' talk to their babies contains these responsive qualities explains the marked differences in vocabulary development between children from different social backgrounds.

Using other resources 1: television viewing

The fact that a carer's responsiveness seems to be so crucial to the baby's cognitive and language development has raised concerns about possible adverse effects on babies of prolonged exposure to television. Indeed, the American Academy of Pediatrics issued guidelines in 2013 urging that children under 2 years should not watch television or similar screen media at all, and they expressed particular concern that parents were being misled by unsubstantiated claims about commercial products allegedly beneficial for child intelligence and learning (notable exceptions are materials produced on the basis of sound developmental evidence, such as those by Annette Karmiloff-Smith and colleagues at The Baby Lab, Birkbeck College, London). Although babies become increasingly able to learn from TV presentations by imitating what they see, in fact such learning does not equal what can be achieved by interacting with a real person until the age of 3 years. Indeed, several reviews show that, for children under 2 years, TV (or similar) viewing is associated with poorer language and cognitive development, including attention and school performance – even when account is taken of important family background factors and parenting quality. Two general pathways seem to be involved in producing these effects. First, there seems to be a direct adverse effect of the stimulation typically presented on TV for young viewers, which in addition to its unresponsive nature is often loud, with frequent and fast-changing images. Such presentations, while designed to attract the baby's attention, may be over-stimulating, difficult to process, and disruptive of the baby's play, even when present only as background stimulation. Second, there may be indirect effects, to do with the fact that the more time the baby spends watching TV, the less time is available for more beneficial, responsive, social interaction. However, given that babies are commonly exposed to screen media from around 6–9 months, it is worth noting that two aspects of its use may help to mitigate the disadvantages. One is that repeated exposure to the same material may help the baby attend to it better, allowing more scope for processing the content. The other is that having a parent or other social partner present, who can interact with the baby while viewing, can confer some of the same benefits of scaffolding and engaging the baby that occur during other kinds of joint focused interactions, including book-sharing.

Using other resources 2: book-sharing

Psychologists and philosophers have long been intrigued by the question of how it is that children come to learn the meanings of words. For example, before a baby knows what the word 'dog' refers to, how does he realize that, when his mother points to a dog running in the park and says 'Look, doggy!' she is referring to the dog itself and not, for example, to its nose or the ball it is holding in its mouth, or the fact that its tail is wagging, or even perhaps to the park bench it runs past as she speaks. After all, the word 'doggy' is just an arbitrary grouping of vocal sounds, without any intrinsic connection to an actual dog. In fact, we now know far more about early brain processing of language and how babies are well-equipped to detect the regularities and patterns in the speech they hear and their relation to the world around them. Many studies have shown how parents, checking that their baby is attending, use clear, simple and repetitive speech, with changing intonation for emphasis, to make the task of word-learning easier. Nevertheless, learning new words for objects, events, actions and feelings, many of which might appear only fleetingly in a baby's everyday life, is still a considerable task. One activity where parental support appears to be especially helpful for the development of language skills such as word-learning, as well pre-literacy skills, is book-sharing.

Special features of baby books

Books for babies usually have some key qualities that make them highly suitable for language learning. The simplest books will show one, or perhaps just a few things on each page, without fussy background detail that could lead to uncertainty about the nature of the main topic, while simple lines and colours are used to emphasize the key features, to the neglect of less important ones. Baby books are also likely to show the same topic over several pages, each fresh illustration differing slightly from the last in terms of detail, but with the same essential features. This repetition of the core elements together with small changes can help the baby to build up the idea of the defining characteristics of the subject of the picture. This is important for the baby's cognitive development since the picture, being like the real-world object in that it shows the essential characteristics, and yet not actually being the real thing, can provide a stepping stone from the baby's immediate, direct experience of the world towards the learned, arbitrary sounds of the words we use to represent it.

Pictures are particularly useful for learning words for things that change in the real world, especially fleeting ones like actions or emotional expressions, which can happen so quickly that they may be difficult for a baby to note and process. By contrast, the baby can look at pictures showing the essentials of such events for as long as he wants, going back to them again and again. Not only can he be helped to grasp what it is that words refer to in this process, but the development of more complex ideas, like what causes things to happen, or what characters' intentions are (say, a mouse trying to run away from a cat), or why different feelings occur (a baby looking happy when being hugged), can also be supported by looking at pictures that illustrate these situations. Then, picture books can be helpful in introducing the baby to things that he does not encounter in daily life – jungle animals, for instance. Last but not least, experience with baby books can of course help to lay the foundations for eventual literacy skills. Such skills include very basic activities, like which way up a book is held, how to turn a page, or the idea that in our culture pages are turned from left to right – all behaviours that do not happen automatically, but which are developed over time.

Proven benefits of book-sharing

There is confirmation that book-sharing is an especially good way to support children's language and cognitive development, from numerous studies which have compared the way parents (usually mothers) talk to their baby or young child in different situations. This research, generally with children aged 9 months to 2 years, has consistently found that book-sharing is quite

naturally treated by parents as a language learning opportunity. Lengthy periods of shared attention take place more commonly with picture books than in other situations and during these sessions, more than in any other context, parents name things for the baby and often acknowledge, extend and elaborate on the focus of the baby's interests or on the sounds they make. Discussing people's thoughts, feelings and intentions also occurs more commonly when sharing picture books than in other kinds of conversation with young children and this kind of talk has been found, in turn, to predict how well children understand other people's experience.

Consistent with the idea that book-sharing is beneficial, other studies have shown that when children often share books with their parents they are likely to have better language and literacy skills later on, an association that still holds when family social class is taken into account. But perhaps the most convincing evidence for the value of supportive book-sharing comes from studies that have tried to increase its use or, more often, improve its quality. This intervention is felt to be important, because parents do not always share books in the most useful way (known as 'dialogic' – more on this below). In some studies the researchers themselves have provided the book-sharing support for the babies, but more often they have trained parents, either one-to-one or in small groups, sometimes using video demonstrations, in programmes typically spanning a number of weeks. The research clearly shows that, compared to other kinds of parent training, book-sharing programmes are associated with greater gains in babies' language skills, as well as their ability to attend and concentrate for longer. Importantly, where it is parents who give the book-sharing support rather than other people, the results seem to be particularly good. So the most important thing to emerge from these studies is that the quality of book-sharing is critical.

Core features of supportive book-sharing

The key quality of book-sharing that we know to be most helpful for babies' language, cognitive and literacy development is referred to by professionals as 'dialogic'. This is where the parent takes their cue from the baby, and supports and encourages the baby's active participation. How this is done changes considerably over time in line with the baby's developing capacities and interests, but one component that is important in the early years and is likely to have a major influence on how motivated the baby/young child is to engage with books, is for the baby to find the experience of book-sharing enjoyable – a time of warm, affectionate contact. By regularly book-sharing early on and by noticing what the baby wants to do and what he is interested in, parents quickly become sensitive to his way of responding. As he develops, their support can become more finely tuned to the baby's behaviour which, in turn, will help him enjoy the experience more. Indeed, it has been shown that the earlier book-sharing is established as a regular pattern (and so the earlier parents can become sensitized to the baby's

cues), the more the child will want to initiate looking at books and sharing them later on.

Changing patterns over time

In the first few months before babies can manipulate things very well they can nevertheless begin to enjoy experiences with books, especially if these are designed with babies' visual preferences in mind – for example, with clear, patterned contrasts and face-like shapes. At this stage, the parent can help simply by holding the book so that the baby can see it clearly, using their tone of voice to support the baby's interest and turning the pages to change the picture if his attention starts to flag (see picture sequence 4.29).

As babies' manipulation skills develop from around 4 to 5 months, they typically like to touch or scratch at the pictures on the page and chew on the corners of the book, as well as grabbing at the pages. Supporting the baby to explore the book in his own way, by holding it

4.29   Naomi aged 4 months

Even small babies enjoy sharing books: Naomi is attracted by the simple face-like forms, and the clear black and white patterns in the book. By giving Naomi time to register and engage with each picture, and supporting her by pointing and talking about them, her mother helps Naomi to sustain her attention and enjoyment, and to establish book-sharing as a positive experience for her.

1 Naomi stills her movements and pays close attention as her mother holds the book for her to see.

2 She becomes animated as she engages with the face-like shape, and reaches towards it as her mother supports her interest with a point.

3 Noticing Naomi's enjoyment, her mother allows her plenty of time to look at the picture, and talks to Naomi about the face-shape.

4 Later, even a pair of plain black circles can hold Naomi's attention, her mother again supporting her interest with pointing and simple comments.

4.30   Adam aged 5 months

As babies' manipulation skills develop, they like to handle and explore books in a variety of ways. Even at five months, babies will make rudimentary efforts to handle the individual pages, and this will gradually develop into skilful page-turning. Other ways of exploring the book also occur early on, but these gradually disappear: for example, babies under a year typically seem to treat a picture in a book as something solid that they might grab, and will scratch at it; they might also like chewing or sucking on the corners, and so sturdy board books that can be wiped clean are useful.

1 Adam is so absorbed that he seems to want to grab the picture from the page, and scratches at it.

2 Adam's mother gives him plenty of time to explore the book, and although he fumbles, he manages to hold one of the pages up, getting an early experience of what can be done with a book.

3 Now he manages to hold a page up, and enjoys bringing the corner to his mouth for a suck.

4 As well as manipulating the book, Adam looks closely at the picture, supported by his mother, who points and warmly comments on what he sees.

steady for him or helping to turn the pages if he seems to want to, will increase the baby's enjoyment and sense of control and his keenness to repeat book-sharing. As well as enjoying the feel of the book, babies of this age already find the pictures interesting, and by noticing the baby's line of gaze the parent can show their own interest in what he is focusing on, pointing to it and using their voice to express their enthusiasm (see picture sequence 4.30).

By around 9 months, the baby's earlier grabbing and scratching at pictures in books has generally evolved to the stage where he is beginning to point at the pictures himself – interestingly, babies point more in the context of book-sharing than at any other time. They also start to be able to follow the direction of another person's pointing, as long as the object of the point is in view, so a parent pointing at a picture and naming it is now easy for the baby to follow. When it is the baby who points at the picture he is signalling his interest and parents generally react as though the baby is inviting them to look at the same thing, again almost invariably responding by naming whatever it is that the baby is pointing to (see picture sequence 4.31). If appropriate, the parent can also support the baby's interest in the named object by animating what is depicted, moving their hand up and down to indicate the bouncing of

4.31 Flora aged 11 months

With routine book-sharing, and repeated use of particular books, babies come to develop clear preferences. Even within a book, if well-known, babies often show a preference for certain pictures; now that page-turning can be managed more smoothly, the baby may go back to a favourite picture again and again. Giving the baby a choice of book to share, following their interest, and supporting them to look at it in their own way, fosters the baby's sense of autonomy and enthusiasm for books.

1 Flora spots one of her favourite books, and points it out to her mother to show that she would like to look at it.

2 Flora's mother checks that it is the right one – it is!

3 As Flora gazes at the picture, her mother supports her interest by pointing and showing her own enthusiasm as she comments expressively on it.

4 Now, Flora loves turning pages, and needs only a little help from her mother to manage it.

5 Flora finds one of the pictures particularly attractive, and she turns the page back to have another look, now pointing at it herself.

a ball perhaps, or making their fingers hop across the page like the movements of a pictured bug. As noted earlier, baby-book illustrations are already well-suited to helping babies develop more abstract representations of things in the real world, so these book-sharing moments, when the topic of interest is clearly identified and also named, help make the task of word learning even easier. Not surprisingly, then, one study found that of a baby's first 20 words, some two-thirds were first encountered in the context of parents' doing such pointing and naming (see picture sequence 4.32).

As babies' language begins to develop and they begin to know what some words mean, parents can support their baby's experience of books in slightly different ways that allow him to be actively involved and practise his new skills. So, for words that the baby understands, instead of pointing and giving the name themselves as they look at the picture together, parents can prompt

4.32   Iris aged 12 months

Iris and her mother regularly share books together, and have built up a stock of firm favourites that can never be shared too often! Iris loves this colourful book, including creatures, and clear pictures of a baby character performing a variety of lively antics, and she is intrigued by turning over the flaps to reveal each one. Iris and her mother have a well-rehearsed set of special noises and gestures that they use to reflect the picture baby's actions; Iris's mother follows her daughter's interest and attention throughout, and provides a simple and animated commentary on what Iris sees. They sit comfortably together, so that it is a close, affectionate, time, as well as one that helps Iris's attention, concentration and other cognitive skills develop.

1 As Iris opens the flap, her mother helps …

2 …and then exclaims to Iris to mark out the discovery of the ladybird picture revealed behind it.

3 As Iris opens the next flap, her mother begins the action game they have come to share at this point in the book, mimicking the picture baby's stretch …

4 … and as Iris too starts the action, her mother reinforces the link to the picture with a point.

5 Iris is fully involved, raising both arms to match the baby in the picture …

6 … and her mother affectionately reaches up again herself, sharing the game with Iris.

the baby to point to a particular object or character, asking questions that begin, 'Where is the . . . ?, or 'Can you find the . . .?' Later on, as the baby begins to be able to say some words himself, the parent can help him practise this new skill too, shifting to questions like, 'What is . . . ?' and pointing to the relevant part of the picture for the baby to name. Babies will particularly enjoy responding when these questions fall just within the limits of their ability and parents can reinforce their success with praise and by repeating the word after the baby has said it. Of course, babies do not always give the right answer when learning these new skills, but rather than telling the baby he is wrong parents can support his learning more positively by simply saying the correct word themselves, and then reinforce that by finding other opportunities to name it for the baby.

Towards the end of the first year, babies' experiences of book-sharing can begin to be enriched and their involvement stimulated by linking the content of the book to their own experience. In its simplest form, this develops naturally from the earlier animation games, as the parent encourages the baby to join in by imitating

the picture character's actions themselves. The baby can also be helped in the process of word-learning by linking what is shown on the page either to himself, or to the person with him. He might be encouraged in a game, for example, in which parent and baby take turns to point to a pictured animal's nose and then find their own and the other person's nose, the parents repeating the word at each point (see picture sequence 4.33). Similarly, the parent can help the baby understand more about what the picture represents and the accompanying words by miming the action, first in relation to the picture itself and then in relation to the baby and, finally, encouraging the baby to do the same (picture sequence 4.34).

As the baby's understanding of words develops and he grows more able to think about things that are not actually present, the parent can enrich the baby's involvement further by linking what is on the page to his wider experience – perhaps the pictured dog is rather like the dog next door, or the picture can be linked to a recent trip to the park when the baby fed the ducks. These linking conversations can include

4.33   Benjamin aged 10 months

Familiarity with a book enables the baby to play a much more active role in using its content to practise their developing cognitive and language skills. Here, Benjamin rehearses his knowledge of

different facial features, using a favourite book with pictures of cats and dogs, and supported by his parents.

1 As the family have their breakfast, Benjamin is looking through one of his favourite books – one with pictures of cats and dogs.

2 Being so familiar with the book, Benjamin's interest has moved beyond simply noting 'cat' and 'dog' to enjoyment of the details of their faces: here, his mother notes this interest, and points to the dog's nose.

4.33   **Benjamin aged 10 months** continued

3 Benjamin shows he now knows what noses are, and reaches up to his mother's nose...

4 ...and she turns this into a game of touching each other's noses.

5 Now Benjamin and his mother point together at the dog's mouth...

6 ...and Benjamin shows her he knows what that is too.

7 Now Benjamin looks across to his father, pointing to the picture, and inviting him to join in.

8 Benjamin's father leans in to see what Ben is looking at, and notes the dog's nose.

9 Now Benjamin reaches up to his father's nose...

10 ...and all three share their enjoyment in looking at the book together, and Benjamin's latest achievement.

quite complex ideas about causes and consequences of actions, as well as feelings, and often mean that the parent is talking to the baby in slightly more advanced language than usual. Accordingly, from the time the young child starts to string words together, their most advanced use of language will often involve phrases they have heard during book-sharing (picture sequence 4.35, learning about the crying baby).

4.34 **Mikhulu aged 14 months**

One important way for parents to support their baby's involvement and enjoyment of books is by linking the content of the picture to the baby's own experience. With babies of around a year old, this can take the form of making a link either to the baby directly, or to something present in the same room; with older babies and small children, links can be made more widely, perhaps to recent experiences they have shared. Helen Oxenbury's books for babies are ideal for this purpose, as they contain attractive, simple, pictures of babies in a range of everyday situations.

Here, Mikhulu is immediately captivated as his mother starts to turn the pages for him, and then engages enthusiastically with the book as his mother carefully watches his response and makes clear links for him.

1 Mikhulu's mother notices that his interest is caught by the picture baby's brightly coloured T-shirt, and she follows his line of gaze, pointing and warmly commenting.

2 His mother then makes the link to Mikhulu himself, by touching his T-shirt, and telling him that the picture baby's T-shirt is like his own.

3 Mikhulu's mother waits until he is ready, and then she turns the page for him.

4 Now the scene is hair brushing, and Mikhulu's mother highlights the place where he is looking, where the mother is brushing the baby's hair . . .

5 . . . and again mimes the action with Mikhulu himself in an affectionate and lively way.

6 Mikhulu now takes his turn, and reaches over to touch the picture babies' heads, his mother warmly supporting his involvement.

7 And now they repeat the miming together . . .

4.34   **Mikhulu aged 14 months** continued

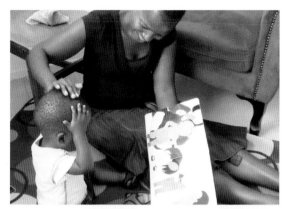

8 …with Mikhulu really making the connection between what is on the page and his own experience.

9 Mikhulu watches quietly as his mother turns to the next page.

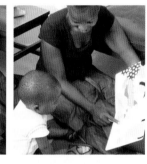

10 Here, it's a picture of a baby sleeping, and Mikhulu's mother points and tells him what is happening…

11 …and then she signals it clearly in a mime to him…

12 …and points again to the picture baby's sleeping face…

13 … checking that Mikhulu is following as she helps him understand the picture…

14 Now Mikhulu gently strokes the sleeping baby's head, and his mother encourages his caring response by clapping.

15 Mikhulu responds with a clap himself…

16 …and together they share their pleasure at what Mikhulu has done.

4.35 Iris aged 14 months

Some events and experiences, like feeling different emotions, can be quite hard to talk about with a baby in ordinary circumstances, particularly if they are fleeting or complex. But picture books can be a useful vehicle for helping a baby or young child think about them, as the parent can monitor the baby's responses carefully, and can take time to explore the picture content. In addition, as babies become more alert to their mothers' emotional reactions to other people and events towards the end of the first year, parents can capitalize on this interest as they share books, and help their baby manage his responses.

1 Iris's mother offers her a choice of books to share.

2 Iris shows a clear wish to see the book of babies showing different expressions.

3 Iris attends closely as each baby is revealed.

4 Iris's mother watches her daughter's face closely as the next picture is shown …

5 … a crying baby.

6 Iris sits down and looks thoughtfully at the picture baby; her mother notes her interest and sober expression, and then takes time to share talking about the baby with her.

7 Iris now watches her mother's face as her mother reflects the picture baby's expression, blended with a look of caring concern …

8 … and invites Iris to think about why the baby might be crying – perhaps he is hungry or has a sore finger – and about what might be done to help him. Iris pays rapt attention throughout.

Studies of repeated sessions with the same book show that the baby's growing familiarity with the material, where much shared understanding of what is depicted can increasingly be taken for granted, is also typically associated with the parent being able to use slightly more complex language with the baby, as they talk about new aspects of the picture. Babies naturally go along with this process, as they develop clear preferences for particular books and even particular pictures within them, which they can want to look at over and over again. Here, a parent's pointing is often used to show how the different parts of the picture link together, and the baby takes his turn to point too, so their shared actions feed into their discussion (picture sequence 4.36). Such familiarity with particular books and pictures is associated with the baby's active

4.36 Ben aged 17 months

Ben's role in sharing this familiar jungle book with his father has become much more active: his page-turning is very assured, and his pointing well-established and more complex. Now, Ben moves his finger deliberately across the page, singling out the details of one creature after another and, as he does so, he accompanies his points with vocalizations, often making the animal's noise. His father's support is closely adjusted to the growing complexity of Ben's responses to the pictures, with well timed prompts, and with pointing that overlaps and takes turns with Ben's, so that their engagement is synchronized. Ben loves to repeat the same sequences again and again, each time practising his newly developing verbal skills.

1 Ben knows what sound to use for the monkey in this picture, and his father encourages him to make it by pointing and asking him what the monkey says ...

2 ... Ben enjoys making the monkey noise ...

3 ... and then he takes the lead, pointing to another monkey and repeating the sound.

4 Ben's father joins in the pointing ...

5 ... and comments on the detail of what the monkey is doing, Ben paying close attention.

6 Ben points back to the first monkey, making the monkey noise once more.

4.36 **Ben aged 17 months** continued

7 …and again his father joins in, following Ben's point with his own.

8 Now Ben turns the page …

9 …and the same process starts once more with the next monkey picture, as Ben points and makes the noise again.

participation, as they practise the routines that have been built up over previous sessions and make use of the words they are starting to know (see picture sequence 4.37). As the baby gains more experience of sharing books with his parents, and where these experiences are positive, he may well want to extend the book-sharing experience to other relationships and even enjoy using the routines and conventions of them more on his own, thus further strengthening a solid foundation for his later developing literacy skills (see picture sequence 4.38).

The wider value of book-sharing

Although this section has concentrated on the benefits to babies and young children of book-sharing in terms of their cognitive, language and preliteracy skills, book-sharing can also be a special time for being close and affectionate, and one where the baby's emotions and imagination can be engaged. Particularly when a baby's ability to think about things that are not present develops, sharing a book can provide opportunities to experiment with ideas and feelings that might not always feel easy or safe to explore in real life. This is

4.37 **Ben aged 24 months**

Books can be fun for babies and young children to share with others, not just for the pleasure of looking at the pictures and talking about them, but for the opportunities they offer for action games and singing rhymes. The strong impulse to identify with the picture figures and imitate them, and the real enjoyment involved in such games, is shown in this sequence of Ben and his mother, as they share a book full of pictures of babies with different expressions and gestures. Ben is very precise in his imitations, reflecting his ability to detect the detailed actions in the images and, with his mother's support, is keen to try every one of them.

1 Ben's mother starts a well-rehearsed game that Ben enjoys a lot, pointing to the first of a series of pictures of babies acting out different expressions and gestures, encouraging him to do what the baby does …

4.37   **Ben aged 24 months** continued

2 ...sitting and smiling...

3 ...Ben copies, adjusting his position, and grinning at the sitting, smiling, baby picture, his mother praising him.

4 Next his mother suggests that Ben copy this little boy...

5 ...and Ben immediately imitates the gesture...

6 ... now Ben's mother shows him a waving child...

7 ...and Ben waves too.

8 And then a clapping baby...

9 ...and Ben immediately claps.

10 Finally, they look at a pointing baby, and Ben pays close attention...

11 ...before raising both his arms to point himself, as his mother praises him again, noting that Ben is just like the picture baby.

4.38 Ben aged 23 months

Even young children can be good at supporting book-sharing. Here, we see Ben with his older brother, Joe, aged 6. Joe shows the key features of good support, like his parents, following Ben's interests as they are reflected in his gaze and pointing, and taking time to let Ben explore the pictures in his own way; he also provides close, affectionate, care, so that Ben is able to feel entirely comfortable.

1 Ben asks Joe if he will read him the Big Digger book.

2 The boys settle down together with it on the sofa ...

3 ... and Joe highlights the action in the picture.

4 The two boys share looking at the same thing, both pointing together ...

5 ... and then Joe draws attention to a different detail, talking to Ben about what is happening.

6 Ben looks up at his brother admiringly ...

7 ... and then points to what the digger is doing on the next page.

8 Ben snuggles in closely to his brother, as they carry on with the story.

4.39   Ben aged 17 months

Babies who repeatedly share books become very familiar with the routines, and they are then able to manage the practicalities of handling books on their own; and close and positive book-sharing experiences are likely to encourage the baby to want to look at books, even when no one else is available. In this uncaptioned sequence, we see Ben thoroughly absorbed in looking at one of his best-loved books, taking on all the habits of page-turning, pointing and naming things that he has been used to when book-sharing with his family.

1   2

3   4   5   6

often the appeal of fairy stories for older children, but even simple books for under-twos can provide rich material for playing with ideas of, say, being frightened, lonely or 'naughty', as well as enjoying wonderment, suspense, delight and amusement. Sharing a book is not just an activity for learning and practising more serious skills, it is a unique opportunity for imaginative sharing of feelings and minds.

Summary of Chapter 4

From birth, babies actively push their cognitive development forward, experimenting to find out what they can do, and how the world works. But babies do not develop their full cognitive potential in isolation, and for their natural abilities to flourish social relationships are of key importance. Relationships where the partner is responsive to the baby's efforts, and in particular to his interests and direction of attention, can enrich the baby's experience and build on his capacities. Different kinds of support are important at different ages, from the close, fine-tuned contingency of early interactions, through facilitating and scaffolding the baby's efforts to manipulate and explore his world, to talking to the baby and sharing picture books with him in ways that are responsive to his interests and his own emerging language skills. At each stage, social interactions can help the baby to see connections between events and to organize his mental experience – thus he can become increasingly competent and gain ever more control over his world.

Notes

References for the text are given by page and paragraph, so 1/1 is page 1, paragraph 1, and so on. Each reference is given in full on first mention in each paragraph; if repeated on the same page, name and short title only are given.

Introduction

Page/Paragraph

5/1   Henrich, J., Heine, S.J. and Norenzayan, A. The weirdest people in the world? *Behavioural and Brain Sciences*, 2012; 33: 61–135.

1 Social understanding and cooperation

7/3   Winnicott, D.W. *Primary Maternal Preoccupation. Through Paediatrics to Psychoanalysis*. London: Hogarth; 1956.
Papousek, H. and Papousek, M. Intuitive parenting. In: M.H. Bornstein, ed. *Handbook of Parenting: Vol 2. Biology and Ecology of Parenting.* Hillsdale, NJ: Erlbaum, 1995, pp. 117–36.

7/4   Kringelbach, M. L., Lehtonen, A., Squire, S., Harvey, A. G., Craske, M.G., Holliday, I.E. et al. A specific and rapid neural signature for parental instinct. PLoS ONE, 2008; 3: e1664.
Caria, A., Falco, S. de, Venuti, P., Lee, S., Esposito, G., Rigo, P. et al. Species-specific response to human infant faces in the premotor cortex. *Neuroimage*, 2012; 60: 884–93.

7/5   Swain, J. E. Baby stimuli and the parent brain: Functional neuroimaging of the neural substrates of parent-infant attachment. *Psychiatry*, 2008; 5: 28–36.

8/1   Bartels, A. and Zeki, S. The neural correlates of maternal and romantic love. *Neuroimage,* 2004; 21: 1155–66.

8/2   Strathearn, L., Fonagy, P., Amico, J. and Montague, P. R. Adult attachment predicts maternal brain and oxytocin response to infant cues. *Neuropsychopharmacology,* 2009; 34: 2655–66.
Feldman, R., Gordon, I. and Zagoory-Sharon, O. Maternal and paternal plasma, salivary, and urinary oxytocin and parent-infant synchrony: considering stress and affiliation components of human bonding. *Developmental Science,* 2011; 4: 752–61.

8/3   Goren, C. C., Sarty, M. and Wu, P.Y. K. Visual following and pattern discrimination of face-like stimuli by newborn infants. *Pediatrics,* 1975; 56: 544–9.
Johnson, M. H., Dziurawiec, S., Ellis, H. and Morton, J. Newborns' preferential tracking of face-like stimuli and its subsequent decline. *Cognition,* 1991; 40: 1–19. 11.
Batki, A., Baron-Cohen, S. and Wheelwright, S. Is there an innate gaze module ? Evidence from human neonates. *Infant Behavior and Development,* 2000; 23: 223–9.
Farroni, T., Csibra, G., Simion, F. and Johnson, M. H. Eye contact detection in humans from birth. *Proceedings of the National Academy of Sciences,* 2002; 99: 9602–5.

8/4   Senju, A. and Csibra, G. Gaze following in human infants depends on communicative signals. *Current Biology,* 2008; 18: 668–71.
Mandel, D. R., Jusczyk, P.W. and Pisoni, D.B. Infants' recognition of the sound patterns of their own names. *Psychological Science,* 1995; 6: 314–7.

8/5   Field, T. M., Cohen, D., Garcia, R. and Greenberg, R. Mother–stranger face discrimination by the newborn. *Infant Behavior and Development,* 1984; 7: 19–25.
Mehler, J., Bertoncini, J., Barrière, M. and Jassik-Gerschenfeld, D. Infant recognition of mother's voice. *Perception,* 1978; 7: 491–7.
DeCasper. A. J. and Fifer, W. P. Newborn preference for the maternal voice: An indication of early attachment. *Southeastern Conference on Human Development*. Alexandria, 1980.

Macfarlane A. Olfaction in the development of social preferences in the human neonate. *Parent-Infant Interactions (Ciba Found. Symp. 33),* Elsevier: New York, 1975; pp. 103–13.

Cernoch J. M. and Porter R. H. Recognition of maternal axillary odors by infants. *Child Development,* 1985; 56: 1593–8.

8/6   Meltzoff A.N., and Moore M.K. Imitation of facial and manual gestures by human neonates. *Science, New Series.* 1977; 189: 75–8.

Simpson, E., Murray, L., Paukner, A. and Ferrari, P. The mirror neuron system as revealed through neonatal imitation: Presence from birth, predictive power, and evidence of plasticity. *Philosophical Transactions of the Royal Society* (in press).

8/7   Ferrari, P.F., Vanderwert, R.E., Paukner, A., Bower. S., Suomi, S.J. and Fox, N.A. Distinct EEG amplitude suppression to facial gestures as evidence for a mirror mechanism in newborn monkeys. *Journal of Cognitive Neuroscience,* 2012; 24: 1–8.

9   Fig. 1a From Meltzoff and Moore, *Science*, 1977; 189: 75. Reprinted with permission from AAAS. Fig. 1b From Ferrari et al., *PloS biology*, 2006; 4: e302. Reprinted with permission from the author.

9/1   Moore, A., Gorodnitsky, I. and Pineda, J. EEG mu component responses to viewing emotional faces. *Behavioural Brain Research,* 2012; 226: 309–16.

9/2   Stern, D.N. *The Interpersonal World of the Infant: A View from Psychoanalysis and Development.* New York: Basic Books; 1985.

[twice] Feldman, R. Parent–infant synchrony and the construction of shared timing; physiological precursors, developmental outcomes, and risk conditions. *Journal of Child Psychology and Psychiatry,* 2007; 4: 329–54.

Condon, W.S. and Sander, L.W. Synchrony demonstrated between movements of the neonate and adult speech. *Child Development,* 1974; 45: 456–62.

Lavelli, M. and Fogel, A. Developmental changes in the relationship between the infant's

attention and emotion during early face-to-face communication: The 2-month transition. *Developmental Psychology,* 2005; 41: 265–80.

Murray, L., Stanley, C., Hooper, R., King, F. and Fiori-Cowley, A., Hooper, R. and Cooper, P.J. The impact of postnatal depression and associated diversity on early mother–infant interactions and later infant outcome. *Child Development,* 1996; 67: 2512–26.

Lavelli, M. and Fogel, A. Developmental changes in mother-infant face-to-face communication: birth to 3 months. *Developmental Psychology,* 2002; 38: 288–305.

Haith, M.M., Bergman, T. and Moore, M.J. Eye contact and face scanning in early infancy. *Science (80–),* 1977; 198: 853–4.

Papousek, H. and Papousek, M. Intuitive parenting. In: M.H. Bornstein, ed. *Handbook of Parenting: Vol 2. Biology and Ecology of Parenting.* Hillsdale, NJ: Erlbaum, 1995; pp. 117–36.

Lavelli and Fogel. Developmental changes . . . birth to 3 months.

Papousek and Papousek. Intuitive parenting . . .

10/1   Lavelli, M. and Fogel, A. Developmental changes in mother-infant face-to-face communication: birth to 3 months. *Developmental Psychology,* 2002; 38: 288–305.

Wolff, P.H. *The development of behavioral states and the expression of emotions in early infancy: New proposals for investigation.* Chicago: University of Chicago Press; 1987.

Legerstee, M., Pomerleau, A., Malcuit, G. and Feider, H. The development of infants' responses to people and a doll: implications for research in communication. *Infant Behavior and Development,* 1987; 10: 81–95.

11   Fig. 1.2 From Murray et al. Mirroring in early mother-infant interactions. Paper given at the British Psychological Society Annual Conference 2013, at the University of Reading.

11/2   Stern, D.N. *The Interpersonal World of the Infant: A View from Psychoanalysis and Development.* New York: Basic Books; 1985.

Trevarthen, C. Communication and cooperation in early infancy: A description of primary intersubjectivity. In: M. Bullowa,

11/2
(cont.)

ed. *Before speech: The beginning of interpersonal communication.* New York: Cambridge University Press; 1979, pp. 321–47.

Blass, E.M. The ontogeny of human infant face recognition: Orogustatory, visual, and social influences. In: P. Rochat, ed. *Early Social Cognition: Understanding Others in the First Months of Life.* Mahwah, NJ, US: Lawrence Erlbaum Associates Publishers; 1999, pp. 35–65.

Haith, M.M., Bergman, T. and Moore, M.J. Eye contact and face scanning in early infancy. *Science* (80–). 1977; 198: 853–4.

Wolff, P.H. *The development of behavioral states and the expression of emotions in early infancy: New proposals for investigation.* Chicago: University of Chicago Press; 1987.

Moran, G., Krupka, A., Tutton, A.N.N. and Symons, D. Patterns of Maternal and Infant Imitation During Play. *Infant Behavior and Development,* 1987; 10: 477–91.

Lavelli, M and Fogel, A. Developmental changes in the relationship between the infant's attention and emotion during early face-to-face communication: The 2-month transition. *Developmental Psychology,* 2005; 41: 265–80.

Trevarthen, Communication and cooperation in early infancy . . .

11/3

Legerstee, M., Pomerleau, A., Malcuit, G. and Feider, H. The development of infants' responses to people and a doll: implications for research in communication. *Infant Behavior and Development,* 1987; 10: 81–95.

Rochat, P., Querido, J.G. and Striano, T. Emerging sensitivity to the timing and structure of protoconversation in early infancy. *Developmental Psychology,* 1999; 35: 950–7.

11/5

Stern, D.N. *The Interpersonal World of the Infant: A View from Psychoanalysis and Development.* New York: Basic Books; 1985.

Moran, G., Krupka, A., Tutton, A.N.N. and Symons, D. Patterns of maternal and infant imitation during play. *Infant Behavior and Development,* 1987; 10: 477–91.

Pawlby, S.J. Imitative interaction. In: H.R. Schaffer, ed. *Studies in mother-infant interaction.* New York: Academic Press; 1977.

13/1

Henning, A., Striano, T and Lieven, E.V.M. Maternal speech to infants at 1 and 3 months of age. *Infant Behavior & Development,* 2005; 28: 519–36.

Gros-Louis. J., Goldstein, M.H., King, A.P. and West, M.J. Mothers provide differential feedback to infants' prelinguistic sounds. *International Journal of Behavioral Development,* 2006; 30: 509–16.

15/1

Winnicott, D.W. *Primary Maternal Preoccupation. Through Paediatrics to Psychoanalysis.* London: Hogarth; 1956.

Stern, D.N. *The Interpersonal World of the Infant: A View from Psychoanalysis and Development.* New York: Basic Books; 1985.

15/2

Keller, H., Kärtner, J., Borke, J., Yovsi, R. and Kleis, A. Parenting styles and the development of the categorical self: A longitudinal study on mirror self-recognition in Cameroonian Nso and German families. *International Journal of Behavioral Development,* 2005; 29: 496–504.

Tronick, E. and Beeghly, M. Infants' meaning-making and the development of mental health problems. *American Psychologist,* 2011; 66(2): 107–19.

16

Figs 1.3a and b Based on Table 1 in Kärtner, J., Keller, H. and Yovsi, R.D. Mother-infant interaction during the first 3 months: The emergence of culture-specific contingency patterns. *Child Development,* 2010; 81: 540–54. With permission from John Wiley & Sons Ltd.

16/1

Keller, et al. Parenting styles and the development of the categorical self…

Kärtner, J., Keller, H. and Yovsi, R.D. Mother-infant interaction during the first 3 months : the emergence of culture-specific contingency patterns. *Child Development,* 2010; 81: 540–54.

Fogel, A., Toda, S. and Kawai, M. Mother-infant face-to-face interaction in Japan and the United States : a laboratory comparison using 3-month-old infants. *Developmental Psychology,* 1988; 24: 398–406.

Wörmann, V., Holodynski, M., Kärtner, J. and Keller, H. Infant behavior and development: a cross-cultural comparison of the development of the social smile. A longitudinal study of maternal and infant imitation in 6- and 12-week-old infants. *Infant Behavior and Development,* 2012; 35: 335–47.

17/1   Stern, D.N. *The Interpersonal World of the Infant: A View from Psychoanalysis and Development.* New York: Basic Books; 1985.
Lavelli, M. and Fogel, A. Developmental changes in the relationship between the infant's attention and emotion during early face-to-face communication: The 2-month transition. *Developmental Psychology,* 2005; 41: 265–80.
Tronick, E. and Beeghly, M. Infants' meaning-making and the development of mental health problems. *American Psychologist,* 2011; 66(2): 107–19.

17/2   Bertin, E. and Striano, T. The still-face response in newborn, 1.5-, and 3-month-old infants. *Infant Behavior and Development,* 2006; 29: 294–7.
Tronick, E., Als, H., Adamson, L., Wise, S. and Brazelton, T.B. The infant's response to entrapment between contradictory messages in face-to-face interaction. *Journal of the American Academy of Child Psychiatry,* 1978; 17: 1–3.
Rochat, P., Querido, J.G. and Striano, T. Emerging sensitivity to the timing and structure of protoconversation in early infancy. *Developmental Psychology,* 1999; 35: 950–7.
Montague, D. P. F. Peekaboo: A new look at infants' perception of emotion expressions. *Developmental Psychology,* 2001; 37: 826–38.
Murray, L. and Trevarthen, C. Emotional regulation of interactions between two month olds and their mothers. In: T.M. Field and N. Fox, eds. *Social Perception in Infants.* New Jersey: Ablex; 1985.
Striano, T. and Stahl, D. Sensitivity to triadic attention in early infancy. *Developmental Science,* 2005; 8: 333–43.

17/3   Nadel, J., Soussignan, R., Canet, P., Libert, G. and Priscille, G. Two-month-old infants of depressed mothers show mild, delayed and persistent change in emotional state after non-contingent interaction. *Infant Behavior and Development,* 2005; 28: 418–25.

Field, T., Nadel, J., Hernandez-reif, M., Diego, M., Vera, Y., Gil, K. et al. Depressed mothers' infants show less negative affect during non-contingent interactions. *Infant Behavior and Development,* 2005; 28: 426–30.
Legerstee, M. and Varghese, J. The role of maternal affect mirroring on social expectancies in three-month-old infants. *Child Development,* 2001; 72: 1301–13.
Bigelow, A.E. and Rochat, P. Two-month-old infants' sensitivity to social contingency in mother-infant and stranger-infant interaction. *Infancy,* 2006; 9: 313–25.

18/1   Field, T., Healy, B., Goldstein, S., Perry, S., Bendell, D., Zimmerman, E.A. et al. Infants of depressed mothers show "depressed" behavior even with nondepressed adults. *Journal of Psychology and Psychiatry,* 1988; 59: 1569–79.
Morrell, J. and Murray, L. Parenting and the development of conduct disorder and hyperactive symptoms in childhood: a prospective longitudinal study from 2 months to 8 years. *Journal of Psychology and Psychiatry,* 2003; 44: 489–508.
Field, et al. Infants of depressed mothers...

20/1   Von Hofsten, C. Developmental changes in the organization of prereaching movements. *Developmental Psychology,* 1984; 20: 378–88.
Feldman, R. Parent–infant synchrony and the construction of shared timing; physiological precursors, developmental outcomes, and risk conditions. *Journal of Child Psychology and Psychiatry,* 2007; 4: 329–54.
Lavelli, M. and Fogel, A. Developmental changes in mother-infant face-to-face communication: birth to 3 months. *Developmental Psychology,* 2002; 38: 288–305.
Legerstee, M., Pomerleau, A., Malcuit, G. and Feider, H. The development of infants' responses to people and a doll: implications for research in communication. *Infant Behavior and Development,* 1987; 10: 81–95.
Striano, T. and Reid, VM. Social cognition in the first year. *Trends in Cognitive Science,* 2006; 10: 471–6.

20/3   Trevarthen, C. and Hubley, P. Secondary

20/3
(cont.)

intersubjectivity: confidence, confiders, and acts of meaning in the first year of life. In: A. Lock, ed. *Action, Gesture, and Symbol.* New York: Academic Press; 1978.

21/1

Hubley, P. A. and Trevarthen, C. B. Sharing a task in infancy. *New Directions for Child and Adolescent Development,* 1979; 1979(4): 57–80.

24/1

Liszkowski, U., Carpenter, M., Henning, A., Striano, T. and Tomasello, M. Twelve-month-olds point to share attention and interest. *Developmental Science,* 2004; 3: 297–307.

25/1

Winnicott, D.W. *The Development of the Capacity for Concern. The Maturational Processes and the Facilitating Environment.* Madison, CT: International Universities Press; 1965, pp. 73–82.

25/2

Baillargeon, R., Scott, R.M. and He, Z. False-belief understanding in infants. *Trends in Cognitive Neurosciences,* 2010; 14: 110–18.
Farroni, T., Csibra, G., Simion, F. and Johnson, M. H. Eye contact detection in humans from birth. *Proceedings of the National Academy of Sciences,* 2002; 99: 9602–5.
Scaife, M. and Bruner, J.S. The capacity for joint visual attention in the infant. *Nature,* 1975; 253: 265–6.
Moore, C. The development of gaze following. *Society for Research in Child Development,* 2008; 2: 66–70.
Carpenter, M., Nagell, K., Tomasello, M., Butterworth, G. and Moore, C. Social Cognition, Joint Attention, and Communicative Competence from 9 to 15 Months of Age. *Monographs of the Society for Research in Child Development,* 1998; 63: 1–174.

25/3

Henderson, A.M.E., Gerson, S. and Woodward, A.L. The birth of social intelligence. *Zero to Three,* 2008; 13–20.
Woodward, A.L. Learning about intentional action. In: A. Woodward and A. Needham, eds. *Learning and the Infant Mind.* Oxford, UK: Oxford University Press; 2009, pp. 227–48.
Cannon, E.N. and Woodward, A.L. Infants generate goal-based action predictions.

Developmental Science, 2012; 15: 292–8.
Paulus, M. How infants relate looker and object: evidence for a perceptual learning account of gaze following in infancy. *Developmental Science,* 2011; 14: 1301–10.

26/1

Behne, T., Carpenter, M. and Tomasello, M. One-year-olds comprehend the communicative intentions behind gestures in a hiding game. *Developmental Science,* 2005; 8: 492–9.
Brunea, C.W. and Woodward, A.L. Social cognition and social responsiveness in 10-month-old infants. *Journal of Cognition and Development,* 2007; 8: 133–58.

27/1

Henderson, A.M.E., Gerson, S. and Woodward, A.L. The birth of social intelligence. *Zero to Three,* 2008; 13–20.
Brunea, C.W. and Woodward, A.L. Social cognition and social responsiveness in 10-month-old infants. *Journal of Cognition and Development,* 2007; 8: 133–58.

27/2

Reddy, V. *How Infants Know Minds.* Cambridge, Mass.: Harvard University Press; 2010.

27/3

Gergely, G. The social construction of the subjective self: The role of affect-mirroring, markedness, and ostensive communication in self development. In: L. Mayes, P. Fonagy, and M. Target (eds), *Developmental Science and Psychoanalysis.* London: Karnac; 2007.

27/4

Senju, A. and Csibra, G. Gaze following in human infants depends on communicative signals. *Current Biology,* 2008; 18: 668–71.
Rohlfing, K.J., Longo, M.R. and Bertenthal, B.I. Dynamic pointing triggers shifts of visual attention in young infants. *Developmental Science,* 2012; 15: 426–35.
Grossmann, T., Johnson, M.H., Lloyd-Fox, S., Blasi, A., Deligianni, F., Elwell, C. et al. Early cortical specialization for face-to-face communication in human infants. *Proceedings of the Royal Society,* 2008; 275: 2803–11.
Reid, V.M., Striano, T., Kaufman, J. and Johnson, M.H. Eye gaze cueing facilitates neural processing of objects in 4-month-old infants. *Cognitive Neuroscience and Neuropsychology,* 2004;

15: 2553–5.

Senju, A., Johnson, M.H. and Csibra, G. The development and neural basis of referential gaze perception. *Social Neuroscience,* 2006; 1: 220–34.

Paulus, M. How infants relate looker and object: evidence for a perceptual learning account of gaze following in infancy. *Developmental Science,* 2011; 14: 1301–10.

Turati, C., Montirosso, R., Brenna, V., Ferrara, V. and Borgatti, R. A smile enhances 3-month-olds' recognition of an individual face. *Infancy,* 2011; 16: 306–17.

28/1   Gaffan, E.A., Martins, C., Healy, S. and Murray, L. Early social experience and individual differences in infants' joint attention. *Social Development,* 2010; 19: 369–93.

31/2   Dunn, J. Young children's understanding of other people: Evidence from observations within the family. In: D. Frye and C. Moore, eds. *Children's Theories of Mind.* Hillsdale, NJ: Erlbaum; 1991, pp. 97–114.

Fivaz-Depeursinge, E., Favez, N., Lavanchy, C., De Noni, S. and Frascarolo, F. Four-month-olds make triangular bids to father and mother during trilogue play with still-face. *Social Development,* 2005; 14: 361–78.

McHale, J., Fivaz-Depeursinge, E., Dickstein, S., Robertson, J. and Daley, M. New evidence for the social embeddedness of infants' early triangular capacities. *Family Process,* 2008; 47: 445–63.

32/1   Reddy, V. Coyness in early infancy. *Developmental Science,* 2000; 3:1, 86–92.

33/2   Reddy, V. *How Infants Know Minds.* Cambridge, Mass.: Harvard University Press; 2010.

34/2   Wellman, H.M., Cross, D. and Watson, J. Meta-analysis of theory-of-mind development: the truth about false belief. *Child Development,* 2001; 72: 655–84.

35/1   Thoermer, C., Sodian, B., Vuori, M., Perst, H. and Kristen, S. Continuity from an implicit to an explicit understanding of false belief from infancy to preschool age. *British Journal of Developmental Psychology,* 2012; 30: 172–87.

35/2   Reddy, V. *How Infants Know Minds.* Cambridge, Mass.: Harvard University Press; 2010.

39/1   Reddy, V. Getting back to the rough ground: deception and "social living". *Philosophical Transactions of the Royal Society,* 2007; 362: 621–37.

Repacholi, B.M. and Meltzoff, A.N. Emotional eavesdropping: Infants selectively respond to indirect emotional signals. *Child Development,* 2007; 78: 503–21.

Repacholi, B.M., Meltzoff, A.N. and Olsen, B. Infants' understanding of the link between visual perception and emotion: "If she can't see me doing it, she won't get angry." *Developmental Psychology,* 2008; 44: 561–74.

44/1   Amsterdam, B. Mirror Self-Image reactions before Age Two. *Developmental Psychobiology,* 1972; 5: 297–305.

46/1   Lewis, M. and Ramsay, D. Development of self-recognition, personal pronoun use, and pretend play during the 2nd year. *Child Development,* 2004; 75: 1821–31.

48/1   Meltzoff, A.N. Understanding the intentions of others: Re-enactment of intended acts by 18-month-old children. *Developmental Psychobiology,* 1995; 31: 838–50.

Meltzoff, A.N. What infant memory tells us about infantile amnesia: long-term recall and deferred imitation. *Journal of Experimental Child Psychology,* 1995; 59: 497–515.

Gergely, G., Bekkering, H. and Király, I. Rational imitation in preverbal infants. *Nature,* 2002; 415: 755–6.

48/2   Rapacholi, B.M. and Gopnik, A. Early reasoning about desires: evidence from 14- and 18-month-olds. *Developmental Psychobiology,* 1997; 33: 12–21.

52/1   Liszkowski, U., Carpenter, M., Striano, T. and Tomasello, M. 12- and 18-month-olds point to provide information for others. *Journal of Cognition and Development,* 2006; 7: 173–87.

Baillargeon, R., Scott, R.M. and He, Z. False-belief understanding in infants. *Trends in*

52/1
(cont.)   *Cognitive Neurosciences,* 2010; 14: 110–18.
Buttelmann, D., Carpenter, M. and Tomasello, M. Eighteen-month-old infants show false belief understanding in an active paradigm. *Cognition,* 2009; 112: 337–42.
Baillargeon et al. False-belief understanding …

52/2   Senju, A., Southgate, V., Snape, C., Leonard, M. and Csibra, G. Do 18-month-olds really attribute mental states to others? A critical test. *Psychological Science.* 2011; 22: 878–80.
Baillargeon et al. False-belief understanding …

53/2   Lewis, M. and Ramsay, D. Development of self-recognition, personal pronoun use, and pretend play during the 2nd year. *Child Development,* 2004; 75: 1821–31.

55/1   Astington, J.W. and Jenkins, J.M. Theory of mind development and social understanding. *Cognition and Emotion,* 1995; 9: 151–65.
Hughes, C. and Dunn, J. "Pretend you didn't know": Preschoolers' talk about mental states in pretend play. *Cognitive Development,* 1997; 12: 477–97.
Youngblade, L.M. and Dunn, J. Individual differences in young children's pretend play with mother and sibling: links to relationships and understanding of other people's feelings and beliefs. *Child Development,* 1995; 66: 1472–92.
Lillard, A. and Witherington, D. Mothers' behaviour modifications during pretense and their possible signal value for toddlers. *Developmental Psychobiology,* 2004; 41: 95–113.

56/1   Brown, J.R., Donelan-McCall, N. and Dunn, J. Why talk about mental states? The significance of children's conversations with friends, siblings and mothers. *Child Development,* 1996; 67: 836–49.

56/2   Dunn, J., Brown, J., and Beardsall, L. Family talk about feeling states and children's later understanding of others' emotions. *Developmental Psychology,* 1991; 27, 448–55.
Denham, S. A., Zoller, D., and Couchoud, E. A. Socialization of preschoolers' emotion understanding. *Developmental Psychology,* 1994; 30; 928–36.

Hughes, C., *Social Understanding and Social Lives.* Hove, Sussex: Psychology Press; 2011.

56/4   Tomasello, M. Cooperation and communication in the 2nd year of life. *Child Development Perspectives,* 2007; 1: 8–12.

2 Attachment

63/2   Bowlby, J. *Maternal care and mental health.* Geneva: WHO Report; 1952.
Bowlby, J. Forty-four juvenile thieves: their characters and home life. *International Journal of Psychoanalysis,* 1944; 25: 107–27.
Robertson, J. and Bowlby, J. Responses of young children to separation from their mothers. *Courier du Centre International de l'Enfance,* 1952; 2: 131–42.
Harlow, H. The nature of love. *American Psychologist,* 1958; 13: 673.
Bowlby, J. *Attachment.* New York: Basic Books; 1982.

65/1   Cassidy, J. The nature of the child's ties. In: J. Cassidy and P. Shaver, eds. *Handbook of Attachment,* 2nd edn. London, New York: Guilford Press; 2008, pp. 3–22.
Bowlby, J. *Attachment.* New York: Basic Books; 1982.

70/1   Ainsworth, M., Blehar, M., Waters, E. and Wall, S. *Patterns of Attachment: A Psychological Study of the Strange Situation.* Hillsdale, NJ: Erlbaum; 1978.
Bowlby, J. *Attachment.* New York: Basic Books; 1982.
Ainsworth, M. *Infancy in Uganda: Infant care and the growth of love.* Baltimore: Johns Hopkins University Press; 1982.

77/1   Ainsworth et al., *Patterns of Attachment* . . .
Main, M. and Solomon, J. Procedures for identifying infants as disorganized/disoriented during the Ainsworth Strange Situation. In: M. Greenberg, D. Cicchetti and E. Cummings, eds. *Attachment in the Preschool Years: Theory, Research and Intervention.* Chicago: University of Chicago Press; 1990, pp. 121–60.

77/2 Spangler, G. and Grossmann, K. E. Biobehavioral organization in securely and insecurely attached infants. *Child Development,* 1993; 64(5): 1439–50.
Zelenko, M., Kraemer, H., Huffman, L., Gschwendt, M., Pageler, N. and Steiner, H. Heart rate correlates of attachment status in young mothers and their infants. *Journal of the American Academy of Child & Adolescent Psychiatry*, 2005; 44(5): 470–6.

77/4 Main and Solomon, Procedures for identifying infants as disorganized/disoriented . . .

78/1 Belsky, J. and Fearon, P. Precursors of attachment security. In: J. Cassidy and P. Shaver, eds. *Handbook of Attachment,* 2nd edn. London, New York: Guilford Press; 2008, pp. 295–316.
Ainsworth, M., Blehar, M., Waters, E. and Wall, S. *Patterns of Attachment: A Psychological Study of the Strange Situation.* Hillsdale, NJ: Erlbaum; 1978.
Cassidy, J. The nature of the child's ties. In: J. Cassidy and P. Shaver, eds. *Handbook of Attachment*, 2nd ed. London, New York: Guilford Press; 2008, pp. 3–22.
McElwain, N. and Booth-LaForce, C. Maternal sensitivity to infant distress and nondistress as predictors of infant-mother attachment security. *Journal of Family Psychology*, 2006; 20: 247–55.

87/1 Meins, E., Fernyhough, C., Fradley, E. and Tuckey, M. Rethinking maternal sensitivity: mothers' comments on infants' mental processes predict security of attachment at 12 months. *Journal of Child Psychology and Psychiatry*, 2001; 42: 637–48.
Slade, A., Greenberger, J., Bernach, E., Levy, D. and Locker, A. Maternal reflective functioning and the transmission gap: A preliminary study. *Attachment and Human Development*, 2005; 7: 283–98.
Koren-Karie, N., Oppenheim, D., Dolev, S., Sher, E. and Etzion-Carasso, A. Mothers' insightfulness regarding their infants' internal experience: Relations with maternal sensitivity and infant attachment. *Developmental Psychology*, 2002; 38(4): 534.

93/1 Belsky, J. and Fearon, P. Precursors of attachment security. In: J. Cassidy and P. Shaver, eds. *Handbook of Attachment,* 2nd edn. London, New York: Guilford Press; 2008, pp. 295–316.
Fearon, P., Campbell, C. and Murray, L. Social science, parenting and child development. In C. Cooper and J. Michie, eds. *Understanding All Our Futures: Why Social Sciences Matter.* Palgrave (in press).

94/2 Bokhorst, C. L., Bakermans-Kranenburg, M. J., Fearon, R. M. P., van, I. M. H., Fonagy, P. and Schuengel, C. The importance of shared environment in mother-infant attachment security: a behavioral genetic study. *Child Development*, 2003; 74(6): 1769–82.
Roisman, G. I. and Fraley, R. C. A behavior-genetic study of parenting quality, infant attachment security, and their covariation in a nationally representative sample. *Developmental Psychology*, 2008; 44(3): 831–9.
Luijk, M. P. C. M., Roisman, G. I., Haltigan, J. D., Tiemeier, H., Booth-LaForce, C., van IJzendoorn, M. H., et al. Dopaminergic, serotonergic, and oxytonergic candidate genes associated with infant attachment security and disorganization? In search of main and interaction effects. *Journal of Child Psychology and Psychiatry*, 2011; 52(12): 1295–307.

94/3 Belsky, J. and Fearon, P. Precursors of attachment security. In: J. Cassidy and P. Shaver, eds. *Handbook of Attachment,* 2nd edn. London, New York: Guilford Press; 2008, pp. 295–316.
Belsky, J. and Pluess, M. Beyond diathesis stress: differential susceptibility to environmental influences. *Psychological Bulletin*, 2009; 135: 885–908.
Cassidy, J., Woodhouse, S., Sherman, L., Stupica, B. and Lejuez, C. Enhancing infant attachment security: an examination of treatment efficacy and differential susceptibility. *Development and Psychopathology*, 2011; 23: 131–48.
Murray, L., Stanley, C., Hooper, R., King, F. and Fiori-Cowley, A. The role of infant factors in postnatal depression and mother-infant interactions. *Developmental Medicine and Child Neurology*, 1996; 38: 109–19.

94/4   Belsky and Fearon, Precursors of attachment security.

94/5   Van IJzendoorn, M. Adult attachment representations, parental responsiveness, and infant attachment. *Psychological Bulletin*, 1995; 117: 387–403.

95/3   Lyons Ruth, K., Bronfman, E. and Parsons, E. Maternal frightened, frightening, or atypical behavior and disorganized infant attachment patterns. *Monographs of the Society for Research in Child Development*, 1999; 64(3): 67–96.

96/1   Martins, C., and Gaffan, E. A. Effects of early maternal depression on patterns of infant-mother attachment: A meta-analytic investigation. *Journal of Child Psychology and Psychiatry*, 2000; 41(6): 737–46.

96/3   Johnson, S., Dweck, C., Chen, F., Stern, H., Ok, S-J. and Barth, M. At the intersection of social and cognitive development: internal working models of attachment in infancy. *Cognitive Science*, 2010; 34: 807–25.

96/4   Main, M., Kaplan, N. and Cassidy, J. Security in infancy, childhood and adulthood: a move to the level of representation. In: I. Bretherton and E. Waters, eds. *Monographs of the Society for Research in Child Development*, 1985; 50(1–2), 66–104. Bretherton, I. and Munholland, K. Internal working models in attachment relationships: elaborating a central construct in attachment theory and research. In: J. Cassidy and P. Shaver, eds. *Handbook of Attachment*, 2nd edn. London, New York: Guilford Press; 2008, pp. 102–30.

96/5   Groh, A.M., Fearon, R.P., Bakermans-Kranenburg, M.J., Van IJzendoorn, M.H., Steele, R.D. and Roisman, G.I. The significance of attachment security for children's social competence with peers: a meta-analytic study. *Attachment and Human Development*, 10.1080/14616734.2014.883636. Berlin, L., Cassidy, J. and Appleyard, K. The influence of early attachment on other relationships. In: J. Cassidy and P. Shaver, eds. *Handbook of Attachment*, 2nd edn. London, New York: Guilford Press; 2008, pp. 333–47. Thomson, R. Early attachment and later development. In: J. Cassidy and P. Shaver, eds. *Handbook of Attachment*, 2nd edn. London, New York: Guilford Press; 2008, pp. 348–65.

97/2   Fearon, R. M. P., Bakermans-Kranenburg, M. J., van IJzendoorn, M. H., Lapsley, A. M. and Roisman, G. I. The significance of insecure attachment and disorganization in the development of children's externalizing behavior: a meta-analytic study. *Child Development*, 2010; 81(2): 435–56. Fearon, R. M. P. and Belsky, J. Infant-mother attachment and the growth of externalizing problems across the primary-school years. *Journal of Child Psychology and Psychiatry*, 2011; 52(7): 782–91.

97/3   Rutter, M., Kumsta, R., Scholtz, W. and Sonuga-Barke, E. Longitudinal studies using a "Natural experiment" design: the case of adoptees from Romanian institutions. *Journal of the American Academy of Child and Adolescent Psychiatry*, 2012; 51: 762–70.

97/4   Berlin, L., Zeanah, C. and Lieberman, A. Prevention and intervention Programs for supporting attachment security. In: J. Cassidy and P. Shaver, eds. *Handbook of Attachment*, 2nd edn. London, New York: Guilford Press; 2008, pp.745–61. Slade, A., Sadler, L. and Mayes, L. Minding the baby: enhancing parental reflective functioning in a nursing/mental health home visiting program. In: L. Berlin, Y. Ziv, L. Amaya-Jackson and M. Greenberg, eds. *Enhancing Early Attachments*. London, New York: Guilford Press; 2005, pp. 152–77. Lieberman, A., Silverman, R. and Pawl, J. Infant-parent psychotherapy: core concepts and current approaches. In: C. Zeanah, ed. *Handbook of Infant Mental Health*, 2nd edn. London, New York: Guilford Press; 2000, pp. 472–84. Cicchetti, D., Rogosch, F. and Toth, S. Fostering secure attachment in infants in maltreating families through preventive interventions. *Development and Psychopathology*, 2006; 18: 623–49. Juffer, F., Bakermans-Kranenburg, M. and Van IJzendoorn, M. *Promoting Positive Parenting: An Attachment Based Intervention*. CRC Press; 2007.

98/2   Cassidy, J., Woodhouse, S., Sherman, L., Stupica, B. and Lejuez, C. Enhancing infant attachment security: an examination of treatment efficacy and differential susceptibility. *Development and Psychopathology*, 2011; 23: 131–48.
Van den Boom, D. The influence of temperament and mothering on attachment and exploration: An experimental manipulation of sensitive responsiveness among lower class mothers with irritable infants. *Child Development*, 1994; 65: 1457–77.
Fearon, P., Campbell, C. and Murray, L. Social science, parenting and child development. In: C. Cooper and J. Michie, eds. *Understanding All Our Futures: Why Social Sciences Matter*. Palgrave (in press).

98/4   (twice) Belsky, J. Early child care and early child development: Major findings of the NICHD study of early child care. *European Journal of Developmental Psychology*, 2006; 3: 95–110.
NICHD Early Child Care Research Network. Early child care and children's development prior to school entry: Results from the NICHD Study of Early Child Care. *American Educational Research Journal*, 2002; 39: 133–64.

98/5   NICHD Early Child Care Research Network. Early child care and children's development prior to school entry . . .
Lamb, M.E. and Ahnert, L. Nonparental child care: Context, concepts, correlates, and consequences. In: W. Damon, R.M. Lerner, K.A. Renninger and I. E. Sigel, eds. *Handbook of Child Psychology, Vol. 4, Child Psychology in Practice*, 6th edn., New York: Wiley; 2006, pp. 950–1016.

99/2   (twice) Ahnert, L., Gunnar, M.R., Lamb, M.E. and Barthel, M. Transition to child care: Associations with infant–mother attachment, infant negative emotion, and cortisol elevations. *Child Development*, 2004; 75: 639–50.
Rauh, H., Ziegenhain, U., Müller, B. and Wijnroks, L. Stability and change in infant-mother attachment in the second year of life: Relations to parenting quality and varying degrees of daycare experience. In: P. M. Crittenden and A. H. Claussen, eds. *The Organization of Attachment Relationships: Maturation, Culture, and Context*. New York:
Cambridge University Press; 2000, pp. 251–76.
Ahnert et al., Transition to child care …

114/1   Ahnert, L., Rickert, H. and Lamb, M.E. Shared caregiving: Comparisons between home and child-care settings. *Developmental Psychology*, 2000; 36: 339.
Booth, C.L., Clarke-Stewart, K.A., Vandell, D.L., McCartney, K and Owen, M.T. Child care usage and mother-infant "quality time". *Journal of Marriage and Family*, 2002; 64: 16–26.
NICHD Early Child Care Research Network. Does amount of time spent in child care predict socioemotional adjustment during the transition to kindergarten? *Child Development*, 2003; 74, 976–1005.
Ahnert, L. and Lamb, M.E. Shared care: Establishing a balance between home and child care settings. *Child Development*, 2003; 74: 1044–9.
Sagi, A., Koren-Karie, N., Gini, M., Ziv, Y. and Joels, T. Shedding further light on the effects of various types and quality of early child care on infant-mother attachment relationship: The Haifa study of early child care. *Child Development*, 2002; 73: 1166–86.
National Institute of Child Health and Human Development Early Child Care Research Network. Child-care and family predictors of preschool attachment and stability from infancy. *Developmental Psychology*, 2001; 37: 847–62.

115/1   Lamb, M. E. Nonparental child care: Context, quality, correlates,and consequences. In: W. Damon, I. E. Sigel and K. A. Reminger, eds. *Handbook of Child Development: Vol. 4. Social, Emotional, and Personality Development* (5th edn). New York: Wiley, 1998; pp. 73–133.

116/1   Owen, M.T, Ware, M.A. and Barfoot, B. Caregiver-mother partnership behavior and the quality of caregiver-child and mother-child interactions. *Early Childhood Research Quarterly*, 2000; 15: 413–28.
Van IJzendoorn, M.H., Tavecchio, L.W., Stams, G-J., Verhoeven, M. and Reiling, E. Attunement between parents and professional caregivers: A comparison of childrearing attitudes in different child-care settings. *Journal of Marriage and the Family*, 1998; 771–81.

116/2 Howes, C., Matheson, C.C. and Hamilton, C.E. Maternal, teacher, and child care history correlates of children's relationships with peers. *Child Development*, 1994; 65: 264–73.
Howes, C. and Hamilton, C.E. The changing experience of child care: Changes in teachers and in teacher-child relationships and children's social competence with peers. *Early Childhood Research Quarterly*, 1993; 8: 15–32.

121/1 Lamb, M.E. and Ahnert, L. Nonparental child care: Context, concepts, correlates, and consequences. In: W. Damon, R.M. Lerner, K.A. Renninger and I. E. Sigel, eds. *Handbook of Child Psychology, Vol. 4, Child Psychology in Practice* (Sixth Edn), New York: Wiley, 2006, pp. 950–1016.

121/2 Lamb and Ahnert, Nonparental child care…

122/1 National Institute of Child Health and Human Development Early Child Care Research Network. Child care and children's peer interaction at 24 and 36 months: The NICHD study of early child care. *Child Development*, 2001; 72: 1478–1500.
Klimes-Dougan, B. and Kistner, J. Physically abused preschoolers' responses to peers' distress. *Developmental Psychology*, 1990; 26: 599–602.
Watamura, S.E., Bonny, D., Jan, A.R. and Megan, G. Morning-to-afternoon increases in cortisol concentrations for infants and toddlers at child care: Age differences and behavioral correlates. *Child Development*, 2003; 74: 1006–20.

122/2 National Institute of Child Health and Human Development Early Child Care Research Network. Child care and children's peer interaction at 24 and 36 months: The NICHD study of early child care. *Child Development*, 2001; 72: 1478–1500.

123/2 Belsky, J. Early child care and early child development: Major findings of the NICHD study of early child care. *European Journal of Developmental Psychology*, 2006; 3: 95–110.
Barnes, J., Leach, P., Malmberg, L., Stein, A., Sylva, K. and the FCCC Team. Experiences of childcare in England and socio-emotional development at 36 months. *Early Child Development and Care*, 2009; 1–15.

123/3 Borge, A.I., Rutter, M., Côté, S. and Tremblay, R.E. Early childcare and physical aggression: differentiating social selection and social causation. *Journal of Child Psychology and Psychiatry*, 2004; 45: 367–76.
Pluess, M. and Belsky, J. Differential susceptibility to rearing experience: The case of childcare. *Journal of Child Psychology and Psychiatry*, 2009; 50: 396–404.

123/5 Winnicott D. W. Transitional objects and transitional phenomena—a study of the first not-me possession. *International Journal of Psycho-Analysis*, 1953; 34:89–97

124/1 Passman, R.H. and Weisberg, P. Mothers and blankets as agents for promoting play and exploration by young children in a novel environment: The effects of social and nonsocial attachment objects. *Developmental Psychology*, 1975; 11: 170–7.

124/2 Van IJzendoorn, M.H., Goossens, F.A., Tavecchio, L.W.C., Vergeer, M.M. and Hubbard, F.O.A. Attachment to soft objects: Its relationship with attachment to the mother and with thumbsucking. *Child Psychiatry and Human Development*, 1983; 14: 97–105.
Donate-Bartfield, E. and Passman, R.H. Relations between children's attachments to their mothers and to security blankets. *Journal of Family Psychology*, 2004; 18: 453–8.
Hobara, M. Prevalence of transitional objects in young children in Tokyo and New York. *Infant Mental Health Journal*, 2003; 24: 174–91.
Gaddini, R. and Gaddini, E. Transitional objects and the process of individuation: a study in three different social groups. *Journal of the American Academy of Child Psychiatry*, 1970; 9: 347–65.
Green, K.E., Groves, M.M. and Tegano, D.W. Parenting practices that limit transitional object use: an illustration. *Early Child Development and Care*, 2004; 174: 427–36.

3 Self-regulation and control

127/1   Kochanska, G. and Knaack, A. Effortful control as a personality characteristic of young children: antecedents, correlates, and consequences. *Journal of Personality*, 2004; 71: 1087–112.
Kim, J. and Cicchetti, D. Longitudinal pathways linking child maltreatment, emotion regulation, peer relations, and psychopathology. *Journal of Child Psychology and Psychiatry*, 2010; 51: 706–16.

127/2   Fox, N.A. The assessment of temperament and self-regulation in infants and young children. In: B. Zuckerman, A. Lieberman, N.A. Fox, eds. *Emotional Regulation and Developmental Health. Pediatric Round Table.* Johnson and Johnson Pediatric Institute, L.L.C., USA; 2002.
Brazelton, T.B. *Neonatal Behavioral Assessment Scale. Clinics in Developmental Medicine N.88.* 2nd edn. London: S.I.M.P.; 1984.
Rothbart, M.K. and Posner, M.I. Temperament and the development of self-regulation. In: L.C. Hartlage and C.F. Telzrow, eds. *The Neuro-psychology of Individual Differences: A Developmental Perspective.* New York, NY: Plenum Press; 1985.
Montirosso, R., Provenzi, L., Tavian, D., Ciceri, F., Missaglia, S., Tronick, E. et al. 5-HTTLPR polymorphism is associated to differences in behavioural response and HPA reactivity to a social stressor in 4-month-old infants. *WAIMH 13th World Congress Babies in Mind – the Minds of Babies: A View from Africa.* 2012.
Talge, N., Neal, C. and Glover, V. and the Early Stress, Translational Research and Prevention Science Network. Antenatal maternal stress and long-term effects on child neurodevelopment: how and why? *Journal of Child Psychology and Psychiatry,* 2007; 48, 245–61.

127/3   Jahromi, L.B., Putnam, S.P. and Stifter, C.A. Maternal regulation of infant reactivity from 2 to 6 months. *Developmental Psychology*, 2004; 40: 477–87.
Albers, E.M., Riksen-Walraven, M., Sweep, F.C. and De Weerth, C. Maternal behaviour predicts infant cortisol recovery from a mild everyday stressor. *Journal of Child Psychology and Psychiatry,* 2008; 49: 97–103.

128/1   St. James-Roberts, I. and Plewis, I. Individual differences, daily fluctuations, and develop-mental changes in amounts of infant waking, fussing, crying, feeding, and sleeping. *Child Development*, 1996; 67: 2527–40.
Jahromi et al., Maternal regulation of infant reactivity…

129/1   Tronick, E., Als, H., Adamson, L., Wise, S. and Brazelton, T.B. The infant's response to entrapment between contradictory messages in face-to-face interaction. *Journal of the American Academy of Child Psychiatry*, 1978; 17: 1–3.
Mesman, J., Van IJzendoorn, M., Marinus, H. and Bakermans-Kranenburg M.J. The many faces of the Still-Face Paradigm: A review and meta-analysis. *Developmental Review*, 2009; 29: 120–62.

131/1   Emde, R.N., Kligman, D.H., Reich, J.H. and Wade, T.D. Emotional expression in infancy: I. Initial studies of social signaling and an emergent model. In: M. Lewis and L.A. Rosenblum, eds. *The Development of Affect.* New York: Plenum Press; 1978, pp. 125–48.
Gianino, A. and Tronick, E. The mutual regulation model: The infant's self and interactive regulation. Coping and defense capacities. In: E.Z. Tronick, T. Field, P. McCabe and N. Schneiderman, eds. *Stress and Coping,194.* Hillsdale, NJ: Lawrence Erlbaum Associates, Inc; 1988, pp. 47–68.
Tronick, E. and Beeghly, M. Infants' meaning-making and the development of mental health problems. *American Psychologist*, 2011; 66: 107–19.

133/1   Murray, L., Cooper, P.J., Creswell, C., Schofield, E. and Sack, C. The effects of maternal social phobia on mother-infant interactions and infant social responsiveness. *Journal of Child Psychology and Psychiatry*, 2007; 48: 45–52.
Brazelton, T.B., Kowlowski, B. and Main, M. The origins of reciprocity: The early mother-infant interaction. In: M. Lewis and L.A. Rosenblum, eds. *The Effect of the Infant on its Caregiver.* New York: Wiley; 1974.
Stifter, C.A. and Moyer, D. The regulation of positive affect: Gaze aversion activity during mother-infant interaction. *Infant Behavior and*

133/1
(cont.)
Development,1991; 14: 111–23.

Tronick, E. Z. The stress of normal development and interaction leads to the development of resilience and variation in resilience. In: E. Z. Tronick, ed. *The Neurobehavioral and Social-emotional Development of Infants and Children.* New York: W. W. Norton and Company Ltd.; 2007, pp. 378–94.

Field, T. Infant arousal, attention, and affect during early interactions. In: L. Lipsitt, ed. *Advances in Infancy*, Vol. 1. New York: Ablex; 1981, pp. 57–100.

133/2
Haley, D.W. and Stansbury, K. Infant stress and parent responsiveness: Regulation of physiology and behaviour during still-face and reunion. *Child Development Today and Tomorrow*, 2003; 74: 1534–46.

Gianino, A., Plimpton, T. and Tronick, E.Z. Infant coping with interpersonal stress: Specificity, developmental changes and stability. *Infant Behavior and Development*, 1986; 9: 138.

Gunning, M., Halligan, S.L. and Murray, L. Contributions of maternal and infant factors to infant responding to the Still Face paradigm: A longitudinal study. *Infant Behavior and Development,* 2013; 36: 319–28.

Morrell, J. and Murray, L. Parenting and the development of conduct disorder and hyperactive symptoms in childhood: a prospective longitudinal study from 2 months to 8 years. *Journal of Child Psychology and Psychiatry*, 2003; 44: 489–508.

Halligan, S. L., Murray, L., Cooper, P. J., Fearon, P., Wheeler, S.W. and Crosby, M. The longitudinal development of emotion regulation capacities in children at risk for externalizing disorders. *Development and Psychopathology*, 2013; 25 (2): 391–406.

Moore, G. A., Cohn, J. F. and Campbell, S.B. Infant affective responses to mother's still face at 6 months differentially predict externalizing and internalizing behaviors at 18 months. *Developmental Psychology*, 2001; 37: 706–14.

135/1
Brazelton, T. B., Kowlowski, B. and Main, M. The origins of reciprocity: The early mother-infant interaction. In: M. Lewis and L.A. Rosenblum, eds. *The Effect of the Infant on its Caregiver.* New York: Wiley; 1974.

136/1
Pacquette, D. and Bigras, M. The risky situation: a procedure for assessing the father-child activation relationship. *Early Child Development and Care,* 2010; 180 (1&2): 33–50.

138/1
Tremblay, R. E. et al. Physical aggression during early childhood: trajectories and predictors. *Pediatrics*, 2004; 114(1): 43–50.

Peterson, J. B. and Flanders, J. Play and the regulation of aggression. In: R.E. Tremblay, W.H. Hartup and J. Archer, eds. *Developmental Origins of Aggression.* New York: Guilford Press; 2005, pp. 133–57.

Flanders, J. L., Leo, V., Paquette, D., Pihl, R.O. and Séguin, J. R. Rough-and-tumble play and the regulation of aggression: An observational study of father-child play dyads. *Aggressive Behavior,* 2009; 35: 285–95.

Pellegrini, A. D. and Smith, P. K. Physical activity play: The nature and function of a neglected aspect of play. *Child Development*, 1998; 69: 577–98.

142/1
Kochanska, G., Murray, K.T. and Harlan, E.T. Effortful control in early childhood: Continuity and change, antecedents, and implications for social development. *Developmental Psychology*, 2000; 36: 220–32.

Kochanska, G., Coy, K.C. and Murray, K.T. The development of self-regulation in the first four years of life. *Child Development*, 2001; 72: 1091–111.

Diamond, A. Neuropsychological insights into the meaning of object concept development. In: S. Carey and R. Gelman, eds. *The Epigenesis of the Mind*. Hillsdale, NJ: Lawrence Erlbaum Associates, Inc; 1991, pp. 67–110.

Posner, M.I. and Rothbart, M.K. Developing mechanisms of self-regulation. *Development and Psychopathology*, 2000; 12: 427–41.

Sheese, B.E., Rothbart, M.K., Posner, M.I., White, L.K. and Fraundorf, S.H. Executive attention and self-regulation in infancy. *Infant Behavior and Development*, 2008; 31: 501–10.

143/1
Kochanska, G., Murray, K.T. and Harlan, E.T. Effortful control in early childhood: Continuity

and change, antecedents, and implications for social development. *Developmental Psychology*, 2000; 36: 220–32.

143/2 Kochanska, et al. Effortful control in early childhood . . .

146/2 Conway, A. and Stifter, C. Longitudinal antecedents of executive function in pre-schoolers. *Child Development*, 2012; 83(3): 1022–36.
Stern, D.N. *The Interpersonal World of the Infant: A View from Psychoanalysis and Development.* New York: Basic Books; 1985.
Sheese, B.E., Rothbart, M.K., Posner, M.I., White, L.K. and Fraundorf, S.H. Executive attention and self-regulation in infancy. *Infant Behavior and Development*, 2008; 31: 501–10.

148/1 Sorce, J.F., Emde, R.N., Campos, J.J. and Klinnert, M.D. Maternal emotional signaling: Its effect on the visual cliff behavior of 1-year-olds. *Developmental Psychology*, 1985; 21: 195.
Murray, L., De Rosnay, M., Pearson, J., Bergeron, C., Schofield, E., Royal-Lawson, M. et al. Intergenerational transmission of social anxiety: The role of social referencing processes in infancy. *Child Development*, 2008; 79: 1049–64.

153/1 Hubley, P.A. and Trevarthen, C.B. Sharing a task in infancy. *New Directions for Child and Adolescent Development*, 1979; 1979 (4): 57–80.
Kochanska, et al. Effortful control in early childhood . . .

155/2 Kochanska, G., Tjebkes, T.L. and Forman, D.R. Children's emerging regulation of conduct: Restraint, compliance, and internalization from infancy to the second year. *Child Development*, 1998; 69: 1378–89.
Maccoby, E.E. and Martin, J.A. Socialization in the context of the family: Parent-child interaction. In: P.H. Mussen and E.M. Hetherington, eds. *Handbook of Child Psychology: Vol. 4. Socialization, Personality, and Social Development.* New York: Wiley; 1983, pp. 1–101.
Gershoff, E. T. Corporal punishment by parents and associated child behaviors and experiences. *Psychological Bulletin*, 2002; 128, 539–79.
Rothbaum, F. and Weisz, J. R. Parental caregiving

and child externalizing behavior in nonclinical samples: A meta-analysis. *Psychological Bulletin*, 1994; 116(1): 55–74.

157/1 Brophy, M. and Dunn, J. What did mummy say? Dyadic interactions between young "Hard to Manage" children and their mothers. *Journal of Abnormal Child Psychology*, 2002; 30: 103–12.

159/1 De Rosnay, M. and Hughes, C. Conversation and theory of mind: Do children talk their way to socio-cognitive understanding? *British Journal of Developmental Psychology*, 2006; 24: 7–37.
Dunn, J. and Brown, J.R. Early conversations about causality: Content, pragmatics and developmental change. *Developmental Psychology*, 1993; 11: 107–23.
Dunn, J., Bretherton, I. and Munn, P. Conversations about feeling states between mothers and their young children. *Developmental Psychology*, 1987; 23: 132–9.
Hughes, C., *Social Understanding and Social Lives.* Hove, Sussex: Psychology Press; 2011.
Gardner, F.E., Sonuga-Barke, E.J. and Sayal, K. Parents anticipating misbehaviour: an observational study of strategies parents use to prevent conflict with behaviour problem children. *Journal of Child Psychology and Psychiatry*, 1999; 40(8): 1185–96.

159/4 Sadeh, A., Tikotzky, L. and Scher, A. Parenting and infant sleep. *Sleep Medicine Reviews*, 2010; 14: 89–96.
Cronin, A., Halligan, S.L. and Murray, L. Maternal psychosocial adversity and the longitudinal development of infant sleep. *Infancy*, 2008; 13: 469–95.
Tikotzky, L. and Sadeh, A. Maternal sleep-related cognitions and infant sleep: A longitudinal study from pregnancy through the 1st year. *Child Development*, 2009; 80: 860–74.
Murray, L. and Andrews, E. *The Social Baby.* London: CP Publishing; 2000.

164/1 Mindell, J.A., Kuhn, B., Lewin, D.S., Meltzer, L.J. and Sadeh, A. Behavioral treatment of bedtime problems and night wakings in infants and young children. *Pediatric Sleep*, 2006; 29: 1263–76. Hiscock, H.K., Bayer, J., Hampton,

164/1
(cont.)
A., Ukoumunne, O.C. and Wake, M. Long-term mother and child mental health effects of a population-based infant sleep intervention: cluster-randomized, controlled trial. *Pediatrics*, 2008; 122: e621–7.

164/2
Murray, L. and Ramchandani, P. Might prevention be better than cure? A perspective on improving infant sleep and maternal mental health: a cluster randomized trial. *Archives of Disease in Childhood*, 2007; 92: 943–4.

165/3
Murray, L., Halligan, S. L. and Cooper, P.J. Effects of postnatal depression on mother-infant interactions, and child development. In: G. Bremner and T. Wachs, eds. *The Wiley-Blackwell Handbook of Infant Development*. New York: Wiley, 2010; pp. 192–220.
Morrell, J. and Murray, L. Parenting and the development of conduct disorder and hyperactive symptoms in childhood: a prospective longitudinal study from 2 months to 8 years. *Journal of Child Psychology and Psychiatry*, 2003; 44: 489–508.
Halligan, S.L., Murray, L., Cooper, P.J., Fearon, P., Wheeler, S.W. and Crosby, M. The longitudinal development of emotion regulation capacities in children at risk for externalizing disorders. *Development and Psychopathology*, 2013; 25(2): 391–406.

165/4
Murray, L., Creswell, C. and Cooper, P.J. The development of anxiety disorders in childhood: an integrative review. *Psychological Medicine*, 2009; 39: 1413–23.
Murray, L., De Rosnay, M., Pearson, J., Bergeron, C., Schofield, E., Royal-Lawson, M. et al. Intergenerational transmission of social anxiety: The role of social referencing processes in infancy. *Child Development*, 2008; 79: 1049–64.

165/5
Brazelton, T.B. *Neonatal Behavioral Assessment Scale. Clinics in Developmental Medicine N.88.* 2nd edn. London: S.I.M.P.; 1984.

166/2
Kagan, J., Reznick, J. S., Clarke, C., Snidman, N. and Garcia-Coll, C. Behavioral inhibition to the unfamiliar. *Child Development*, 1984; 55: 2212–25.

Fox, N.A., Henderson, H.A., Rubin, K.H., Calkins, S.D. and Schmidt, L.A. Continuity and discontinuity of behavioral inhibition and exuberance: psychophysiological and behavioral influences across the first four years of life. *Child Development*, 2001; 72: 1–21.
Calkins, S.D., Fox, N.A. and Marshall, T.R. Behavioral and physiological correlates of inhibition in infancy. *Child Development*, 1996; 67: 523–40.

166/3
Morrell, J. and Murray, L. Parenting and the development of conduct disorder and hyperactive symptoms in childhood: a prospective longitudinal study from 2 months to 8 years. *Journal of Child Psychology and Psychiatry*, 2003; 44: 489–508.
20. Halligan, S.L., Murray, L., Cooper, P.J., Fearon, P., Wheeler, S.W. and Crosby, M. The longitudinal development of emotion regulation capacities in children at risk for externalizing disorders. *Development and Psychopathology*, 2013; 25 (2): 391–406.
St James-Roberts, I. and Plewis, I. Individual differences, daily fluctuations and developmental changes in amounts of infant waking, fussing, crying, feeding and sleeping. *Child Development*, 1996; 67: 2527–40.
Belsky, L. and Pluess, M. Beyond diathesis stress: Differential susceptibility to environmental influences. *Psychological Bulletin*, 2009; 135: 885–908.
Blair, C. Early intervention for low birth weight, preterm infants: The role of negative emotionality in the specification of effects. *Development and Psychopathology*, 2002; 14: 311–32.

167/1
Suomi, S.J. Attachment in rhesus monkeys. In: J. Cassidy and P. Shaver, eds. *Handbook of Attachment*, 2nd edn. London, New York: Guilford Press; 2008, Ch. 8.

167/2
Murray, L., Pella, J., De Pascalis, L., Arteche, A., Pass, L., Percy, R., Creswell, C. and Cooper, P. J. Socially anxious mothers' narratives to their children and their relation to child representations and adjustment. *Development and Psychopathology*, in press.

167/3
Tremblay, R.E., Hartup, W.H. and Archer, J.

Developmental Origins of Aggression. New York: Guilford Press; 2005.

Hay, D.F., Hurst, S.L., Waters, C.S. and Chadwick, A. Infants' use of force to defend toys: the origins of instrumental aggression. *Infancy*, 2011; 16: 471–89.

Webster-Stratton, C. Preventing conduct problems in Head Start children: Stengthening parenting competencies. *Journal of Consulting and Clinical Psychology*, 1998; 66: 715–30.

Hutchings, J. and Gardner, F. Support from the start: effective programmes for three–eight-year-olds. *Journal of Children's Services*, 2012; 7: 29–40.

167/4   Rothbaum, F. and Weisz, J. R. Parental caregiving and child externalizing behavior in nonclinical samples: a meta-analysis. *Psychological Bulletin*, 1994; 116(1): 55–74.

Patterson, G.R. *Coercive Family Process*. Eugene, OR: Castalie; 1982.

170/1   Grusec, J.E. and Goodnow, J.J. Impact of parental discipline methods on the child's internalization of values: A reconceptualization of current points of view. *Developmental Psychology*, 1994; 30: 4–19.

Smetana, J.G. Toddlers' social interactions in the context of moral and conventional transgressions in the home. *Developmental Psychology*, 1989; 25: 499–508.

170/2   Gardner, F.E.M. Inconsistent parenting: Is there evidence for a link with children's conduct problems? *Journal of Abnormal Child Psychology*, 1989; 17: 223–33.

171/1   Murray, L., De Rosnay, M., Pearson, J., Bergeron, C., Schofield, E., Royal-Lawson, M., et al. Intergenerational transmission of social anxiety: The role of social referencing processes in infancy. *Child Development*, 2008; 79: 1049–64.

Creswell, C., Murray, L., Stacey, J. and Cooper, P. J. Parenting and child anxiety. In: W. Silverman and A. Field, eds. *Anxiety Disorders in Children and Adolescents: Research, Assessment and Intervention*. Cambridge University Press; 2011, pp. 299–345.

Cooper, P. J., Fearn, V., Willetts, L., Seabrook,

H. and Parkinson, M. Affective disorder in the parents of a clinic sample of children with anxiety disorders. *Journal of Affective Disorders*, 2006; 93: 205–12.

Creswell, C., Apetroaia, A., Murray, L. and Cooper, P. Cognitive, affective, and behavioral characteristics of mothers with anxiety disorders in the context of child anxiety disorder. *Journal of Abnormal Psychology*, 2012; 122: 26–38.

Thirwell,K., Cooper. P. J. and Creswell, C. The treatment of child anxiety disorders via guided parent-delivered CBT: A randomised controlled trial. *British Journal of Psychiatry*, 2013; doi: 10.1192/bjp.bp.113.126698.

4 Cognitive development

173/2   Johnson, M. H. *Developmental Cognitive Neuroscience*. Chicago, Wiley; 2010.

173/3   Diamond, M. C., Krech, D. and Rosenzweig, M. R. The effects of an enriched environment on the histology of the rat cerebral cortex. *Journal of Comparative Neurology*, 1964; 123: 111–19.

174/1   Champagne, D., et al. Maternal care and hippocampal plasticity: evidence for experience-dependent structural plasticity, altered synaptic functioning, and differential responsiveness to glucocorticoids and stress. *Journal of Neuroscience*, 2008; 28(23): 6037–45.

Liu, Diorio, J., Francis, D. and Meaney, M. Maternal care, hippocampal synaptogenesis and cognitive development in rats. *Nature Neuroscience*, 2000; 3 (8): 799–806.

174/2   Hubel, D. H. and Wiesel, T. N. Receptive fields in cells in striate cortex of very young visually inexperienced kittens. *Journal of Neurophysiology*, 1963; 26: 994–1002.

175, Box E Kuhl, P. K. Early language acquisition: cracking the speech code. *Nature Reviews Neuroscience*, 2004; 5: 831–43.

175/1   Johnson, M. Functional brain development in humans. *Nature Reviews Neuroscience*, 2001; 2: 475–83.

175/4 Castiello, U., Becchio, C., Zoia, S., Nelini, C., Sartori, L., Blason, L. et al. Wired to be social. *Public Library of Science,* 2010; 5: e13199.
Craig, C. M. and Lee, D.N. Neonatal control of sucking pressure: evidence for an intrinsic tau-guide. *Experimental Brain Research,* 1999; 124: 371–82.
Von Hofsten, C. Eye-hand coordination in newborns. *Developmental Psychology,* 1982; 18: 450–61.
Meltzoff, A. The 'like me' framework for recognizing and becoming an intentional agent. *Acta Psychologica,* 2007; 124(1): 26–43.
Van der Meer, A. L. H. Keeping the arm in the limelight: advanced visual control of arm movements in neonates. *European Journal of Paediatric Neurology,* 1997; 4: 103–8.
Meltzoff, The 'like me' framework . . .

176/1 Von Hofsten, C. An action perspective on motor development. *Trends in Cognitive Sciences,* 2004; 8: 266–72.
Bremner, A., Holmes, N. and Spence, C. Infants lost in (peripersonal) space? *Trends in Cognitive Sciences,* 2008; 12: 298–305.
Held, R. and Bauer, J. Visually guided reaching in infant monkeys after restricted rearing. *Science,* 1967; 155: 718–20.
Bonini, L. and Ferrari, P. F. Evolution of mirror systems: a simple mechanism for complex cognitive functions. *Annals of the New York Academy of Sciences,* 2011; 1225: 166–75.

181/1 Baillargeon, R., Li, J., Weiting, N. G. and Yuan, S. An account of infants' physical reasoning. In: A. Woodward and A. Needham, eds, *Learning and the Infant Mind.* New York, Oxford University Press; 2009.

185/1 Falck-Ytter, T., Gredebäck, G. and Von Hofsten, C. Infants predict other people's action goals. *Nature Neuroscience,* 2006; 9: 878–9.
Kochukhova, O. and Gredeback, G. Preverbal infants anticipate that food will be brought to the mouth: An eye tracking study of manual feeding and flying spoons. *Child Development,* 2010; 81: 1729–38.
Sommerville, J.A., Woodward, A.L. and Needham, A. Action experience alters 3-month-

old infants' perception of others' actions. *Cognition,* 2005; 96: B1–B11.
Meltzoff, A. The 'like me' framework for recognising and becoming an intentional agent. *Acta Psychologica,* 2007; 124: 26–43.
Meltzoff, A. 'Like me': a foundation for social cognition. *Developmental Science,* 2007; 10(1): 126–34.

185/3 Farroni, T., Csibra, G., Simion, F. and Johnson, M.H. Eye contact detection in humans from birth. *Proceedings of the National Academy of Sciences,* 2002; 99: 9602–5.

186/2 Barr, R. and Hayne, H. It's not what you know it's who you know: Older siblings facilitate imitation during infancy. *International Journal of Early Years Education,* 2003; 11: 7–21.

186/3 Nagy, E. and Molnar, P. Homo imitans or homo provocans? Human imprinting model of neonatal imitation. *Infant Behavior and Development,* 2004; 27: 54–63.
Meltzoff, A. N. and Moore, M.K. Explaining facial imitation: a theoretical model. *Early Development and Parenting,* 1997; 6: 179–92.
Ferrari, P. F., Paukner, A., Ruggiero, A., Darcey, L., Unbehagen, S. and Suomi, S. J. Interindividual differences in neonatal imitation and the development of action chains in rhesus macaques. *Child Development,* 2009; 80: 1057–68.

186/4 Meltzoff, A. and Moore, M. K. Early imitation within a functional framework: The importance of person identity, movement, and development. *Infant Behavior and Development,* 1992; 15(4): 479–505.
de Waal, F. and Ferrari, P. Towards a bottom-up perspective on animal and human cognition. *Trends in Cognitive Sciences,* 2010; 14(5): 201–7.

187/1 Meltzoff, A. Understanding the intentions of others: re-enactment of intended acts by 18-month-old children. *Developmental Psychology,* 1995; 31: 838–50.

189/1 Johnson, S. C. The recognition of mentalistic agents in infancy. *Trends in Cognitive Sciences,*

2000; 4: 22–8.

Hanna, E. and Meltzoff, A. N. Peer imitation by toddlers in laboratory, home, and day-care contexts: Implications for social learning and memory. *Developmental Psychology,* 1993; 29: 701.

192/1   Bauer, P. and Mandler, J. Putting the horse before the cart: The use of temporal order in recall of events by one-year-old children. *Developmental Psychology,* 1992; 28(3): 441–52.

192/2   Meltzoff, A. N. and Moore, M. K. Imitation of facial and manual gestures by human neonates. *Science, New Series,* 1977; 189: 75–8.
Meltzoff, A. N. and Moore, M. K. Newborn infants imitate adult facial gestures. *Child Development,* 1983; 54: 702–9.
Meltzoff, A. N. and Moore, M. K. Imitation, memory and the representation of persons. *Infant Behavior and Development,* 1994; 17: 83–99.

194   Double video experiment based on Murray, L. PhD Thesis, The sensitivities and expressive capacities of young infants in communication with their mothers, University of Edinburgh, 1980.

194/2   Watson, J. S. Smiling, cooing and "the game". *Merrill-Palmer Quarterly,* 1972; 18: 323–39.
Markova, G. and Legerstee, M. Contingency, imitation and affect sharing: Foundations of infants' social awareness. *Developmental Psychology,* 2006; 42: 132–41.
Murray, L. and Trevarthen, C. Emotional regulation of interactions between two month olds and their mothers. In: T.M. Field and N. Fox, eds. *Social Perception in Infants.* New Jersey: Ablex; 1985.
Nadel, J., Carchon, I., Kervella, C., Marcelli, D. and Reserbat-Plantey, D. Expectancies for social contingency in 2-month-olds. *Developmental Science,* 1999; 2: 164–73.
Legerstee, M. and Varghese, J. The role of maternal affect mirroring on social expectancies in three-month-old infants. *Child Development,* 2001; 72: 1301–13.

196/1   Legerstee, M. Contingency effects of people and objects in subsequent cognitive functioning in three-month-old infants. *Social Development,* 1997; 6: 307–21.
Dunham, P. and Dunham, F. Effects of mother-infant social interactions on infants' subsequent contingency task performance. *Child Development,* 1990; 61: 785–93.
Dunham, P., Dunham, F., Hurshman, A. and Alexander T. Social contingency effects on subsequent perceptual-cognitive tasks in young infants. *Child Development,* 1989; 60: 1486–96.
Murray, L., Arteche, A., Fearon, P., Halligan, S., Croudace, T. and Cooper, P. The effects of maternal postnatal depression and child sex on academic performance at age 16 years: a developmental approach. *Journal of Child Psychology and Psychiatry,* 2011; 51: 1150–9.

197/1   Casile, A., Caggiano, V. and Ferrari, P.F. The mirror neuron system: a fresh view. *The Neuroscientist,* 2011; 17: 524–38.
Meltzoff, A.N. 'Like me': a foundation for social cognition. *Developmental Science,* 2007; 10: 126–34.
Fogassi, L. and Ferrari, P.F. Mirror systems. *WIREs Cognitive Science,* 2010; 2: 22–38.

197/2   Stern, D., Spieker, S. and Mackain, K. Intonation contours as signals in maternal speech to prelinguistic infants. *Developmental Psychology,* 1982; 18: 727–35.
Kaplan, P., Bachorowski, J. and Zarlengo-Strouse, P. Child directed speech produced by mothers with symptoms of depression fails to promote associative learning in 4-month-old infants. *Child Development,* 1999; 70: 560–70.

198/1   Gergely, G. and Watson, J.S. Early socio-emotional development: Contingency perception and the social-biofeedback model. In: P. Rochat, ed. *Early Social Cognition: Understanding Others in the First Months of Life.* Mahwah, NJ: Lawrence Erlbaum Associates; 1999, pp. 101–36.

201/1   Vygotsky, L. *Mind in society: The development of higher psychological processes,* Cambridge, MA: Harvard University Press; 1978.

202/2   Trevarthen, C. and Hubley, P. Secondary intersubjectivity: confidence, confiders, and acts

202/2
(cont.)
of meaning in the first year of life. In: A. Lock, ed. *Action, Gesture, and Symbol.* New York: Academic Press; 1978.
Striano, T., Reid, V. and Hoehl, S. Neural mechanisms of joint attention in infancy. *European Journal of Neuroscience,* 2006; 23: 2819–23.
Gaffan, E.A., Martins, C., Healy, S. and Murray, L. Early social experience and individual differences in infants' joint attention. *Social Development,* 2010; 19: 369–93.

212/1
Page, M., Willhelm, M.S., Gamble, W.C. and Card, N.A. A comparison of maternal sensitivity and verbal stimulation as unique predictors of infant social-emotional and cognitive development. *Infant Behavior and Development,* 2010; 33: 101–10.
Trevarthen, C. B. The Musical Art of Infant Conversation; Narrating in the Time of Sympathetic Experience, Without Rational Interpretation, Before Words. *Musicae Scientiae Special issue* 2008, 15–46.
Marwick, H.M. and Murray, L. The effects of maternal depression on the 'Musicality' of infant directed speech and conversational engagement. In: S. Malloch and C. Trevarthan, eds. *Communicative musicality.* Oxford, UK: Oxford University Press; 2010, pp. 281–300.
Gros-Louis, J., Goldstein, M.H., King, A.P. and West, M.J. Mothers provide differential feedback to infants' prelinguistic sounds. *International Journal of Behavioral Development,* 2006; 30: 509–16.

212/2
Singh, L., Nestor, S., Parikh, C. and Yull, A. Influences of infant-directed speech on early word recognition. *Infancy,* 2009; 14: 654–66.
Thiessen, E.D., Hill, E.A. and Saffran, J.R. Infant directed speech facilitates word segmentation. *Infancy,* 2005; 7: 53–71.
Kaplan, P., Bachorowski, J. and Zarlengo-Strouse, P. Child directed speech produced by mothers with symptoms of depression fails to promote associative learning in 4 month-old infants. *Child Development,* 1999; 70: 560–70.
Marwick and Murray, The effects of maternal depression . . .
Gros-Louis, J., Goldstein, M.H., King, A.P. and

West, M.J. Mothers provide differential feedback to infants' prelinguistic sounds . . .

213/1
Huttenlocher, J., Haight, W., Bryk, A., Seltzer, M. and Lyons, T. Early vocabulary growth: Relation to language input and gender. *Developmental Psychology,* 1991; 27: 236–48.
Kuhl, P., Tsao, F. and Liu, H. Foreign-language experience in infancy: Effects of short term exposure and social interaction on phonetic learning. *Proceedings of the National Academy of Sciences,* 2003; 100: 9096–101.

213/2
Scarr, S. and Weinberg, R. The influence of "family background" on intellectual attainment. *American Sociological Review,* 1978; 43: 674–92.
Tamis-LeMonda, C.S., Bornstein, M.H. and Baumwell, L. Maternal responsiveness and children's achievement of language milestones. *Child Development,* 2001; 72: 748–67.
Page, M., Willhelm, M.S., Gamble, W.C. and Card, N.A. A comparison of maternal sensitivity and verbal stimulation as unique predictors of infant social-emotional and cognitive development. *Infant Behavior and Development,* 2010; 33: 101–10.
Tamis-LeMonda et al., Maternal responsiveness... (twice) Masur, E.F., Flynn, V. and Eichorst, D.L. Maternal responsive and directive behaviours and utterances as predictors of children's lexical development. *Journal of Child Language,* 2005; 32: 63–91.

213/3
Tamis-LeMonda et al., Maternal responsiveness...

213/4
Zammit, M. and Schafer, G. Maternal label and gesture use affects acquisition of specific object names. *Journal of Child Language,* 2011; 38(1): 201–21.
Shimpi, P.M. and Huttenlocher, J. Redirective labels and early vocabulary development. *Journal of Child Language,* 2007; 34: 845–59.
Hoff, E. The specificity of environmental influence: Socioeconomic status affects early vocabulary development via maternal speech. *Child Development,* 2003; 74: 1368–78.

213/5
American Academy of Pediatrics, Where we Stand: TV viewing time, October, 2013,

healthychildren.org.

214/1   Zimmerman, F. J. and Christakis, D.A. Children's television viewing and cognitive outcomes: A longitudinal analysis of national data. *Archives of Pediatrics and Adolescent Medicine,* 2005; 159: 619–25.
Pagani, L. S., Fitzpatrick, C., Barnett, T.A. and Dubow, E. Prospective associations between early childhood television exposure and academic, psychosocial, and physical well-being by middle childhood. *Archives of Pediatrics and Adolescent Medicine,* 2010; 164: 425–31.
Wass, S., Porayska-Pomsta, K. and Johnson, M. H. Training attentional control in infancy. *Current Biology,* 2011; 21(18):1543–7.
Barr, R. and Hayne, H. It's not what you know it's who you know: Older siblings facilitate imitation during infancy. *International Journal of Early Years Education,* 2003; 11: 7–21.
Christakis, D.A., Zimmerman, F., DiGiuseppe, D.L. and McCarty, C.A. Early television exposure and subsequent attentional problems in children. *Pediatrics,* 2004; 113: 708–13.
McCollom, J.F. and Bryant, J. Pacing in children's television programming. *Mass Community and Society,* 2003; 6: 115–36.
Schmitt, M.E., Pempek, T.A., Hirkorian, H.L., Lund, A.F. and Anderson, D.R. The effect of background television on the toy play behaviour of very young children. *Child Development,* 2008; 79: 1137–51.
Mendelsohn, A.L., Berkule, S.B., Tomoupolos, S., Tamis-LeMonda, C.S., Huberman, H.S., Alvir, J. et al. Infant television and video exposure associated with limited parent-child verbal interactions in low socioeconomic status households. *Archives of Pediatrics and Adolescent Medicine,* 2008; 162: 411–17.

214/2   Quine, W. *Words and Objects.* New York: Wiley; 1960.
Kuhl, P. Early language acquisition: Cracking the speech code. *Nature Reviews Neuroscience,* 2004; 5: 831–43.
Dunn, J. and Wooding, C. Play in the home and its importance for learning. In: B. Tizard and D. Harvey, eds. *Biology of Play.* Philadelphia: Lippincott; 1977, pp. 45–58.

214/3   Moerk, L. Picture book reading by mothers and young children and its impact upon language development. *Journal of Pragmatics,* 1985; 9, 547–66.

215/1   Bus, A.G. and Van IJzendoorn, M.H. Affective dimensions of mother-infant picture book reading. *Journal of School Psychology,* 1997; 35: 47–60.

215/3   Fletcher, K. and Reese, E. Picture book reading with young children: a conceptual framework. *Developmental Review,* 2005; 25: 64–103.
Ninio, A. Joint book reading as a multiple vocabulary acquisition device. *Developmental Psychology,* 1983; 19: 445–51.
Adrian, J., Clemente, R., Villanueva, L. and Rieffe, C. Parent-child picture-book reading, mothers' mental state language and children's theory of mind. *Journal of Child Language,* 2005; 32: 673–86.

215/4   Bus, A., Van IJzendoorn, M. and Pellegrini, A. Joint book reading makes for success in learning to read: a meta analysis on intergenerational transmission of literacy. *Review of Educational Research,* 1995; 65: 1–21.
Huebner, C. and Meltzoff, A. Intervention to change parent-child reading style: a comparison of instructional methods. *Applied Developmental Psychology,* 2005; 26: 296–313.
Reese, E., Sparks, A. and Leyva, D. A review of parent interventions for preschool children's language and emergent literacy. *Journal of Early Childhood Literacy,* 2010; 10: 97–117.
Cooper, P. J., Vally, Z., Cooper, H., Sharples, A., Radford, T.,Tomlinson, M. and Murray, L. Promoting mother-infant book-sharing and child cognitive development in an impoverished South African population: a pilot study. *Early Childhood Education Journal,* 2013; DOI 10.1007/s10643-013-0591-8
Mol, S., Bus, A., de Jong, M. and Smeets, D. Added value of parent-child dialogic readings: a meta-analysis. *Early Education and Development,* 2008; 19: 7–26.

216/1   Moerk, L. Picture book reading by mothers and young children and its impact upon language

216/1
(cont.)
development. *Journal of Pragmatics,* 1985; 9: 547–66.

DeLoache, J.and DeMendoza, O. Joint picture book interactions of mothers and 1-year-old children. *British Journal of Developmental Psychology,* 1987; 5: 111–23.

Bus, A.G. and Van IJzendoorn, M.H. Affective dimensions of mother-infant picture book reading. *Journal of School Psychology,* 1997; 35: 47–60.

Llytenin, P., Laasko, M. and Poikkeus, A. Parental contributions to child's early language and interest in books. *European Journal of Psychology and Education,* 1998; 8: 297–308.

Oritz, C., Stowe, R. and Arnold, D. Parental influence on child interest in shared picture book reading. *Early Childhood Research Quarterly,* 2001; 16: 263–81.

Fletcher, K. and Reese, E. Picture book reading with young children: a conceptual framework. *Developmental Review,* 2005; 25: 64–103.

Bus, A. G. and Van IJzendoorn, M. H. Mothers reading to their three-year-old children: The role of mother-child attachment security in becoming literate. *Reading Research Quarterly,* 1995; 30: 998–1015.

216/3
Bus and Van IJzendoorn, Affective dimensions of mother-infant picture book reading . . .

Murphy, C. Pointing in the context of a shared activity. *Child Development,* 1978; 49: 371–80.

217/2
Bus, and Van IJzendoorn. Mothers reading to their three-year-old children . . .

DeLoache, J.and DeMendoza, O. Joint picture book interactions of mothers and 1-year-old children. *British Journal of Developmental Psychology,* 1987; 5: 111–23.

Ninio, A. and Bruner, J., The achievement and antecedents of labelling. *Journal of Child Language,* 1978; 5: 1–15.

218/1
Bus and Van IJzendoorn, Affective dimensions of mother-infant picture book reading . . .

Fletcher and Reese, Picture book reading with young children: a conceptual framework . . .

Moerk, L. Picture book reading by mothers and young children and its impact upon language development. *Journal of Pragmatics,* 1985; 9, 547–66.

220/1
Ninio, A. Joint book reading as a multiple vocabulary acquisition device. *Developmental Psychology,* 1983; 19: 445–51.

Snow, C. and Goldfield, B. Turn the page please: situation-specific language acquisition. *Journal of Child Language,* 1983; 10: 551–69.

225/1
Snow and Goldfield, Turn the page please . . .

229/1
Rustin, M. and Rustin, M. *Narratives of love & loss: Studies in modern children's fiction.* London: Verso; 1987.

Index